ロニ・ホーン：水の中にあなたを見るとき、
あなたの中に水を感じる？
Roni Horn: When You See Your Reflection in Water,
Do You Recognize the Water in You?

2021年9月18日［土］—2022年3月30日［水］ ポーラ美術館
September 18, 2021 – March 30, 2022 Pola Museum of Art, Hakone, Japan

主催：公益財団法人ポーラ美術振興財団 ポーラ美術館
後援：アメリカ大使館
協力：Hauser & Wirth／ヤマト運輸株式会社
Organizer: Pola Museum of Art, Pola Art Foundation
In association with: United States Embassy
Support: Hauser & Wirth／YAMATO TRANSPORT CO., LTD.

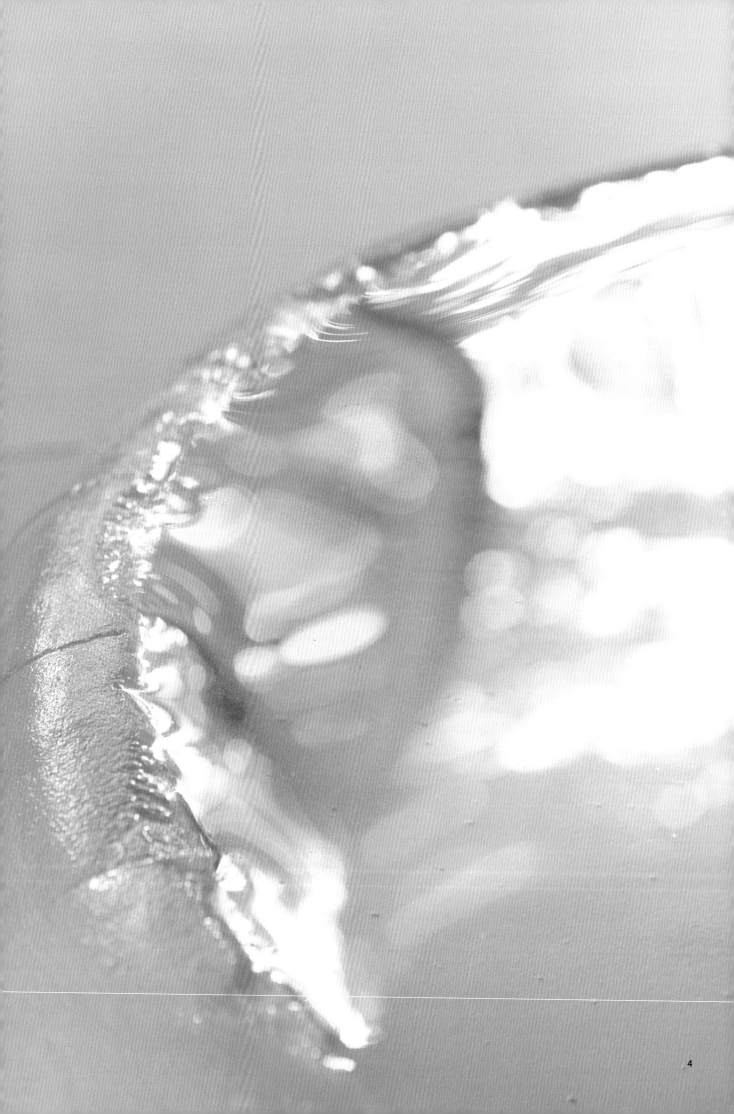

ロニ・ホーンは、アメリカの現代美術を代表するアーティストです。本展は、国内の美術館におけるホーンの初個展となるとともに、2002年の開館以来、ポーラ美術館における大型企画展としては初めて、同時代の作家を単独で取り上げる機会となります。

イギリスのテムズ川やアイスランドの温泉、島の地図、水鏡を思わせるガラスなど、ロニ・ホーンの作品の多くは自然と密接に結びつきながら、極めてシンプルに削ぎ落とされた形式で展開されています。作品は、写真、彫刻、ドローイング、パフォーマンスや本など多岐にわたりますが、一つの概念が多様な作品へと形を変えて表れる様は、環境や周囲との関わりによって姿を変える、「水」の性質を想起させます。また東洋思想において人間の精神のあり方や無常観を表してきた水や川は、展覧会のタイトルにもある通り、ホーンが作品の重要なモティーフやテーマとして用いるものです。

本展では、ロニ・ホーンの近年の代表作であるガラスの彫刻作品をはじめ、1980年代から今日に至るまでの約40年間におよぶ実践の数々を紹介します。1975年に初めてアイスランドを旅して以来、ホーンはこの島に魅せられて訪問を繰り返し、その厳しく荒涼とした自然に対峙し続けるなかで、独りでいることを「自ら選び取った」と言います。人々が孤立や不確かさを恐れる時代において、その作品は曖昧さや変化のなかに潜む力をあえて利用してみせるのです。

「真実」や「現実」のあり方がめまぐるしく入れ替わるこの世界で、差異、アイデンティティ、物事の意味についての思索を続け、絶えず制作を続けるホーンの姿は、静かに流れゆく川のようです。本展はこのような作家の思索へと誘い、その体験は、私たちに強く生きるヒントとReflection（内省）の時間を与えてくれるでしょう。

最後になりましたが、本展開催にあたり、惜しみない協力を賜りましたロニ・ホーン氏に心より御礼申し上げます。また、貴重なご所蔵作品をご出品いただきました美術館、機関、個人の所蔵家の皆様、ご後援をいただきましたアメリカ大使館、本展覧会の開催にあたりご協力をいただきました関係各社、ハウザー&ワース、ロニ・ホーン・スタジオの皆様に厚く御礼を申し上げます。

公益財団法人ポーラ美術振興財団
ポーラ美術館

Roni Horn is one of America's preeminent contemporary artists. This is Horn's first solo show at a Japanese museum as well as the first major exhibition by a contemporary artist at the Pola Museum of Art, which opened in 2002.

Many of Horn's works are inextricably linked to nature, with sources including the waters of the River Thames, hot springs in Iceland, and the water-like, liquid of glass. Horn employs a wide range of media, including photography, sculpture, drawing, performance, and books, and often presents her work in paired or sequenced form. The recurrence of motifs across widely varied media is reminiscent of the nature of water, with its form and appearance changing as the local environment and surroundings change. Water and rivers, which represent the human spirit and transience in East Asian philosophy, are at the heart of Horn's œuvre, as suggested by the title of this exhibition.

The exhibition is an in-depth survey of Roni Horn's practice spanning almost 40 years, from the 1980s to the present, exploring a multifaceted body of work including the glass sculptures that are among her most prominent pieces in recent years.

Captivated by Iceland since first traveling there in 1975, Horn has continually returned to the island with its spartan and wild landscape, suggesting that being alone is "very much a choice." Horn's art harnesses the undertow of ambiguity and change in an era in which people are uneasy with isolation and uncertainty.

In a world where ideas about truth and reality change rapidly Horn is a quietly flowing river, addressing notions of difference, identity, and meaning in the varied yet specific nature of her work. This exhibition invites viewers to do the same, offering inspiration and time for reflection.

In closing, we would like to extend our heartfelt gratitude to Roni Horn for her untiring efforts to bring this exhibition to fruition. We would also like to express our sincere appreciation to the museums and collectors who kindly agreed to lend us important works, the U.S. Embassy, Hauser & Wirth, and Roni Horn Studio for their support and assistance, and all of the many others who helped us realize this exhibition.

Pola Museum of Art, Pola Art Foundation

日本の美術館での初めての大規模な個展となる本展は、私の人生の重要な節目をなすものです。その大半は翻訳や翻案、あるいは想像を通して体験したものですが、日本文化は私の作品に長きにわたり、深い影響をもたらしてきました。

私は図書館や博物館などで、俳句、文楽、生け花、折り紙、刀鍛冶、木工、織物、日本庭園といった伝統を学びながら育ちました。特に工芸や伝統に顕著な、具体的なもの、抽象的なもの、実在的なものに対する日本文化の研ぎ澄まされた感性を実感しました。こうした意識が生み出す経験に心を奪われ、また、無常の存在に潜むものに触れるための直感的な知識や理解に心を惹かれました。

この度、日本のみなさんをお迎えし、意義深い展覧会をお届けできることを大変喜ばしく思います。

2021年　ロニ・ホーン

This first large museum show in Japan marks an important moment in my life. The influence of Japanese culture on my work, though mostly vicarious—through translation, transposition and imagination, is long standing and deep.

When I was growing up, I learned, largely through libraries and museums, of haiku, bunraku, ikebana, origami, sword making, woodworking, textiles, and garden traditions. I recognized the culture's exquisite sensitivity, especially evident in the artifacts and traditions, to the physical, the metaphysical, and the actual. I was drawn to the experiences created by this awareness. I was drawn as well to the intuitive knowledge and understanding needed to access the potential present in insentient things.

I am happy for this opportunity to have a Japanese audience and for a meaningful setting in which to share the work with you.

Roni Horn, 2021

目次 | Contents

失くした部分たちを集めて

ブリオニー・ファー

　かつてマルグリット・デュラスは、映画についての著作でこう言ったことがある。自分がなにを観たかようやくわかるのは、それを観た翌朝のことなのだと。スクリーンに映ったものは彼女の記憶のなかで、じっさいに経験するのとはまた違ったしかたでかたちづくられる。それはあたかも彼女の感覚が、一夜のうちにふたつできるかのようだ。しかもこのふたつの出現は双方向に起こる。いっぽうではそれは集合であり、他方ではそれは分岐だ。たぶんこの状況はどうやっても解消しない。それとも、ひとつの溢れんばかりの経験というのは、こうしてあらためて心に思い起こそうにも、とうてい手に負えないものとなるのだろうか? そしてわたしに言わせるなら、この点を確かめることによってこそ、もっとも微かなものではあるにせよ、ロニ・ホーンの作品を理解する手がかりを得ることができる。これはわたしの信仰告白でもなければ、声明〔ステイトメント〕でもない。じっさいこの手がかりをそのまま摑んでおくのは至難の業だ。つぎの瞬間にはもうそれはこの手をすり抜けてしまうのではと、わたしたちは怯えることになる。

　このような危うさは、まずホーンの作品が多岐にわたることに関わっているように思う。たとえばごく簡素な彼女の一点のドローイング〔＝線描〕作品は、どうして同じホーンのガラス彫刻から溢れ出す官能性に見合うものとなるだろう? もちろん、今日では同じひとりの芸術家が多様な媒体〔メディウム〕によって、多様な作品を数多く制作している例も数多くある。彼女の作品で経験するそのほかのものも、概念的〔コンセプチュアル〕であることと官能的であることとの対立を、すっかりそのままにしておくことはない。なるほど彼女の作品では色彩が重要な役割を果たすが、それも〔古典的な芸術理論で言われるように〕線描に対立してはいない。このように彼女の作品のありようはきわめて不安定で、わたしの手をすり抜けようとするばかりか、作品それ自体としての統一も保ちえないでいる。そのときもっと効果的で、もっと鋭く、もっといろいろなものと共鳴し、もっと肯定的ななにかを形容する言葉があるとすれば、それは「かそけき〔tenuous〕」という一語に尽きるだろう。彼女の作品のことを思い出そうとするほどに、わたしの脳裏にはその語が甦る。「かそけき」とは「細い」あるいは「薄い」を意味する語だが、これこそそれぞれにはっきりと種類の異なるホーンの作品たちのあいだにある、つながりのようなものを示すのにふさわしいのではないかと思う。もちろん、心に沁み入るようなその特徴をぴったり言い当ててもいるだろう。現実にわたしが手中にすることのできるかそけき手がかりは、毛一本ほどの太さしかない。けれどそれはとてつもない力に溢れた経験であり、見すごすことはできない。ドローイング作品にごく微かに書きつけられた鉛筆による線、あるいは信じられないような強度を持った透き通る青さのガラスが、その経験の引き金となる。いっぽうの美しさが囮〔デコイ〕で、それはもういっぽうの微かさが囮であるのと同じなのかもしれないが。

　ではわたしの考察を、ホーンのドローイングに集中させてみよう。それこそが彼女の営みの中心にあるものだから。こう言うとまるでドローイングがなにかしら彼女の作品すべての鍵になっているように聞こえるかもしれないが、それは違う(たったひとつの要素をもってこれが鍵だなんていうことがあるだろうか?)。彼女の作品は、まさにそれ自体を、ある場所を、ある形状を、「中心にしよう」と企てるものだ。ここで「中心」がなにを意味するにせよ、それによって啓示のような単一の真理を見出そうと言うつもりはない。彼女はいろいろな作品を手がけながらも、いっぽうでアトリエをはじめいたるところでドローイング作品を制作してきた。このドローイングの実践を、彼女は「語彙を日々呼吸すること」[1]になぞらえる。あたかもドローイングは引き受けざるをえない務め〔タスク〕だと、しかもその衝動のもっとも本質的なところは、それがもっとも日常的だということにあると、言っているかのようでもある。このときわたしの目指すところは単純に、それが求めているような方法で、このドローイング作品に思考を集中すること、そしてこのかそけき手がかりについて、なにごとかを理解してみることの、ふたつだけである。そしてこの手がかりを摑んでしまったばかりに、わたしはいやおうなく観客として、彼女の作品の前に立たざるをえなくなる。

悲しき北極地帯

わたしはいくつかの風景を標本として選び、切り取ってみる。この木だと言うのか？ この花だと言うのか？ そんなものはほかにもあるだろう。これもまた嘘だと言うのか——わたしを夢中にさせたあの全体は、各部分をひとつひとつ取ってみれば、わたしになにも語ろうとしない。[2]

クロード・レヴィ＝ストロース『悲しき熱帯』

1982年、ホーンはアイスランドの海に面した村ディルホゥラエイを訪れ、そこから少し離れた場所にある灯台でひとり過ごした。今日よく知られる彼女の作品の多くはアイスランドをめぐるものだが、それはあたかも、芸術が延々と続く旅日記に転じたかのようだ。それは日々の行程を、実時間と実空間を基準に特定の場所へと図表化してゆくばかりか、彼女自身の脳裏にも刻み込んでゆく。ホーンが自身をエミリ・ディキンスンと重ね合わせるのも無理はない。この詩人はわずか二度の機会を除いて生涯自宅を離れることがなく、日々その心のうちで旅を続けた。灯台とは遠く海を見つめるためのものだが、またひとりになることのできる場所でもある——そしてまさにこのふたつの面が、《ブラフ・ライフ》（1982年）と題された、灯台滞在時の彼女のドローイングに合流している。外を見ることは内を見ることであり、逆もまたしかりだ。この苛烈な自己反省の側面を、「瞑想的」などといった一語で片づけはするまい。アグネス・マーティンがたゆまず続ける抽象の探求は、ある特定のしかたでそれを見るよう要求するが、それをそんな一語で片づけられないのと同じことだ。それではあまりに柔和に響く。ニュー・メキシコの砂漠であれ、一本の木も生えない索漠としたアイスランドの風景のただなかであれ（それもまた別種の砂漠であるだろう）、そうした場所での孤独な実存の探求は、極度の集中を伴う。それに比べればロバート・スミッソンの砂漠紀行など散漫で気ままなものに感じられるし、じっさいもそうだっただろう。

ホーンによるドローイング作品、《ブラフ・ライフ》（1982年）は一枚ずつはがすことができるメモ用紙に描かれている。シリーズ中の作品総数は13点。それぞれ線描によるかたちが、一枚の白紙の中央に、まるで地質学の標本のようにつつましく座す。もちろんどれも自然の観察記録に類するものではなく、さまざまな線と印が動物の巣のように絡み合う線描だ。そのうち3点はオレンジ色の水彩で描かれ、残りでは黒またはそれに近い色彩の鉛筆が塗り重ねられている。作品一点一点はたがいに微妙に異なり、あたかも標本として、それぞれに固有の鉱床の存在を示しているようだ。岩石の組成ではなく、長い時間と自然の力によって侵食を受けた岩石を描いたもののように見えるが、それも地殻変動の産物というよりは、作者の身体のリズムや圧力が痕跡として残ったものだろう。

地質学からミニマル・アートのあの外観が、すぐに思い出されるということはないし、その基本単位を組み合わせる構成や連続的な配置、工業素材については言うまでもない。それでもロバート・スミッソンがドナルド・ジャッドについての試論、「結晶の大地」の冒頭をどう切り出していたか、ここで思い起こしてみる価値はあるだろう。スミッソンはそのとき彼とジャッドのふたりが地質学に対する関心を共有していたこと、そしてふたり連れ

fig.1：ドナルド・ジャッド（1928-1994）《100点の圧延アルミニウム板による無題の作品》（部分）
1982-1986年、アルミニウム、各104.1×129.5×182.9cm　チナティ財団、マーファ、テキサス

立ってニュー・ジャージーまで鉱物採集に出かけたことを引き合いに出すところから、話を始めているのだ。ス
ミッソンはまた「精神の堆積」というべつの試論でも、人間の精神生活を地層ができるときのような堆積作用に
よるものとし、さらにそれを、エントロピーの法則にしたがって崩壊してゆく状態に置いて描き出している。このス
ミッソンのディストピア〔＝反理想郷、暗黒世界〕的な世界観は、J. G. バラードが〔1969年の『結晶世界』
のような〕SF小説に進出したことと呼応している。バラードはそのとき、世界のすべてが精神的な衰亡に向かう
さまを思い描いた。[3] スミッソンはこの世界観をジャッドの作品に投影したのだ。いっぽうジャッドはジャッドで、
のちにマーファ——ジャッドはテキサス州のこの街にあった旧軍用施設を住居と制作の場の複合体に転用し
た——で展開した作品によって、これとはみごとに異なる砂漠に対する感性を示している。彼のマーファでの
試みはその場所の風景に、とりわけ強烈な陽射しのありように、鋭く反応する。ある特定の場所にどのように作
品を設置するかという問いに取り憑かれたジャッドは、自作のなかでも金属製の作品の表面仕上げに熱中す
ることになった。その結果この表面は、かの地の自然環境がもたらす目も眩むような光に応じたものとなったの
である[fig.1]。

　ジャッドはごく初期からホーンの作品を収集していた人物のひとりで、1991年にはその彫刻作品のひとつ
《再来するもの》(1986年) [figs.2 and 3] をマーファに設置している。ホーンは折にふれこの地に彼を訪ね、当時
ふたりでテキサスの砂漠についてアイスランドと比較しながら話したことを、いまも思い出す。かつてホーンはミニ
マリズムの遺産(レガシー)の傘のもとで制作していると説明され、またいまでもよくそう言われるが、それでもそのとき彼女が
ジャッドの作品をこのマーファの地で経験したことがどれだけ重要であったか、強調しておくことは無意味では
あるまい。それはホーンにとって、スミッソンが幻想のなかに思い描いた、風景をつぎつぎと通過してゆくふるまい
（彼はひとところに長く止まったりはしない）よりもはるかに重要だった。アイスランドのように荒涼とした火山地の美しさと
は、なにもないように見えてひとたびその場所の細部に眼をこらせば、あらゆることがそこで起こっている、と気づく
ことにある——ちょうど暗闇に慣れてしまえば、砂漠の風景や夜の世界の振幅を知覚できるよう感覚が調整さ
れるのと同じように（ホーンがディルホゥラエイをよく散歩したのは夜だった）。

　つまり、たんに作品の形態の上でのつながりや影響関係だけがここで重要なのではない。ミニマル・アートと
ある種の出会いを果たした思い出が、いわば心理学と地質学が独特のしかたで重なり合ったものとして、彼
女の作品の随所に組み込まれていることが重要なのだ。たとえばホーンのガラス彫刻のひとつは〔多くのミニマ
ル・アートと同じく台座を経ずに〕床にじかに置かれている[fig.4]。鋳造ガラスによるその直方体の塊は、光沢
のない側面の内側に、周囲の光を屈折させまた反射する、透き通った深い琥珀色を孕んでいる。けれどその
意味はどろどろになった溶岩や、鉄分が溶け出て赤茶色になった水といった、さまざまに、そして刻々と移り変
わる連想を通じて〔文法用語で言うところの〕屈折変化をする。《彼女の瞳》(1999/2005-2007年)と《白のディ
キンスン》(2006-2007年)は、抽象的な作品として見ればアルミニウム製の棒に、白いプラスティックで不規則
に連なる飾り模様を刻み込んだものである。その棒が壁の高い位置に水平に据えられ、あるいは壁に対して
垂直に、つっかえ棒のようにして立て掛けられている。どれも見過ごしてしまいそうなくらいにそこにそっけなく置か
れているようなのだが、見ればひとつひとつの棒に埋め込まれているのは言葉である。2006年の《白のディキ

figs.2 and 3：《再来するもの》1986年、チナティ財団（マーファ、テキサス）での展示風景
2つの銅、直径：各29.2-43.2cm、長さ：各88.9cm　ジャッド財団

ンスン》ではこう読める。「もっともつかみどころのないものは、もっとも記憶から消しがたいものです」。これはエミリ・ディキンスンの遺したある手紙の冒頭の一行だ［fig.5］。《白のディキンスン》の設置された場所がどれほどなにもない空っぽな空間のようであっても、そこには依然として濃厚な事件の気配が漂っており、この一行のような言葉の連なり（クラスター）をいくつも含んでいるのである。

　もし美術史研究が博物学の一形式であるとすれば――多分にそうあるべきだと思うが――根本的にかけ離れた例どうしを結びつけることもそれほど奇異とは思われるまい。たとえばジャッドとマーティンが砂漠に対して示した感受性を、ヴィヤ・セルミンスのような芸術家と関連づけてみてもよいだろう。1970年代に始まるセルミンスのドローイングの企ては総体として、自然宇宙に存在する生物種たちを、ホーンのドローイングとも密接に関わる手法で鮮やかに示すことにあった。セルミンスはかつてこう言っている。「ドローイングは乾いた世界だ」と。あたかも彼女がその込み入ったドローイングを描くための黒鉛や黒炭もまた、踏査を待つ砂漠であるかのようだ。[4] 水溜まりや砂原の小石のようなごく微かな部分さえ見逃さない視線が、一葉の紙の全面を彼女の刻んだ印で覆いつくしている［fig.6］。小石と砂塵の複雑に織りなす大地はまた、ドローイングのための素地でもある。こうしたすべてが、水面と砂漠を行き来するセルミンスのドローイングの場合とは方法がまったく違うものの、ホーンによるそのふたつのあいだにある密接な協働の理解にも関連している――というのも、ホーンはそのふたつのあいだを行き来するのではなくひとつに撚り合わせるのであり、そのことが彼女の制作の大部分を形成しているのだ。《ブラフ・ライフ》でオレンジ色の水彩が溜まったところは、方法はどうあれ直截に水を湛えた風景を喚起するが、ホーンの作品の要所はそこにはない。もっと広範な発想、つまりドローイングはひとつの場所を表象しない、あるいはその場所をドローイングに翻訳することさえしない、という発想にある。ホーンにとってドローイングはそれ自体がひとつの場所、アイスランドの荒地を織りなす溶岩地や水溜まりの複雑な配置に劣らず、自分を捉えて離さない場所なのだ。セルミンスにとってその手で一枚の紙の表面を踏査しつくすことが、時間を要すること、そしてまたその時間を刻み込むことだったのと同じように。

　ホーンの作品が際立って感じられる理由のひとつは、それがいちどきに二重の動作（ダブル・アクション）をすることにある。たとえばそれは、内心に起こった強烈なできごとを続けざまに吐露するような孤独な独白とまったく同時に、その状況をめぐる身体的な感覚をも呼び起こす。彼女の作品を経験することとは十字砲火をまさにそれが交差する場所で浴びるようなもので、だからそれは最終的に、ミニマリズムの作品がよく引き起こすと言われる「現象学的転回」[5] とはまったく異なった経験になる。なにごとか直接的な経験をしているという感覚が、作品に埋め込まれた言語や文章を介して起こるというだけではない。いつでもそうとはかぎらないが、文章がそこにあるときにも文字のかたちは簡素にされているし、あるていど抽象形態のようになっていて文字として判読できないこともある。それはあたかも、経験が現象学にぶつかっていっているかのようだ。

　ここからわたしは、まったく偶然にもクロード・レヴィ=ストロースが『悲しき熱帯』と題した紀行文に書きつけた、ある思い出話のことを想起する。それによれば後々の彼の知的な展開を決定づけたのは、子供のころ、小石が集まってできたある部分に気づくか気づかないかの区分を見つけたことだという。フランス、ラングドックの石

左
fig.4：《疑念のかたまり》2005-2006年、
ハウザー・アンド・ワース（チューリヒ）での展示風景
鋳造ガラス、55.2×106×128.9cm
シルヴィー・ウィンクラー、ブリュッセル

右
fig.5：《白のディキンスン、もっともつかみどころのないものは、もっとも記憶から消しがたいものです》2006年
アルミニウム、成型した白いプラスチック、229×5.1×5.1cm
Courtesy of the artist and Hauser & Wirth

灰岩高原で、地層どうしの接面が線のように見えていることに気づいたのだ。[6] 彼はそれを、そのときまで経験と現実の連続を理解するのに用いていた、現象学という手法の限界を示すものと思ったようだ。ホーンはほかのものをすべて締め出して、地質学をめぐる込み入った隠喩の山を積みあげている、と私は言っているのではない。ひとかけらの岩や溶岩の質感のうちにあって注目しなければならないのは、そのごく微かな軋みにこそひとつの莫大な変動の痕跡が刻まれているということであり、また彼女にはそういう感覚があると言いたいのだ。この力に満ちた変動は視野にも等しく起こる。めまいのようななにかが、空間と同じくすでに時間のスケールの歪みのうちにもある。つまりその微かな線には何千年もの時間が一気に圧縮されているのである。

乱気流

　　　空ではなにかが進行している——それは依然として静寂を保っている大気の分解、あるいは崩壊と言えるようなものである。

ジョセフ・コンラッド『陰影線』[7]

　ホーンのドローイングはごく小さいものから始まり、やがて大きくなるに至る。1980年代に始まる、《ブラフ・ライフ》の余波として生まれた紙に描いた作品は、不規則で閉じた形態を輝くような色彩によって描き出している。彼女が近年制作しているドローイングに比べれば、それはほとんど宝石のように見える。分厚く塗られた絵の具は、芸術家の心情をその手が表現した印というよりは心情の集積が物質となったものだろう。そこにはただ稠密な色彩の肌理だけがある——ざっくりとした手つきで盛り上げられたその肌理は美的な機微や所作とは無縁だ。じっさいそこにある形態はどれも小さいわりに落ち着きが悪く、不格好といってもよいものである。紙の素地にしても、新品同様の白というにはわずかにだがあちこち染みがある。そうした特徴から言ってもこれらのドローイングは単体では成立しない。ふたつひと組になるのもよくあること、三つが隣り合わせに置かれればそこにひとつの連続性がほのめかされることになるが、これも規則的な進行や特定の論理に従うものではない。そこには反復的な要素がごくわずかな変化とともに組み込まれており、その変化がひとつひとつの作品を区別することを可能にしている。ホーンにはそもそもドローイングを切断して組み替えることがあり、ひとつながりに見えてもじっさいにはそれは途切れ途切れで、紙に差し挟まれた薄片が形態を分断している。ときにほんのかすかな違いを梳いてほぐす必要があるが、これは時間のかかることだ。ところどころがわずかにぼやけた色斑はドローイング全体の大きさとは不釣り合いで、あたかもその用紙には荷が重すぎるかのようだ。けれど紙の切り口のほうはじっさい信じられないくらいに鮮明で、分厚さに対してかろうじて知覚できるような薄さを拮抗させる。このように

fig.6：ヴィヤ・セルミンス（1938年生まれ）《無題（砂漠）》1971年
リトグラフ、シート：56.8×73.7cm、イメージ：53.3×70.5cm
メトロポリタン美術館、ニューヨーク；ジョン・B・ターナー・ファンド1972.501.5

fig.7：ロニ・ホーンのスタジオ（ニューヨーク）の壁面、2008年

分厚くしたり薄くしたりすることが、彼女のドローイングを突き動かしているように思える。すでに鑑賞者としてわたしが摑んだかそけき手がかりとは、この原動力のまたべつの部分にすぎない。

　たがいに極めて相似しているふたつの形態が組み合わせられるとき、相互の対称性がそこにあるのではと考えるのは無理からぬことだ。それだけにいっそう、《分身3.9》(1990年)に見るようなかたちの組み合わせが、対称性の効果——わたしがこの言葉で言いたいのは、ふたつの事物が平衡した状態にあって完璧なバランスを保っているということだ——を発揮できないままにあるのには驚かされる。かわりにいっぽうはもういっぽうの分身としての役割を担っており、逆の効果を発揮する。つまり不均衡だ。ふたつのドローイングはいくつかの点ではほとんど同一なのかもしれないが、それだけに右手にある作品で着彩された垂直線が右へ右へとずれてゆくという劇的な結果を生じている。パウル・ツェランがごく簡潔に嘆いてみせたとおり、「この世界の／読みがたさ。すべては二重になって」いる。[8] 二本の線。ふたつのガラスの塊。二匹の白いフクロウ。そして二重の動作が、単独の作品であろうと、二点一組の、あるいはもっと多数を組み合わせたものの一部としての作品であろうと、その内部で増殖してゆく。この効果は積み重なり、やがてそういった部分に収まらなくなる。事物と事物のあいだに起こるこの変動の曖昧さは、二重性の増殖過程でいっそうひどくなってゆく——そしてこの曖昧さははっきりと意図されているのである(うやむやにされようとしているというよりも)。

　これまでもホーンは自身が分身や二重化に心奪われていることを、有無を言わさない調子で文字にしてきた。それこそが彼女の作品の第一条件であり、ひいてはそれ自身を見るための条件なのだと。同形のふたつの金属塊が壁一枚を隔てて置かれているインスタレーション作品《再来するもの》は、あるときひとが見るもの、そしてふたたび見るものに基づいている。見ているものの記憶はかつて見たものに影響し、またそれを変える。すっかり別様に変形してしまうと言ってもよい。そのときはじめに見たもののほうは、魔法にかかったかのように原型（オリジナル）ということになるのだが、しかしそれはたんに、あとからそこにやってきたなにかがあるから、もともとあったものがそうなるということにすぎない。こうしてわたしたちが反復を知覚するときはいつでも、底流に一時的な分裂があることが明らかになる。それがこのうえなく鮮明になる場所が、たとえば彼女が1980年代の終わりに始めた〈二重の距離〉シリーズだ。二点のドローイングがそれぞれ別の部屋に架かっている。ふたつめのドローイングを見るとき、それははじめに見たものと同一だということがわかるだろうが、絶対に同一だという保証はない。ただしどれほど強調しても足りるまいが、二点のドローイングがいちどきに複製されたとして、それを見てたしかにここがちょっと違うというところを特定してみせるのは、ホーンのじっさいの作品が有するのとは真逆の効果を見い出しているにすぎない。この作品はむしろなにかを正確には思い出せないことをめぐるものであり、あるいは少なくとも、思い出せることと思い出せないことの区別はいつも不確かだとほのめかしているのである。かつて同じものをいちど見ていること、つまり既視（デジャヴュ）であることはそのものを身近に感じさせはするだろう。けれどそれをどうやって見たのかを正確には思い出せないときには、かえってずっと遠ざけてしまう。空間上の距離を一皮剝けば、時間上の非対称が現れる。

　すると、こういうことになる。ホーンのドローイングをひとつの時系列に沿った進歩という枠組みに当てはめて見るのは、美術史研究の観点からは想像力を搔きたてることであっても、有効ではない。というのも彼女の作品は変化すればするほど、それ自身に立ち返ってゆくからだ。いまなお彼女は折をみてごく初期の作品にさかのぼっては、それを再利用する。ホーンは同一の作品を再制作することもあるが、それは必ずしもはじめの作品が失敗に終わったからではなく、そのような再制作こそが彼女にとっては制作そのものだからなのだ。この制作の論理には作品の一部を取り外すことや、その全体をばらばらにすることも含まれる。これはそうした変化が重要ではないということではなく、彼女の制作の論理を根本から逸脱するものではない、ということだ。そのなかでもっともはっきりした変化はサイズに現れたそれと、かたちが閉鎖的というよりは開放的なものに移行したことだろう。1993年以降の《あれⅥ》は、閉じたかたちを紙の中央にひとつ置くのではなく、小さくゆるやかに曲ったⅤ字形を作品の表面上に不規則なパターンで配置することで成立している。それが描かれる紙の地は、垂直方向に細長く伸びる短冊状に切り裂かれていて、この短冊は互いにしっかりと縫い合わされている。ここでは地は——なにも描かれていないうちからすでに——裂け目だらけなのだ。そこにはまさに根本的な解体が刻まれている。とりたてて語る必要のあるかたちもない。またべつのドローイングでは、各要素が撒き散らすように配列されている。これらの要素は単独の、あるいはふたつの中心の周囲を循環することもあり、それによって構

成の中心という発想を内側から突き崩す。《またも V》（2000年）では、描き出された形状はまるで遠心分離機が発生させた渦のようになる。そのスケールは観客を、さきほどの小さなスケールのドローイング作品とはまったく異なる立ち位置に置く――観客はこのばらばらになった場所の力によって引きずり込まれるのだ。

　ニューヨークにあるホーンのスタジオには、彼女が「板」と呼ぶもので覆われたとてつもなく広い壁面がある［fig.7］。この語には地質学の用語としての含みがある（地球の表層を移動するあの岩盤のことだ）。けれどその語はまた、版画や写真の版を暗示するものでもある（たんに像を仲介する、あるいは移行させるための要素のことだ）。こうした版はすでにドローイングであるが、やがて彼女のドローイング作品にもなる。なかにはルイーズ・ブルジョワの不眠症のドローイングを彷彿させるものもあるにしても、ほかはそれとはまったく別物だ。［figs.8 and 9］これらはまったく未完成のままに、《ほか 9》（2010年、pp.148-149）のような作品を構成してゆくことになるのだろう。2、3、あるいは4枚の紙をひとまとめにしたものがいくつかあって、壁を覆っている。螺旋や同心形の楕円、あるいはほどけた色彩の結び目が、ばらばらにされてはふたたび集められ、大きなスケールの作品になってゆく――ほぼ素材のままのものから完成品まで、さまざまな状態にある作品がスタジオのあちこちを占めている。ホーンはそうやって多数の作品に一度に取り掛かる。けれどすべてが完成するまでには長い時間が必要で、1年かそのくらいかかることもある。なぜそんなにかかるのか、制作の過程がこうしてどれほど複雑で労を要するものかを実感できれば、理由はすぐにわかる。ただ重要なのは技術ではない。技術のあとを辿っていったとしても、その作品の源泉は少しもわからないし、それはあたかも、そうして紙片がふたたび集められたにせよ、そんな状態は吹き飛ばしてしまってほしいと望むこともできるかのようだ。この意味ではドローイングで覆われた壁面を示してみたところで、それは事態を明確にするどころかむしろ錯綜させる。けっきょくその「板＝版」を見ているか見ていないかにかかわらず、ドローイングそれ自体のうちにつねにあるのは、この版の配置はそれが元あった場所からはるか遠い場所まで、かなりの遠回りをしながら旅してきたのだという感覚である――あちこち行ったり来たりしながらここまでやってきたのだ。

　一定の距離をとれば、《を通じて 4》（2007年）は途切れ途切れの青いジグザグ形が二重の花のように開いたかたちに見える。小刻みな線の数々はまったくかたちを成さないように見えて、そこにはしっかりとした形態がある。振りまかれたような線は、大ぶりでゆるやかな円形のパターンをふたつつくっているのがわかる。線は星座のように配置され、ふたたび集まったり集められたりしながら、繊細極まりないカットによって削り出された結晶構造を白い紙一面に刻みつける。わたしたちはそんな線の集まりにさえ、丸ごと引き込まれる。表面にあるのはごく質素で、広大な紙面を覆うにはおよそ不充分なものでしかないのに。わたしたちは概念としてその全体を把握することができるが、細部はどうしても抜け落ちる。この効果はアイスランドの風景がもたらすそれとは真逆にあるもののようだ。アイスランドの効果をホーンはこう説明していた。「自分を見失えるだけの大きさだし、自分を見つけられるだけの小ささだ」。[9] ここにはまたべつの回り道がある。その小ささを望遠鏡で覗き込むほどに、そこで見えるものは維持できなくなる。近寄るほどに一度は摑んだと思ったかもしれないものも、そこにある複雑な視覚情報に直面してしまうと、そのままに保っておくことはどんどん難しくなってゆく。最初の、そして最大ので

figs.8 and 9：ルイーズ・ブルジョワ (1911-2010)《不眠症のドローイング》(部分)、1994-95年
220点の多様なサイズのミクストメディア作品からの2点、インク/紙、22.9×30.2cm (左)、30.5×22.9cm (右)
ダロス・コレクション、チューリヒ

きごとは着彩された形態の暗号化（スクランブル）が解けることだ。そしてこの過程の論理を突き止めようとするほどに、わたしたちはしだいに足場を失ってゆくことになる。

　紙の一面には鉛筆で刻まれた印の余白さえも美しく散りばめられていて、あちこちにある結節点の大半の位置を測定できるようになっている。二重になった線がふたつの縁を示しつつ整列させることもあれば、べつのどこかではふたつの単語がたがいに隣接して、どの地点で合流すればよいかを示すこともある。これらは複数の紙片を束ねておくための印だが、作品全体に対してはすこし取り乱したような効果を加える（落ち着かせるのとは逆の効果だ）。加えてピンで開けた小さな穴がいたるところに散りばめられているのだが、これはばらばらの紙片を、壁面上の紙が織りなす重量級のパズルにうまく嵌め込もうとしてつけたり外したりするうちにできたものだ。指紋や、足跡さえもついていて、こちらはすべてを物理的にひとつに束ねるときにできた、物質的な指標記号（インデクス）としての痕跡である。その痕跡は紀行文のもっとも端的な要約であるかもしれないが、唯一それだけが少なくともその効果として、このような作品制作の過程を鮮明に示すというよりむしろ曖昧にする。

　鉛筆による書き込みはふたつひと組で登場する——二重線、あるいは単語やものの名前をふたつひと組にしたものとして。ある作品ではいっぽうに「ローラ」、もういっぽうに「パーマー」と書かれており（デヴィッド・リンチ監督『ツイン・ピークス』（1990–1991年）の登場人物からの引用）、べつの作品の「アンス・アンス」はなにかを召喚しようとしているかのようだ。「boo-boo（ブー・ブー）」「who-who（フー・フー）」「you-you（ユー・ユー）」のように韻を踏（ライム）んだ短い語句が記されることもある。こうした語は暗号化された記号のようにも読めるが、まったく、そして不可避的に、意味ははっきりしない。それはむしろ意識の流れに似て、でたらめに浮かんだ単語が連鎖しているようなものだ。だからすべてを測る印は、主体としてのわたしたちのうちに不連続を刻みつける——「grow grow〔育て、育て〕」「vow vow〔誓え、誓え〕」「claw claw〔足掻け、足掻け〕」「crab crab〔横に歩け、横に歩け〕」というように。鉛筆またはクレヨンで書き込まれた印は、蝶番のもっとも脆い箇所のように不安定なままの状態を保っている。くりかえせば、その印がなにか突き止めようとするほどにすべてが眼前で崩壊してゆくのだ。暗号を（しかもそんな暗号などないところに）解読しようとすれば、作品を見る喜びは失われてしまう。

　ホーンの《静かな水（テムズ川、例として）》（1999年、pp.94–101）では、写真に映った水面に、いくつも数字が散りばめられている。まるで小さな泡が集まって水面をたゆたっているようだ。そこには水の純粋さよりも、その汚染や毒性が暗示されているという感じが拭えない。無数のたゆたう水のパターンにはすべて文字で脚註が付され、画像の下部に連ねられる。小さな印を散らしたところはドローイングのようにも見える。脚註とそこに記された註釈の内容はしだいに焦点を絞り、細部を穿ち、ごく微かな点も刻明に描き出してゆく。ときに問いが投げかけられることもあるが、答えはどこにも示されない。「これは黒か？」というのは、数字で示された水上の小さな一区画に安置された者に投げかけられた問いだ。ほかに「（これは何色？）」と読める部分もある。ジョセフ・コンラッド『闇の奥』（1902年）中の1ページやエミリ・ディキンスンの詩への参照を促す箇所も。もし脚註が伝統的に、本文の内容を例証し、また引用の典拠を示すために学者たちが使う綿密なしくみなのだとすれば、ここで脚註は本文にあたる水それ自体の動きに合わせて駆け足で流れてゆく註釈の姿を借りて、つぎつぎと問いを提起してゆくことになるだろう。

　ある脚註にさらにつけられた脚註で、ホーンはこう書いている。「写真の上に散りばめられた数字は、この光景を構成する星座だ」。ところが続く脚註では、その数字は「ゴミ」とされ、せっかくの「光景」をぶちこわしにするものとして語られる。これはたぶん、ステファヌ・マラルメがひとつのページに文字を配置するときの発想に通じる——つまり言語を組み立ててゆく作業は、まさにそれを解体するために行われるのだ。水の流れはほんのわずかに乱れるだけで、水面に新たな肌理を創出する。それは静かなときも荒々しいときも、流れの方向や重なりに応じて大小の渦をかたちづくってゆく。もちろん水面の様子というのは、写真のなかで静止しているのを見るのとじっさいのものを見るのとでぜんぜん違う。じっさいには死んだように静かな水面でさえ、突然まるごと濁流に呑み込まれることだってある。これはホーンのドローイングともごく近い性質であるように思える——あちこちに配された色とりどりの印も、水面のごく狭い部分に現れた渦へとやがて呑み込まれてゆくのだ。

　ここでジョン・ラスキンの『素描の基礎（ドローイング）』を想起するのは少々強引にすぎるだろうか——19世紀半ばに著された、素描を学ぼうとする人々のための手引きである。けれどその水の描きかたの説明を通じて溢れ出てくるのは、むしろラスキンの感受性のあまりの鋭さのほうだ。彼は読者に一日中水面を見つめるよう奨めるが、その

教えは飽くなき妄想のような夢想（ヴィジョン）を孕んでいる。水面上の同一点が、異なる光を受けて見えかたを変えてゆくさまをどう描くか。ラスキンはその方法を考察するのに何ページも割く。「震えるような絵の具の染み」[10]がわずかな数でもあればそれを摑みとることはできる。だがそのときこの重要な課題を前にして震えているのは、むしろ彼の感受性なのである。その描法を習得しようとする人々に、ラスキンはある訓練法を提案する。まず大きなたらいを用意したら、そこにプルシアン・ブルー〔＝紺青〕の溶液を溶いた水を張る。さらにその水面にくるみの殻のかけら（ホーンがいう破片あるいはごみ屑としての脚註のようなものだ）をいくつか落とし、それを浮かべたまま光のもとでかき混ぜ、その方向に応じて水面の反射に起こる変化をよく研究しなさい、というのである。もちろんここに美術アカデミー流の訓練法を読み取ることもできるだろう。だがラスキンの細部に注ぐ愛情の強さ、そして水面に落ちた光の交錯のひとつひとつまで見逃すまいとする欲望の強さには、なにかわたしたちを釘づけにするものがある。それはホーンに劣らず強烈な水への偏愛（ハイドロフィリア）ではないか。もっともわたしの想像では、ラスキンはホーンと違って水に入りたいとは思わなかったろうけれど（「温かなお湯、思い出、エロティックな小説や絵——はほぼ同じものだ」とはホーンがアイスランドの温泉について書いたことだ[11]）。

　冒頭でも述べたが、彼女のガラスに対する関心はドローイングの簡素さに比べて驚くほど官能的なものであるように感じられる。ガラスの色彩というのは独特で、外部からそれを照らす光の効果にことごとく左右されながら、そういった状況を丸ごと呑み込んで自らのものにもしてしまう。色彩とはよく美術にあって最大の表現力を持つ要素だと思われているが（それは美という感情の芳香を湛えている）、ホーンの作品で際立っているのはその色彩の用法が、表現のための言語としてそれを用いることからみごとに分離しているところだ。彼女の作品では、色彩はもっと天気のような役割を果たしている。それはまた天気のようにさまざまな物語を伝え、あるいは「あなたのことを教えてくれる」。《無題（ジョージア）》（2005年）の色彩はまさに目まぐるしく変わり、それが連想させるものも同様にすばやく切り替わる。あるときにはそれは液状の溶岩だが、つぎの瞬間にはもう赤錆の侵食である。透明ガラス製の透き通った円柱状の塊は側面に砂吹き加工（サンドブラスト）を施されたかのようで、それによって不透明と半透明のあいだを行き来する最小限のグラデーションを奏でる——まるで巨大なレンズのようだ。ホーンが「黒い水は黒いミルクだ」[12]と記すとき、その毒性の含意は死へ、そしてナチスの強制収容所へと転じる（パウル・ツェランの謳った「明け方の黒いミルクぼくたちはそれを晩に飲む」[13]という一行に切り替わる）。けれどそれなら「ミルクのような黒」のほうがむしろ《無題（イエス）》[fig.10]の色彩の効果を説明するにはうってつけだろう。ルートヴィヒ・ウィトゲンシュタインならそれを「輝く灰色」と同じだから、そして一種のカテゴリー錯誤（ミステイク）だから、概念上は存在するはずのないものだと考えたかもしれないが。[14]ある意味ではウィトゲンシュタインの言うとおりだけれど、じっさいにそれこそがわたしたちの見るものなのだ。黒いミルクとミルクのような黒は、わたしたちが思うほどにかけ離れているわけではないのかもしれないし、あるいはやはりかけ離れているのかもしれない。いずれにせよ色彩によって、わたしたちはこういった矛盾のうちに棲まうのである。

　ひとたびそれがわかれば、熱心に書き込まれたいくつかの註釈と同じくらいに色彩が気にかかってくるし、紙の地にふりそそぐ微かな鉛筆の線や色彩も、ガラスやそのほかの素材と同じように官能的なものになりうる。ときにはまず気づかないような要素が、わたしたちをふと立ち止まらせる。たとえば艶やかなガラス面に落ちる光の効果や、同じ表面に思いがけずできてしまった極小の傷には厳しすぎるくらいの精度があって、とくにこの傷は

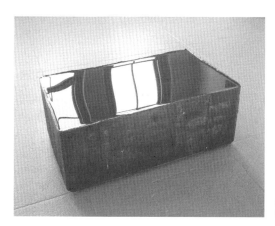

fig.10：《無題（イエス）》2001年、ディア・アート・センター（ニューヨーク）での展示風景　鋳造ガラス、43.2×73.7×122.2cm　個人蔵、バーゼル

特定の光のもとでとてつもない乱流を起こす効果を発揮する。けれどそんな効果も少し光が変わればまったく現れることはない。ガラスの表面は見る角度に応じて剃刀のような切れ味を発揮することもあれば、無限の深さを湛えることもある。そしてある瞬間には、ガラスの表面はあの床に敷かれた《ペアになった黄金のマット──ロスとフェリックスのために》(1994年)のように金箔と同じくらい薄く、きらめいているように見える。しかしまたべつの瞬間にはガラスは完全に透明になる。知覚に起こるこの変化を見てとることはできない。唯一それが見えるのは、不意にある種の表面が見えないままに別種の表面へと切り替わるときの効果としてだけである。なるほどガラスの表面の奥底を覗いてみることはできる。だがそのあと突然光が変わり、ガラスの内側にはなにもなくなる──ただ一枚の表面と外界を反映した輝きが残るだけなのだ。ふたつの状態のあいだを横切る線はあまりに微かで、知覚上はもはや存在しない。だがわたしたちの経験こそが、ほんの一瞬そこにひびを入れる。

　ここで断片化のことを、あるいは精神分析の諸理論にいう部分対象（パート・オブジェクト）や、ジークムント・フロイトが固く信じていた「分身は不気味なものだ」という考えのことを話題にしてみれば、議論も落ち着くのかもしれない。少なくともそれで用語がひとつ、それから文脈がひとつ得られる。けれどホーンの場合、そこまで断片というわけではない。この断片たちが精神の動揺を引き出すこともあるが、それでもとくに不気味ということはない。大ぶりなドローイングのひとつひとつは、2、3、あるいは4つの版＝板（プレート）を再調整して合体させたもので、まるで大きすぎて調整しようにも手に負えない電気回路を納めた箱のようだ。結果として得られるのはひとつの全体からの一部分ではない。逆にすべてはそこにあり、すべては紙の板なのだが、それがさまざまに異なったしかたでまとめ上げられている。描き損じはあるにしてもごくわずかだ。あたかもそこからはなにも失われていないかのようだが、統一感は例外だ。ここで失われるのはたぶん分割された時間の一部であって、このパズルを構成する物理的な部分ではない。このようにホーンのドローイングの制作過程はすべて明らかなのだが、しかしそれは見えはしていても読み解けはしないのだ。記憶とは一部を選び出して作られるだけでなく、穴だらけでもある。1949年、タル・コアットという芸術家をめぐるジョルジュ・デュテュイとの対話を、サミュエル・ベケットはこう説くところから始めている。「完全な対象を、部分的な対象の代わりに失くした部分をかき集めて作り上げるんだ。程度の問題ではあるけれど」。[15]「失くした部分をかき集めて作り上げる」とはホーンの作品を説明しているようでもある。謎めいていようがじっさいそういう作品なのだ。それはすべてを呑み込む完全な対象という感覚を捉えてはいるものの、そのときこの対象は同時にいくつかの点では扱いがたく、したがっていつも不完全である。このようにあらゆるものごとをたやすく、すみやかに運ぶことを拒む以上、わたしたちは速度を落としてじっくり考えなければならない。このかそけき手がかりを手放さないために。それでいい、それはそういうものだよね、という理解のしかたにはなにか幸福に満ちたものがある。

fig.11: クリス・マルケル (1921–2012)、『サン・ソレイユ』1983年
35mm、カラー、白黒、音声：100分　配給：アルゴ・フィルム、スイイ＝シュル＝セーヌ、フランス

fig.12:《水、選ばれた》2007年
氷河から採取した水を満たした24本のガラスの柱　柱の直径：各30.5cm、高さ：各279.4cm、
全体：約457㎥　ヴァトナサフン（水の図書館）（スティッキスホールムル、アイスランド）に恒久設置

アイスランド効果

　　なにかを失くしている、というのは美しいユートピアの定義ですね。なにかが失くなっていればそれは不
　　完全だということですか？ それとも、なにか失くしたものがあるからこそ、それは完全だということでしょうか？ [16]
　　　——ロニ・ホーン

だれもがユートピアについて、こんな考えを抱いているわけではない。

　ユートピア〔＝理想郷；原義は「どこにもない場所」〕というのはふつう、失くした部分をなにか満たされたイメージで置き換えたり、あるいは少なくともそれで代用したり埋め合わせたりするものだ。ユートピアこそがみごとに歴史に残る過誤や社会的不平等、あるいは心理的な傷（トラウマ）をもたらす。いつでもそれはよりよい未来の方向を見失った現在を離れて、どこに進むべき道があるかを考える方法だった（そしてよく昔はよかった、というような想像上の過去に重ね合わせられてきた）。ホーンがそれとなく示しているのは、完全ななにかというのはすでに失くしてしまったものも含めて、部分を集めて作られるということだ。これはベケットの言う完全な対象という観念に近い。ただ彼はそれをユートピアとは呼ばなかった。むしろ彼はユートピアという理念の挫折を言葉にした世代の人間であり、それは先行する20世紀初期の歴史的なアヴァンギャルドたちが、この理念をテクノロジーの面でも心理の面でも自分たちの思い描いた夢の国（ドリームランド）に投影していたからだった。このときもともと信仰があった場所に代わって置かれたのは不条理であり、よりよいなにかへの希求があった場所に置かれたのは薄寒い虚無だった。そしてこの虚無の空間こそがスミッソンのような芸術家にはほとんど悦楽をもたらすものへと転じ、そのとき彼は完全な崩壊に向かう風景という、あのディストピア的な夢想に取り憑かれたのである。わたしが本稿のはじめで説いたことの一部を繰り返せば、ホーンの作品はスミッソンよりはジャッドに、〔スミッソンがよく作品を制作した場所である〕ユカタンよりはマーファに、多くを負っている。というのも彼女は、初期のアヴァンギャルドの芸術家たちが抱いていた理想的なモデルに対して、たとえばベケットやスミッソンが（それは長いあいだ）唯一これなら対抗できると考えて選び取った批評的な視点から、さらに根本的（ラディカル）に決別しているからだ。かわりに彼女の作品はまた別に可能なものの地平を示す。それも一種のユートピアだ、とわたしは思うのだが、しかし一度ディストピアを経由してから舞い戻ってきたユートピアなのだ。

　アイスランドとは彼女にとってたんなる場所ではなく、ひとつの理念である。《ブラフ・ライフ》とは異なって、わたしが議論してきた彼女の大ぶりのドローイング作品がアイスランドではなくニューヨークのアトリエで制作されたのは事実だが、それもこの主張の論理を損なうものではない。芸術とは、ユートピアに近似しながらしかしそれとは一致することのないひとつの理念なのだ。というよりそれはたぶん、距離を置いて現れた分身によく似ている。ホーンはアイスランドをわたしのオズの国と呼ぶ。これによってわたしは彼女がアイスランドを理想化していると言いたいわけではない。ただそれをきめて的確に位置づけた、と言いたいのである。彼女の制作の背景にある地質学の視点から、アイスランドが占める場所はどのように定められたのかを思うとき、わたしはクリス・マルケルが「時の脆さ」をめぐって1983年に制作した素晴らしい映画、『サン・ソレイユ〔＝太陽のないところで〕』と題された一作を思い出す［**fig.11**］。忘れられないのは東京とカーボベルデ諸島という対になったふたつの場所を結びつけるこの映画が、どの場所から始めてどの場所で終わることもできるということだ。つまりアイスランドから始まっても、あるいはそこで終わってもかまわない。幕開け早々、まだ作品のタイトルも示されないうちに登場するごく短いくだり（シークエンス）は、陽光に照らされた三人の子供たちがたがいに手を取りあい、道に沿って歩いてゆくところだ。そこに女性のナレーターの声が重なる。ひとりの写真家の物語を、わたしたちはこれから聞くことになるのだという。この写真家はずっと前にこの幸せに満ちた映像を撮影していながら、それを別のフィルムと組み合わせようとして果たせなかった。まったくうまく収まらないからだ。そこでこの映像はここに加えられることになった。これから始まる映画のちょっとした前日譚のように、後続する数秒間の暗転の前に置かれ、さらにそのあと続く残りのフィルム全体から切り離されたのだ。このアイスランドの映像は、ナレーターがさらに語るところによれば「胸がときめくもののリスト」のひとつに含まれていた。映像の推移とそれが展開する場所はある時間、あるいはある場

所に対する欲望をくっきりと描き出す。けれどそれがいつなのか、あるいはどこなのかははっきりしない。

　ホーンのアイスランドとは、つかの間のイメージや失われた対象をはるかに上回るなにかである。それは郷愁（ノスタルジア）や憂鬱（メランコリー）よりもむしろ欲望によって燃え上がり、また欲望を燃え上がらせる。彼女がアイスランドで制作してきた作品は、西端にあるスティッキスホールムルという小さな街で最近制作された《ヴァトナサフン（水の図書館）》の作品（2007年）のように、その場所と住民たちへの愛着をよく示している。24ヶ所の氷河から水を集めてきた彼女は何本もの透き通ったガラスの柱にそれを収めたあと、さらにかつての図書館を転用した建物の内部に並べた[**fig.12**]。ゴム製の床には天気を表す用語が英語とアイスランド語で刻まれており、彼女はそれを二ヵ国語（バイリンガル）のドローイングと呼ぶ。「おだやかな」とか「荒れた」とか、「蒸し蒸しする」といった単語が、天気を記述するものとして二度繰り返される。ホーンはこの作品を灯台になぞらえ、見る者はその光に照らされるのだと言う。けれどそれはまたある種の巨大な光学機器のようにも作用して、歪曲レンズとなった列柱はそこに残留あるいは沈殿した物とまったく同じように、ばらばらの断片となった室内の眺めを切り取ってみせる。その断片に見えるのは水の内部、つまりわたしたち自身の内側であり、そして、水の外部である。

　《水の図書館》は、広々した窓の向こうに一望できる港の風景へと開けたインスタレーション作品だとはいっても、そこに入る体験は少しだけ、彼女のドローイング作品へと入るそれに似ている。作品がそこからばらばらに分かれてゆくと思われるまさにその点——紙に入った切れ目にせよ、インスタレーションで視野に入ったそれにせよ——がまた、作品の各部を統合し、さらにわたしたちをその作品にかそけく、そして執拗に繋ぎ止める。偶然とは思えないが、ホーンのドローイング作品の題名はそのじつに多くがごく短い単語である。しかも「too〔…もまた〕」、「was〔それは…だった〕」、そして「were〔それらは…だった〕」といった、ひとつの文（センテンス）を内部から繋ぎとめるのに用いられるような単語なのだ。これらの単語はまた多くの場合、言語の内部で時制全体の変化を、ということは潜在的には莫大な時間の推移を決定する最小単位でもある。題名中の語は、言うまでもないがほかの諸要素とまったく同様に彼女の作品を構成する一部であり、さらには切断と接合——連続ではなく隣接の論理だ——の徴候である。そしてこの切断と接合こそが作品全体を統合する。つまり収まりの悪さこそそれが収まりをつける方法なのだ。それも、完璧に。

終章（コーダ）

　フランス語、ロシア語、そして英語でタイトルが画面に入ってきて、ようやく『サン・ソレイユ』は本格的に幕を開ける。場所はアイスランドではない、日本だ。冒頭の場面は北海道、つまり日本の最北にある島を発って本州へと向かうフェリー船を舞台に始まる。この日は重い雲が垂れ込めていて、本州も遠く霧のなかに溶けている。画面からは湿った空気が感じられる。先ほどの前奏曲（プレリュード）のフィルムに登場した陽射しのなかの子供たちの姿はすでになく、はかない記憶と化している。かわって画面に登場するのはもっと年嵩（としかさ）の日本人女性たちで、船のデッキに出てたがいに話しかけながら、はるか遠方を見つめている。しかしなにを見ているのか、そして見

fig.13：クリス・マルケル、『サン・ソレイユ』1983年
35mm、カラー、白黒、音声：100分
配給：アルゴ・フィルム、ヌイイ＝シュル＝セーヌ、フランス

えているのはからっぽの空間か、海か、あるいはその両方か、いずれにしてもそれはさして重要ではない。海越しに遠くを見ている彼女たちをさらに見ることに、どこか引き込まれるものがあるのだ。島から島へと移るように海を渡る船の航路はやがて中断され、この女性たちがフレームの外を覗き込むとき、彼女たちもそこから切り離されたままの、ある時間の流れに棲まうことになる。また別の失くした部分だ、そう言ってもよい。

ロニ・ホーンの作品を見ることは、少しだけ水を眺めることに似ている。それは水を眺めることがぼんやりとした体験だからではなく、むしろなにかを眺める技術に磨きをかけるよう強いてくるものだからである。水はたえず変化し、また進化する。この芸術家はこう書きつけている。「わたしが何度も何度も立ち返る水をめぐるひとつの逆説は、どれほどそれに近くまた親しんだとしても、つねになじみのないものとして現れてくるということだ…水というのはどこまでも摑みどころのない、恒久的な関係を超えた状態にあるものなのだ」。[17] この言葉は「水という／鉱石の簡潔な独白」[18] とそれを説明したイギリスの詩人、アリス・オズワルドにこだまする。ホーンにとって水はさまざまな様態をとりながら、つねに自作に現れるものである。たとえばそれはアイスランドの温泉の水蒸気であり、やがて流動と循環とに分類されながら、水彩によるドローイングの液状性へと至る。けれど彼女はそこに括弧に入れてこう付け加える。「（水を見るというがそのときほんとうはなにを見ているのか、わかったものではない）」。[19] 水紋を、その流れを見ようと視線を調整するということは、じっさいにはその動きを警戒することだ。短い通り雨、波立つ水路、水管の通過、渦巻、引き波。こうやって水を眺めていると、天気を見るように少し緊張する思いをすることもあるけれど、そのさきに彼女が「わたしのオズ」と呼んだものも、そしてそこにある自由の可能性も、垣間見ることができるはずだ。[20]

ホーンはまた時間をその作品の潜入捜査員（アンダーカヴァー）として導き入れる。大文字の‘T’で始まるTime〔時間〕ではないが、わずかな迂回路を、あるいは隠し通路を通ってそこに辿り着いた時間だ。そのひとつの方法が先行するドローイングや版画のめった斬りと再編成（カットアップ）であり、またそれを独自のしかたで元に戻しつつ変形することである。どちらも彼女がどうやって多数のドローイングを制作しているかはもちろん、延々とかかるその制作過程に含まれる複雑な時間の性質についても率直に説き明かしてくれる。それはホーンがいつもアイスランド内の同じ場所に戻るのを習慣にしていることに、喩えることができる——あるいはその延長？にあるのかもしれない。彼女はこうも書いている。「それを必要としていることはもうわたしの一部なのだ」と[21]。彼女はどんな天気のときもアイスランドに戻ってくるし、だからこの島も霧や靄越しにそのつど異なる部分を見せてくれる——そして彼女の作品に戻れば、それは状況や文脈の変化に敏感であり、さらに言ってみればその変化に晒されている。つまり「時の脆さ（ヴァルネラブル）」に対しても傷つきやすいと同時にしなやか（レジリエント）なのである。[22]

《火山現象》（1990／2014年）のシリーズでは、初期の地図を用いたドローイングや《トゥー・プレイス：ブラフ・ライフ》（1990年）から採られた版画の一群が複雑な方法で切断され、相互に織り込まれている（pp.78-83）[23]。これは彼女が《ほか》（4：2009年／9：2010年、pp.148-149）のようなスケールの大きなドローイングを制作するにあたり、何年ものあいだ使ってきた方法だ。同じ方法を彼女はそこから派生した紙の作品のシリーズ、《ハック・ウィット》でも用いている。この作品は日常会話にありふれた言い回しや慣用句、あるいは引用を二つ重ね合わせて貼り、慣れ親しんだ意味を破壊するとともに新しい意味の組み合わせを創造する作品である。「蛤（はまぐり）のように幸せ〔「最高に幸せ」の意〕」とか「空中を歩く〔「うきうきする」の意〕」といった言葉がつなぎ合わされ「空中の蛤を歩くように幸せ」という一節になったり、「キュウリのように冷たく〔「落ち着いて」の意〕」と「不在は心を深く掘り下げる〔「会えない時間が想いを強くする」の意〕」が合成され、また一部が入れ替わって、「不在のように冷たい」と「キュウリは心を深く掘り下げる」という一節がそれぞれ生まれたりする。ほかにも言葉の切れ端のもっとも薄い部分に入った切り込みが、ときには判読不可能な地点に至るまでそれを解体する。[24]《北極圏の自信》（v.1：pp.82-83／v.2、1990／2016）では、あたかもドローイングは地質学的な意味でのその土地の岩盤が移動する場であるかのようだ（pp.78-83）。これらはコラージュ〔collage；フランス語の原義は「糊付け」〕による作品だが、それは文字通り糊がそこに用いられているからではなくて、さまざまな様相や実体が予想外の方法でたがいにくっついたようになっているからである。しかも、そしてこちらがたぶんより重要だが、それら様相や実体はホーンがアイスランドについてそう記した意味において「べったりくっついてる」。彼女が言おうとしているのは、アイスランドはたんに人をある場所に繋ぎ止めるのではなく、むしろ人にべったりと貼り付く、ということなのである。[25]

シリーズはさらにシリーズを生んでゆく。しかもそれぞれが——紙の作品だけでなく彫刻でも——たがいに接

続しあい、さらにそのあいだにも他所参照はつぎつぎ増殖してゆく。十字砲火に囲まれたように思われた作品の題名たちにしても、その残骸はどこかで息を吹き返すことになるのだ。語、つまり言語活動の素材となる単位は、いつでもホーンに日常会話の周辺を掘り下げつつ偶然にしたがって用語を探り当てる手段をもたらしてきた。典型的な皮肉交じりのものとしては「ハック・ウィット」がある。これは「三流記者」という意味を持つ名詞の「ハック〔hack〕」と、高熱のトーチで金属を焼き切るとか、コンピューター・システムに不法に侵入するという意味を持つ、動詞の「ハック〔hack〕」を合成ででっち上げた職業について説明する手がかりになってくれる。そして「機智〔wit〕」という語のほうにも、ひとを楽しませるというだけでなく痛烈だったり辛辣だったりする意味もある。[26] シリーズや個々の作品の題名が言葉による説明を与えてくれるわけではないし、まして図像が持つ意味内容や主題を示してくれるわけでもない。むしろこうした言語のちいさなかけらたちは、作品の素材という役割を担っている。引用や格言をどこかで見つけてきた素材として——そして多くは括弧でくくって——用いることも、作品を貫く論理のうちに保たれている。口語による言い回しや常套句も、あまりに身近になってしまえばあとは陳腐になるだけだ。使いすぎればその言い回しや常套句の意味も空っぽになる。そして反復は、そんな言葉を合挽肉にし、またかしこまった言葉遣いや使い古されたお馴染みの格言をごった煮にする。その過程で穏当と思われていた表現もひとを不安に陥れたり、ときには邪悪でさえあるような裏側を露呈する。どれも愉快なものではないが、かといってそこに教訓的な意味があるわけでもない。

　シリーズや組作品が経済的なのは反復が元になっているからである。生成する形態にも解体に向かうそれにもこの反復が用いられるが、その経済性がたえず移り変わる全体に関連してたえず移り変わる部分をいつでも駆動し、ホーンがこの40年以上ものあいだ作り続けてきた作品の総体を駆り立てている。まったく同じことの繰り返しは最大限まで変化形の数を増やし、いっぽう各シリーズはさらに複数のかたちに変化して、それ自体から多数の異なる版を生み出してゆく。これを明白に示すものとして、今回ポーラ美術館で展示されるガラス彫刻にまさるものはない (pp.50-58)。この作品はどれもみな高さ11インチ×直径48インチ〔27.9×直径121.9cm〕と同じ大きさの背の低い円筒形で、ずっしりとした鋳造ガラス製であるところも同じだが、色が違う。ひとつは黒、ひとつは透明、そしてほかはいずれも一点の曇りもない、淡いピンクや黄色、緑といった色を与えられている。これはこの組み合わせと正式に決定されているわけではなくて、それぞれが単独で作品として成立しているものをひとつの単位として集めて作り上げたものである。ガラスの鋳造はかなり複雑な工程を経るので、極小の気泡にせよ表面に吹いた緑青の皮膜の質感の変化にせよ、同じ効果はけっして生まれてこない。淡い色はアグネス・マーティンの後期作品における色遣いを思わせ、知覚可能なニュアンスの範囲を拡大する。わたしたちのほうが時間をかけて、そうした微かなちがいでも気づけるようにと知覚を調整しなおすからだ。

　ずっしりとしたガラスの塊として鋳造されることによって、ホーンの彫刻はわたしたちの視野をマーティンの絵画とはまた違ったしかたで圧倒する。ただホーンの場合その方法は、周囲の環境に依拠してもいる。照明や天候の状況に左右されることで、多かれ少なかれその存在を消したり示したりできるのである。同じ彫刻があるときにはほとんどそこから消えてしまったり、あるいはまたべつのときには灯台の光のようにひとを引き寄せる、光を取り込んだ罠になったりする。床に低く横たわるそれらガラスの塊は、自らを主張するような彫刻とは対極にあり、むしろためらいがちにわたしたちの視野をよぎりながら広がってゆく。わたしたちはふとそれと出会う。すると作品のほうが**わたしたちに**沁みこんでくる。見下ろしてその中を覗き込むときの感覚は、ついで光輝く水溜まりを思い出させる。まるで水を眺めているときのように、周囲の眺めがそこに映し出されたまま囚われる。観客の注意はある種の空白といっそう不確かになった観察結果のあいだを、そして表面を見ることと深みを見ることのあいだを往還する。

　《無題》と題されたそれぞれのガラス彫刻には、カッコに入った引用の小片がまるで付属装置のように接続されている。ガラスの色彩は繊細で段階的に変わり、ひとつがごくわずかだがほかに比べて透き通ったかと思えば、ひとつがほかよりもわずかに明るくなったり暗くなったりする。ある作品 (pp.50-51) ではものものしい引用文中の語句が、純然たる官能的な美しさを湛えた肌理細かなガラス面に刻み込まれている。もとは真円形の透明なガラスの全面に磨り加工が施されているかのようなのだが、それよりその引用文はチェルノブイリ、つまりウクライナ国内（当時はソヴィエト連邦領内）にある、1986年に原子力発電所が爆発事故を起こした場所のことを記述している。「ビニールですっぽりおおわれた雌牛」というのがそこにこびりついた言葉だ。死を仄めかすも

のが欲望の場面に持ち込まれている。どこまでも淡い黄色——曙光の予兆に満ちた——は突然に光を失い、不穏な気配を湛え始める。黄色は地図中の放射能汚染地域の色を思わせるからだ。牛とビニールもひとたび心に刻まれれば、たとえ作品という物理的な実体から取り除かれたとしても、記憶からは拭いがたいものになる。放射能はまた危険なもの、希望を打ち砕くものともなりうる。ツェランの「黒いミルク」もチェルノブイリの撒き散らした放射能の霜を被って黄変してしまった。それは環境を、そしてこの惑星をあまねく覆う災害の予兆であり、まさにいまもわたしたちはその災害の掌中にある。

　ある彫刻の状況しだいで変わる部分というのは、徹底して逆説的であるとは言わないまでもそもそも不安定である。ホーンの作品の題名も——ほんの一部分だが——ちょっとした打ち明け話のようなもので、屈折変化していたり、なにかの仄めかしだったりする。いずれにしてもなにかをまとめあげるというよりは脱線させるのがふつうだ。霜の降りたようなピンクのガラス彫刻はたとえば導火線の紙のようなもので、その場所の気配や歌の一節、周囲に近い将来起こりうる事件に繋がっている（pp.50-51）。括弧に収められた断章「必要なニュースはすべて天気予報から手に入れる」は、有名でよくカヴァーもされるサイモン＆ガーファンクルの歌、『ニューヨークの少年』[27]から採った一節であるだけでなく、彼女自身の少し前の作品、《天気があなたのことを教えてくれる》（2006年）のことを示してもいる。1994年から95年にかけて制作された彼女の独創的な写真のシリーズ《あなたは天気》では、若いアイスランド人女性の顔が、火山性の温泉が発散する湯気によって見え隠れしており、彼女が見えるか見えないかは完全に水蒸気の濃度にかかっている。つまりお湯の熱さが空気の冷たさとどう出会うかにかかっているのだ。巨大なピンクのガラス・レンズは光を吸収もすれば発散もするが、実体として見れば展示室を一周する写真のシリーズとは明らかにまったく別種のものだ——だがどちらの作品もきっと、周囲を取り囲む環境や大気の条件へとそれら作品が晒されていることを、劇的に示している。

　《鳥葬（箱根）》（2017-2018年、pp.182-184）という重さ5トンのガラス単体の作品は全体に白く霜が降りたようであり、ポーラ美術館とともに国立公園に立つ、完全に天候と自然の力の慈悲のもとにあるような作品だ。ホーンはこのグループに属する作品を2013年から制作しており、それぞれ設置されている場所は異なるものの、いずれもチベットの葬送の儀式のことを示している。この儀式では山頂に置かれた死者の体はしだいに腐敗して大地に帰ってゆく。鋳造ガラスによるずっしりとした塊もまた、気温の変動に晒されたりゆっくりと風雪に濯がれたりすることで、時とともにわずかずつ崩壊してゆくことだろう。つまりエントロピーの法則に従って衰亡してゆくことはたしかなのだが、じっさいそれまでにどれだけの時間を要するかは、それぞれが置かれた場所の生態系や、その素材に気候が与える影響の大小に左右されるだろうから、事前にはわからない。けれどそれよりさきに《鳥葬》のような作品は気圧計（バロメーター）として作動する。つまり気圧や湿度、そして気温に鋭く反応するのである。それはちょうどこの作品の溶けて輝くような上面部分が、周囲の空や木々を映し出すのと同じことだ。そして鬱蒼とした森林地帯に立てば、それは地表面にひそかに置かれた道標のように光を集めるだろう。重苦しい曇天下に生じる最小限の光にも反応し、ひとたび陽射しを捉えれば劇的なまでに輝き始める。それ自体が光る点として、また方位を示す点として、《鳥葬》は奇妙なことにわたしたちをディルホゥラエイの灯台へと、そしてホーンが1982年以降の《ブラフ・ライフ》のためのドローイングに描いた、苔や地衣類へと連れ戻す。そのあいだにある、そう感じられる時間もどういうわけかどこかへ行ってしまった。

　野心的な芸術というものは、すでに知っていることを確かめるというよりは、違ったふうに考え、感じることをわたしたちに要求する。ホーンの作品では思考様式の変化は——視野に起こる小さな変動のように——微かなものだがやがて大きくなってゆく。この芸術を打ち立てるだけの場所は必要だが、それはその意味をすべて詳らかにし、わたしたちにもわかるよう整理して示すためではない。40年にわたってホーンという芸術家が生み出してきた作品の本体にあって、時間こそが彼女にとって最大の媒体（メディウム）だということを、その場所が明るみに出しているからだ。読者は覚えているだろうか。マルグリット・デュラスはたった一晩前に観た映画について、自分がそこで観たものはなんだったのかと問いかける。けれどどうだろう、もし一夜ではなく、何ヵ月とか何年も先、あるいは何十年も先に同じことを問うと考えてみたら？ ロニ・ホーンが自身の作品に組み込んできた一時的な回帰や遅延、そして不確かさによって、わたしたちは、そんなふうに時代を超え、そして各時代を通じて散りばめられたさまざまな部分が集まって、ひとつの巨大ななにかを構成しているのでは、という問いに思いを馳せられるようになる。部分たちを散り散りにしてはまた集めるという彼女のやりかたは、けっして滑らかに前へ進んでゆくことはなく、い

つでも不揃いでむらのあるものだ。自ら引き返すこともありうるし、邪魔もたくさん入るだろう。それでも彼女の作品がたえず進展しているからこそ、その作品の〈いつ〉、そして〈どこ〉もたえず問いに付される──言わば、不確かさそのものをまさに土台として、失くした部分たちの倫理が打ち立てられるのである。

（ユニヴァーシティ・カレッジ・ロンドン教授〔美術史〕）

［翻訳：林 卓行（はやし・たかゆき）］

［原著者註］
この小論の第一部はもともとアメリカ、ホイットニー美術館での『ロニ・ホーンまたの名をロニ・ホーン』（2009年）展のカタログ（シュタイデル出版刊）に掲載されたものである。今回ポーラ美術館での展覧会（2021年）のために「終章」を加筆した。

［訳者註］
訳註は最小限にとどめ、本文中に〔　〕によって示した。また引用された文章のうち既訳のあるものについては参照し、その典拠を示した。各引用文の原訳者諸氏に感謝申し上げる。なお本文に合わせて訳文を一部変更したところがある。

1　Roni Horn in *Art and Architecture*, James Ackerman et al. (Marfa, Texas: Chinati Foundation, 2000), p. 70.
2　Claude Lévi-Strauss, *Tristes Tropiques* (1955; repr., London: Penguin, 1976), p. 437.（クロード・レヴィ＝ストロース、『悲しき熱帯』（Ⅱ）、川田順造訳、中央公論新社、2001年、265ページ）
3　Robert Smithson in *Robert Smithson: The Collected Writings*, ed. Jack D. Flam (Berkeley: University of California Press, 1996), pp. 7–9, 100–113.
4　Vija Celmins "Interview with Ann Seymour" in *Vija Celmins: Drawings of the Night Sky*, Anthony D'Offay (London: Phaidon, 2003).
5　Alex Potts, *The Sculptural Imagination: Figurative, Modernist, Minimalist* (New Haven: Yale University Press, 2000), p.209.
6　Lévi-Strauss, p. 68.（レヴィ＝ストロース、『悲しき熱帯』（Ⅰ）、82ページ）
7　Joseph Conrad, *The Shadow-Line: A Confession* (New York: Vintage 2007), p.101.（ジョウゼフ・コンラッド「シャドウ・ライン」、『シャドウ・ライン 秘密の共有者』、田中勝彦訳、八月社、2005年、101ページ）
8　Paul Celan, *Snow part/Schneepart*, trans. Ian Fairley (Manchester, England: Carcanet Press, 2007), pp. 14–15.（パウル・ツェラン、「雪の声部」、『パウル・ツェラン全詩集 第Ⅱ巻』、中村朝子訳、2012年、565ページ）
9　Roni Horn, *To Place: Pooling Waters*, 2 Vols. (Cologne: Walther-König, 1994), p.23.
10　John Ruskin, *The Elements of Drawing* (1857; repr., London: George Allen, 1902).
11　Roni Horn in *Art and Architecture*, James Ackerman et al., p.64.
12　Roni Horn, *Another Water (The River Thames, for Example)* (London: Scalo, 2000), n.p.
13　Paul Celan, "Death Fugue", *Poems of Paul Celan*, trans. Michael Hamburger (New York: Persea, 2002), p.31.（パウル・ツェラン「死のフーガ」、『パウル・ツェラン全詩集 第Ⅲ巻』中村朝子訳、2012年、110ページ）この詩との関連についてわたしに話してくれたマーク・ゴドフリーに感謝する。
14　Ludwig Wittgenstein, *Remarks on Color* (Oxford: Basil Blackwell, 1977), p.7.（ルードウィヒ・ウィトゲンシュタイン、『色彩について』、中村昇、瀬嶋貞徳訳、新書館、1917年、30ページ）
15　Samuel Beckett and Georges Duthuit, *Three Dialogues* (1965; repr., London: John Calder, 1999), p. 101.
16　Hans Ulrich Obrist, *Interviews* (Florence: Charta/Fondazione Pitti Immagine Discovery, 2003).
17　Roni Horn, interview with James Lingwood, *Some Thames*, Steidl, 2003 as cited under 'Water' in *Roni Horn aka Roni Horn* (Göttingen: Steidl; New York: Whitney Museum of American Art, 2009), p.165.
18　Alice Oswald, *Nobody* (Cape Poetry, Jonathan Cape, 2019), p.63.
19　Roni Horn *Still Water*, 1999, as extracted in *Roni Horn aka Roni Horn*, op. cit. p.165.
20　ロニ・ホーンはアイスランドを長い間「わたしのオズ」と考えているが、これはジュディ・ガーランド主演の映画版に登場する、「虹の彼方に」ある極彩色のユートピアを想起させる。ホーンはかつてレイキャビク大学での講演で、彼女の作品に気候が果たす役割と、どうやってそれをアイスランドで見出したかを語っている。「天気こそがわたしたち人間の生活にとって重要なのです…もうただの会話のきっかけですませられるような、単純な問題ではありません」。これは気候〔の変動〕が今日のように大きなニュースになるずっと前のことだ。(Roni Horn, *Island Zombie Iceland Writings* (Princeton and Oxford: Princeton University Press, 2020), p.127).
21　Roni Horn, *ibid*, p.1.
22　クリス・マルケル『サン・ソレイユ』(1983年)。この映画のナレーションはフロランス・ドゥレイによる。
23　二重になった日付はこの一時的な二重性をよく示している。一面にわたるその文字の「下敷き」になっているのは版画作品《ブラフ・ライフ》の特別版である。
24　わたしは別のところで 'More War: The Disaster Series' シリーズでのロニ・ホーンのドローイングに対する取り組みについても書いている。以下を参照。'More War: The Disaster Series' in Roni Horn, *Dogs' Chorus*, (Göttingen: Steidl, 2019) and in 'Words in the Wild'.
25　Roni Horn, 'An Adhesive Feeling', *Island Zombie*, op cit, p. 89.
26　この《ハック・ウィット》のシリーズについては、詩人のアンヌ・カーソンがつぎのようなすばらしい反応を返している。Anne Carson, 'Hack Gloss' in Roni Horn, *Hack Wit* (Göttingen: Steidl, 2015).
27　サイモン＆ガーファンクル『ニューヨークの少年〔原題：The Only Living Boy in New York〕』はポール・サイモンが作詞作曲して1970年に発売された一曲。アルバム『明日に架ける橋』に収録されている。エヴリシング・バット・ザ・ガールも1993年にこの曲をカヴァーした。またテナーズによるこの曲のレゲエ版『天気予報〔Weather Report〕』(1973年) はタイトル部分のフレーズを「故郷にたったひとりの小さな女の子（the only little girl in my hometown）」に変えて歌っている。

Complete with Missing Parts

Briony Fer

In her writings on cinema, Marguerite Duras once said that she only knew what she saw the morning after she had watched a film. In her memory, what she saw on screen took shape in a way it did not as she was actually experiencing it, as if her entire sense of it could be cut in two by a single night. This split could work two ways: a coming together or a falling apart. Maybe it never resolves one way or the other. Or is it possible for an experience that is already hard to contain to become even more unwieldy as you try to recall it in your mind? Using this test, I have only the most tenuous grip on Roni Horn's work. This is not a confession on my part so much as a statement about the work. It is difficult work to hold on to. It can make you feel in danger of losing your grip.

At first this may seem to do with the different kinds of work that Horn makes: how to match the spareness of a drawing, for example, with the sensuality of some of her glass sculpture. But a lot of artists make a lot of different kinds of work in different media. Something else in the experience of the work does not quite allow an opposition between the conceptual and the sensual to be kept in place. Color plays an important role, but it does not work in opposition to drawing. There is an extreme precariousness not only in my hold on it but to what holds it together. Of all the words that might be more effective, more accurate, more resonant, more of a positive *something*, it is the word "tenuous" that keeps coming back, insinuating itself in my attempt at recollection. Tenuous means "slender" or "thin" and seems somehow apt for the kinds of connections that exist between the manifestly different kinds of Horn's work as well as the feeling they instill. If I have a tenuous grip on reality, I am holding on to it by a hair's breadth. That is a very powerful experience, not a negligible one. A pencil mark that is hardly there or a translucent blue glass of incredible intensity can trigger it. The beauty of one might be as much of a decoy as the slightness of other.

To say that I am concentrating on Horn's drawing because it is at the center of what she does sounds as if drawing is somehow the key to all her work, which it is not. (What single element could be?) Her work has been precisely about what it means "to center": oneself, a place, a shape. And whatever a center means, it is not about finding a single revelatory truth. Whatever else she has done, she has always made drawings in her studio or elsewhere. She has compared her practice of drawing to "a kind of breathing vocabulary on a daily level."[1] This sounds like an imperative, as if the most essential impulse is also the most everyday. My aim is simply to concentrate on the drawings in the way I think they demand and to try to understand something about that tenuous grip that endangers me as a viewer of her work.

> I can pick out certain scenes and separate them from the rest; is it this tree,
> this flower? They might well be elsewhere. Is it also a delusion that the whole
> should fill me with rapture, while each part of it, taken separately, escapes me?
> —Claude Lévi-Strauss, *Tristes Tropiques*[2]

In 1982 Horn traveled to Dyrhólaey on the coast of Iceland to spend time by herself
in a remote lighthouse. Much of her work, as is well known, revolves around Iceland
as if art could be a long series of travel notes, charting not only a journey in real
time and space to a particular place but also inside her head. It is not surprising
that she identifies with Emily Dickinson, who only left her home on two occasions
during her life but traveled every day in her mind. A lighthouse is a lookout, but it
is also a solitary place—these two aspects combine in the series of drawings she
made while there called *Bluff Life* (1982). Looking outward is a way of looking inward
and vice versa. I would not call this aspect of fierce self-reflection contemplative,
just as I would not call the kind of looking demanded by Agnes Martin's relentless
pursuit of abstraction contemplative. It sounds too soft when the pursuit of a solitary
existence, whether it is in the desert of New Mexico or in the barren, treeless
Icelandic landscape (another kind of desert), has a concentration about it that makes
Robert Smithson's desert itineraries feel as distracted and freewheeling as they no
doubt were.

The *Bluff Life* drawings are on notepad paper. There are thirteen in all. They
sit at the center of a plain page like geological specimens; of course they are not
observational studies of nature but intricate nests of lines and marks. Three of them
are orange watercolor while the rest are layered black and nearly black graphite, all
slightly different, as if each is its own peculiar mineral deposit. They may not be
images of rock formations, but it is as if the images could be eroded by time and the
elements, the product not so much of the earth's convulsions as the body's rhythms
and pressures leaving their traces.

Geology may not immediately bring to mind the look of Minimal art, let alone
its modular formats, its serial arrangements, or its industrial materials. But it is
worth remembering how Robert Smithson began his essay on Donald Judd, "The
Crystal Land," by invoking their shared interest in geology and their rock-hunting

fig.1: Donald Judd (1928–1994), *100 untitled works in mill aluminum* (detail), 1982–86.
Aluminum, 104.1 × 129.5 × 182.9 cm each. Cinati Foundation, Marfa, Texas

excursions in New Jersey. Then in "The Sedimentation of the Mind," Smithson imagined a multilayered stratification of mental life in a state of entropic disintegration.[3] Smithson's dystopian visions, echoing J. G. Ballard's literary forays into a science fiction where he imagined a whole world in mental breakdown, projects quite a lot on to Judd. On the other hand, the work that Donald Judd made later at Marfa—the vast complex of home and studio and exhibiting space that he converted from a former military base in Texas—has its own very distinctive desert sensibility, one that is acutely responsive to the landscape and, most of all, to the light of that place. Judd's obsession with how to install work in a particular situation led him to think intensely about how the surfaces of his own work, often metallic ones, react to the spectacular lighting of a natural environment [fig. 1].

Judd was one of Horn's first collectors, installing one of her sculptures at Marfa in 1991 [figs. 2 and 3]. She visited him there on several occasions and remembers their conversations comparing the desert to Iceland. When Horn is described, as she often is, as an artist who has worked through a legacy of Minimalism, it is worth stressing how important the Marfa experience of Judd was for her, much more so than Smithson's more hallucinatory musings on passing through such landscapes (without stopping there too long). A bleakly beautiful volcanic landscape like Iceland's, which seems so empty, is full of incident once you adjust to the detail of the place — just as you can adjust to perceive the amplitude of a desert landscape or a nocturnal world once you become accustomed to the dark (Horn took to taking night walks at Dyrhólaey).

Merely formal links or influences are not the point here. Instead, the memory of a certain kind of encounter with Minimal art is built into her work as part of its own psycho-geology, if I can put it that way. One of her glass sculptures, for instance, sits directly on the floor [fig. 4]. It is a rectangular block of cast glass with matte sides and a clear, deep amber interior, refracting and reflecting the light of its surroundings. But it is also *inflected* through multiple and momentarily changing associations to molten lava or iron-tainted water. *Her Eyes* (1999/2005–2007) and *White Dickinsons* (2006–2007), viewed abstractly, are aluminium bars with irregular sequences of white plastic frets, placed horizontally high on the wall, or propped vertically against it. They are barely there at all, yet each is embedded with words. Horn's 2006 *White Dickinson* reads, "the most intangible thing is the most adhesive," which is the first line from one of Emily Dickinson's letters [fig. 5]. However empty an installation of *White Dickinsons* appears, it is still thick with incident, including many word clusters like this one.

figs. 2 and 3: *Things That Happen Again*, 1986 (installation view at Chinati Foundation, Marfa Texas). Two solid copper forms, diameter 29.2–43.2 cm each, length 88.9 cm, each. Judd Foundation

If art history were a form of natural history—and maybe it should be—it would perhaps not seem so odd to make connections between radically diverse examples. It would allow us to link the desert sensibilities of Judd and Martin with an artist like Vija Celmins, whose whole approach to drawing since the 1970s marked out species of natural spaces in ways that relate closely to Horn's work. Celmins once said, "drawing is a dry world," as if the graphite and charcoal that she uses to make her intricate drawings is also a kind of desert to be explored.[4] The attention to the infinitesimal detail of a patch of water or the rubble of a desert floor fills the whole surface of a sheet of paper with her marks [fig. 6]. A complex ground of small rocks and dust is also the ground of drawing. All of this, not in the least the way Celmins's drawing alternates between water and desert, relates to Horn's understanding of the intimate correspondence between them—a twinning that has come to shape so much of her work. The point is not that a pool of orange watercolor in *Bluff Life* invokes a watery landscape in any direct way; it is the larger idea that drawing does not represent a place, or even translate it, but drawing itself becomes a place that is as captivating as a lava field or an intricate pattern of pools that make up Iceland's wilderness. As it had been for Celmins, the exploration of a surface through touch takes time and marks time.

One of the striking features of Horn's work is the double action it sets in motion: at once invoking a solitary monologue, like a particularly intense inner-thought train, and at the same time a bodily sense of the situation. The experience of her work is what it is like to be caught in the crossfire between these two things, so it ends up being very different from what has often been referred to as "the phenomenological turn"[5] taken by Minimalism. It is not just that a sense of direct experience is mediated through language and the presence of text embedded in the work. This is not always the case, and when text is there, the shape of the letters becomes simple and to some extent abstract. It is as if experience is pitched against phenomenology.

This reminds me, entirely coincidentally, that Claude Lévi-Strauss, in his memoirs as travel notes called *Tristes Tropiques* (1955), noted that the most formative moment in his intellectual development was his childhood discovery of the almost imperceptible difference in rock fragments that marked the line of contact between geological strata on a limestone plateau in the Languedoc.[6] It seemed to him to show the limits of phenomenology, which he understood as the continuity of experience and reality. I am not saying that Horn mounts elaborate metaphorics around geology

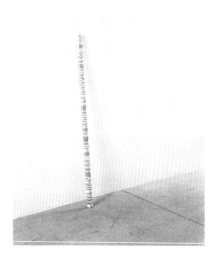

to the exclusion of anything else, but there is a sense that what is remarkable about texture in a piece of rock or lava is that its miniscule ructions mark the trace of an immense disturbance—equally powerful disturbances of the visual field. There is already something vertiginous in that disproportion of scale that is as much temporal as it is spatial, suddenly compressing several millennia in the finest of lines.

Turbulence

> There is something going on in the sky like a decomposition, like a corruption of the air, which remains as still as ever.
>
> —Joseph Conrad, *The Shadow-Line*[7]

Horn's drawings started out very small and have become very large. Her works on paper from the 1980s that were done in the aftermath of *Bluff Life* tend to contain uneven, enclosed shapes in glowing color. They look almost gemlike by comparison with her more recent drawings. The way the pigment is layered on thickly is not an expressive mark of a touch so much as a material deposit of one. There is just a dense texture of color—thickened by pure touch but untrammelled by aesthetic nuance or gesture. In fact the shapes can be quite awkward, ungainly even, although they are small. And the ground is often slightly smudged rather than pristine white. Characteristically they do not come singly. They often come in pairs. When three are placed next to each other a beginning of a sequence is implied, but it is not a progressive or a particularly logical one. They have a built-in repetition, with minor variations differentiating one from another. From the outset, Horn cut the drawings and rearranged them, so a sequence is in fact discontinuous, with faint slices in the paper dissecting the shapes. Sometimes fairly subtle differences need teasing out, which takes time. The sometimes slightly mottled patches of the color are at odds with the size of the drawings, as if they are almost too heavy for the paper. But the cuts, incredibly fine as they are, counter the thickening with a barely perceptible thinness. Thickening and thinning like this seems to be their main dynamic. The tenuous hold that I might have as a viewer is just another part of that dynamic.

fig. 6: Vija Celmins (b.1938), *Untitled (Desert)*, 1971.
Lithograph, sheet 56.8 × 73.7 cm, image 53.3 × 70.5 cm.
The Metropolitan Museum of Art, New York; John B. Turner Fund, 1972.501.5

fig. 7: Wall of plates in Roni Horn's New York studio, 2008

When two shapes are combined that resemble each other very closely it would be reasonable to think they might be in a symmetrical relation with each other. It is all the more striking how a pair of shapes like those of *Double 3.9* (1990) fail to have the effect of symmetry—by which I mean the perfect balance of two things in equilibrium with each other. Instead one functions as the double of the other and has the reverse effect: disequilibrium. Two drawings may be in some respects nearly identical, but the drift of the colored vertical further to the right in the right-hand work becomes all the more dramatic as a consequence. As the poet Paul Celan succinctly lamented: "Unreadable this/world. All doubles."[8] Two lines. Two glass blocks. Two white owls. Add all the double actions proliferate within each work, whether it is single or part of a pair or a larger group. The effect is cumulative and greater than its parts. The obscurity of the movements between things is exacerbated in the process of proliferation—an obscurity that is meant (rather than *meant* to be explained away).

Horn has written very compellingly about her own preoccupation with doubles and doubling. It is the prime condition of work and, by extension, of viewing itself. Two identical metal solids are divided by a wall: the installation of *Things That Happen Again* is predicated on what you see and what you see again. Remembering what you see affects and changes what you saw before, transforming it entirely. The first part you see magically becomes the original but only because it has been made so by coming upon another. It becomes clear that a temporal splitting underlies all repetitions as we perceive them. Nowhere is this more vivid than the *Distant Double* series that she began at the end of the 1980s, for instance. Two drawings are hung in different rooms. When you encounter the second it may seem identical to the first, but you can't be entirely sure. It cannot be stressed enough that the subtle differences you identify with certainty when they are reproduced together is the opposite of the effect of the actual works. Rather, the work seems to be about a failure to remember with precision or at least suggests that any distinction between remembering and misremembering is insecure. The déjà vu of having seen something once before brings it close, but the failure to recall precisely how puts it at an even greater distance. Spatial distance flips over immediately into a temporal asymmetry.

It follows that it is not that useful to impose a chronological progression on Horn's drawings despite its appeal to the art historical imagination. Because as much as the works have changed, they also double back on themselves. Even now she occasionally goes back to very early drawings and reuses them. Horn reworks things not because they have necessarily failed but because that is how she makes work. The logic of making involves dismantling and disassembling. This is not to say the changes have not been significant but that they do not fundamentally divert from that logic. The most obvious changes have been in their size and the move to open rather than closed configurations. Rather than an enclosed shape at the center of the paper, *That VI* from 1993 consists of small chevrons distributed across the surface of the work in irregular patterns. The paper ground is cut into thin vertical strips, which neatly suture one against the other. It is a ground—empty as it is—full of slits. This marks a radical decomposition. There is no form to speak of. In other drawings, there are configurations of elements that scatter and disperse. Some of these become circular, with single or double centers, which make the idea of a compositional center collapse in on itself. In *Too V* (2000), the configurations become like a vortex or a centrifuge. The scale of it places the viewer in an entirely different position from the small-scale drawings—you get sucked in by the force of the shattered field.

There is a large wall in Horn's New York studio covered with what she calls "plates"[fig.7] The word has geological connotations (the plates that move on the earth's surface). It also suggests printing or photographic plates, (merely intermediary or transitional elements). These are the drawings that will become her drawings. Some invoke Louise Bourgeois's insomnia drawings [figs.8 and 9], others not at all. They will be completely undone in order to become her large composites like *Else 9* (2010, pp.148–149). Groups of two or three or four paper the wall. Patterns of spirals or concentric ovals or dispersed knots of color get dismantled and reassembled into the large-scale pieces—several of which are in various states of completion around the studio. She works on a number of them at the same time, and they take a long time to make, sometimes a year or so. You can see why when you realize how intricate and laborious the process is to make them. But the point is not about technique. It doesn't really help to trace them back to their origins, as if all the reassembly that has occurred can be somehow wished away. In this sense even showing the wall of drawings potentially confuses rather than clarifies matters. After all, whether or not you have seen the plates, there is always a sense in the drawings themselves that these configurations have traveled some way from their point of origin and in a fairly circuitous route—that they have been away and come back again.

From a distance, *Through 4* (2007) looks like a double bloom of discontinuous blue zigzags. Although the markings are quite amorphous, there are shapes, two large roughly circular patterns of scattered marks, to be perceived. These constellations have been reassembled and regrouped, and the faint crystalline cuts in the white paper ground splinter the whole surface. We can take in all of this even though the surface is extremely spare with barely enough on it to fill such a large expanse of paper. We can conceptually grasp all of this except the detail of it. It is like the opposite of the Iceland effect, which Horn has described as: "Big enough to get lost on. Small enough to find myself."[9] Here it is the other way round—the more you telescope into the smallness of it, the less you are able to retain. As you go in closer, that hold you can think you have gets more and more difficult to maintain in the face of the complexity of the visual information that is there. What happens first and foremost is that the colored shapes unscramble. The more you try to figure out the logic of the process, the more you end up losing your footing.

There is a fine scattered residue of pencil markings all over the surface,

figs. 8 and 9: Louise Bourgeois (1911–2010). *The Insomnia Drawings* (details), 1994–1995. Two of 220 mixed-media works on paper of varying dimensions, ink on paper, 22.9 × 30.2 cm (left), 30.5 × 22.9 cm (right). Daros Collection, Zurich

calibrating most of the joins at one point or another. Sometimes a double line marks and aligns two edges, and elsewhere two words are placed adjacent to one another to signal where a join should be. These are marks to fix the pieces together, and they add to the frenetic effect of the whole thing (the opposite of fixing it). Alongside them, scattered all over, are pin pricks where the separate pieces have been pinned to the wall in the process of fitting the whole massive puzzle of paper together. There are fingerprints, even footprints, which are indexical traces of physically putting the whole thing together. Maybe they are the briefest of travel notes but they only, in their effect at least, obscure more than manifest the process of execution.

The pencil annotations come in pairs—a double line or pairs of words or names. In one there is "laura" on one side and "palmer" on the other (from David Lynch's *Twin Peaks* (1990–1991)) while in another "anne anne" is like an invocation. Or there are short words that rhyme: "boo-boo," "who-who," "you-you." The words read as encrypted signs, but they are totally and necessarily obscure. It is more like a stream of consciousness, the kinds of chains of words that come to mind randomly. So marks that measure the whole thing inscribe the discontinuities within us as subjects— "grow grow," "vow vow," "claw claw," and "crab crab." The pencil or crayon marks precariously keep hold like the most fragile of hinges. Again, try to figure them out, and the whole thing disintegrates before your eyes. Try to break the code (where there is none) and you lose the rapture of them.

The images in Horn's *Still Water (The River Thames, For Example)* (1999, pp.94–101) are scattered with numbers superimposed over the water, like tiny bits of foam floating on the surface. Rather than purity, the implication of pollution and toxicity is never far away. In all its myriad movements and patterns, water has footnotes, which are listed at the base of the image. The pattern of dispersal of tiny marks is like the drawings. The footnotes and annotations represent a kind of tapering off into smaller and smaller details, finer and finer points. Some are questions, none are answers. "Is this black?" asks one that is placed on a tiny section of water. Others read: "(what color is this?)" There are also references to a page of Joseph Conrad's *Heart of Darkness* (1902) or a poem by Emily Dickinson. If footnotes traditionally verify and cite sources, an elaborate scholarly apparatus, here they raise questions in a running commentary as fluid as the movements of the water itself.

In a footnote to another footnote, Horn writes, "this litter of numbers on the photograph is a constellation composing the view," and then in the next that it breaks it up. Maybe this is similar to Stéphane Mallarmé's idea of constellating a page— the operation of composing language precisely in order to decompose it. The smallest disturbance in water creates texture. It is still or rough, it forms little eddies or vortexes depending on the currents and cross currents. Of course the textures look quite different when still in the photograph than when you actually look at water. It breaks up the whole surface into a turbulent field, even where it is dead calm. This comes to seem very close to the drawings—the configurations of colored marks swirling into the kind of vortex you might find in a tiny section of water.

It might seem a little wayward to invoke John Ruskin's *Elements of Drawing*— a handbook for people wanting to learn to draw, which he wrote in the mid-nineteenth century. But it is Ruskin's hypersensitivity that comes through in his descriptions of how to draw water. There is a kind of restless and obsessive vision involved as he advises his readers to look at water all day long. He spends several pages speculating on how to draw the same spot of water in different lights. A few "tremulous blots"[10] could capture it, but it is also his sensibility that is tremulous before the enormity of the task. In order to try to master it, he suggests an exercise that involves filling a very large basin with a solution of Prussian blue in water, putting in bits of walnut shell (like Horn's litter or debris of footnotes) to float on the surface and break it up in the light, and studying the changes in the reflections depending on the direction of the light. Of course you can read this as an academic exercise, but there is something riveting about that level of love of detail and his desire to follow every vicissitude of the light on water: a hydrophilia no less intense than Horn's, except I imagine Ruskin did not like being in it as much as she does ("hot water, memory, erotica—more or less the same thing," she has written of Iceland's hot pools[11]).

Her interest in glass, as I said at the start, seems startlingly sensual when compared with the spareness of her drawings. The color of glass has a unique quality in that it is entirely contingent upon the light effects outside it, yet it absorbs those conditions entirely. Color is often seen as the most expressive element in art (redolent of aesthetic feeling), but what is striking in Horn's work is how detached her use of color is from that language of expression. Color functions more like the weather. Color also tells stories or "reports you" like the weather. The color of *Untitled (Georgia)* (2005) changes just as instantaneously and so do its associations; one moment it is like molten lava, the next corrosive rust. The clear round block of transparent glass, with its sandblasted circumference, plays on the slimmest gradations between opacity and translucency—like a giant lens. When Horn writes, "Black water is black milk,"[12] toxicity turns to death and to the concentration camp (cut to Paul Celan's line "Black milk at daybreak we drink at evening"[13]). But milky black is a rather apt description of the chromatic effect of *Untitled (Yes)*[fig.10] even though Ludwig Wittgenstein might have thought it to be as conceptually implausible as a glowing grey[14] and a kind of category mistake. In a sense it is, yet that is precisely what we see. Black milk and milky black may or may not be as far apart as we would wish. Through color, we live inside these contradictions.

As it turns out, color can be as fraught as a few frenetic annotations, and a drizzle of fine pencil marks and colors raining down on a paper ground can be as sensual as glass or any other material. Sometimes it is the barely noticeable element that stops you in your tracks. For example, there is an almost unbearable precision in the effect of the light on the smooth surface of glass or an accidental but infinitesimal flaw in the surface that creates an effect of massive turbulence in certain lights and absolutely none in others. Depending on the angle of view, glass has a surface of

fig.10: *Untitled (Yes)*, 2001
(installation view at Dia Center for the Arts, New York).
Solid cast glass, 43.2 × 73.7 × 122.2 cm. Private collection, Basel

either razor sharpness or infinite depth. At one moment its surface can seem as thin and dazzling as the gold leaf laid out on the floor of *Gold Mats, Paired—for Ross and Felix* (1994), at another it is purely transparent. You cannot see the change happening in perception; it is only visible in its sudden effect when one kind of surface has switched invisibly into another. You can see into it and then suddenly the light changes, and it has no inside at all—only a surface and a shine that reflects outward. The line between the two is so fine that in perception it no longer exists. But it is our experience that fractures in an instant.

It would almost be reassuring to talk about fragmentation, to talk about the part object or Sigmund Freud's belief that doubles are uncanny. This would at least provide a vocabulary and a context. But these are not really fragments. And while they provoke a disturbance, they are not particularly uncanny. In each large drawing, two or three or four plates have been rearranged and reassembled, like a vast and unruly circuit box. The result is not a part of a whole. On the contrary, everything is there, all the plates, but they are put together in a different arrangement. There is little if any waste. It is not as if anything is missing, except a sense of unity. Perhaps what has been lost is a segment of time rather than a physical piece of the puzzle. The evidence of the process of making the drawings is visible but also illegible. Memory is not just selective but full of blanks. In a dialogue from 1949 with Georges Duthuit about the artist Tal Coat, Samuel Beckett began by asserting: "Total object, complete with missing parts, instead of partial object. Question of degree."[15] "Complete with missing parts" sounds like a description of Horn's work. It is enigmatic, but so is the work. It captures the sense of a total object that is all absorbing yet at the same time intractable in some way and, therefore, always incomplete. This refusal to deliver everything easily or quickly forces us to slow down and reflect: to hold on to that tenuous hold. There is something euphoric in the recognition that that is okay: that is what it is like.

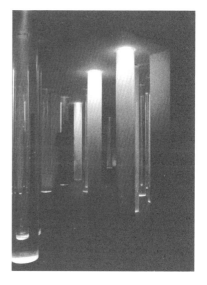

fig. 11: Chris Marker (1921–2012), *Sans Soleil*, 1983. 35mm, color and black and white, sound; 100 minutes. Distributed by Argos Films, Neuilly-sur-Seine, France

fig. 12: *Water, Selected*, 2007. Twenty-four glass columns filled with water from glacial sources, column diameter 30.5 cm each, height 279.4 cm each, approximately 457 square m overall. Permanent installation at VATNASAFN/LIBRARY OF WATER, Stykkishólmur, Iceland

"Something is missing" is a beautiful definition of utopia. Would you say that if something is missing it is incomplete, or would you say it is complete because there's something missing?

—Roni Horn[16]

This is not everybody's idea of utopia.

Utopias usually replace the missing parts or at least substitute or compensate for them in an image of plenitude. They make good historical failures or social inequities or psychic trauma. Utopias have always been a way to think your way out of a present that is lacking in the direction of a future that will be better (and so often merges with an imagined past that was better). Horn suggests that something that is complete comprises all its parts including the missing ones. This is close to Beckett's idea of the total object, except Beckett did not call it utopia. He was of a generation to give voice to the failure of the utopian ideal as it had been projected on to either a technological or a psychological dreamland by the historical avant-gardes of the early twentieth century. Instead there was absurdity where there had been faith, a bleak void where there had been the hope of something better. This void space turned into something almost ecstatic for an artist like Smithson, in thrall to dystopian visions of a landscape in total disintegration. Part of my earlier insistence that Horn's work owes more to Judd than Smithson, more to Marfa than the Yucatán, is because she radically departs from what (for a long time) had seemed to be the only viable critical alternative to those earlier ideal models. Instead, her work offers another terrain of possibility, a kind of utopia, I suppose, but one that has been to dystopia and back.

Iceland is not just a place for her but an idea. The fact that, unlike *Bluff Life*, all the large-scale drawings I have discussed were made in her New York studio rather than in Iceland is immaterial to this logic. And as an idea it is close to, but not identical to, utopia. It is more like a distant double perhaps. She calls Iceland her *Oz*. By this I don't mean that she idealizes Iceland, but she positions it in a very precise way. Her configuration of the place that Iceland occupies in the geography of her work reminds me of Chris Marker's great film from 1983 about the "infirmities of time" titled *Sans Soleil*. It is impossible to forget that the film that engages with the twin sites of Tokyo and the Cape Verde Islands actually begins and ends elsewhere: Iceland. The brief opening sequence, even before the title of the film comes up on the screen, is of three sunlit children, arms interlocked, walking along a road [fig. 11]. We are told by a female narrator that the photographer, whose story we are about to hear, had shot this image of happiness long before but had never been able to incorporate it into a film. It never fit. So it is added on here like a bit of prehistory, separated from the rest of the film by a black screen that lasts several seconds. The image of Iceland was, as the narrator relates, one of "the list of things that quicken the heart." The movement and the placement of it figures desire for a time or a place, but it is unclear when or where.

Horn's Iceland is much more than a fleeting image or lost object. It is fuelled by and fuels desire rather than nostalgia or melancholy. Works that she has made in Iceland, like her recent *VATNASAFN/LIBRARY OF WATER* (2007) in the small town of Stykkishólmur on the country's western tip show her intimacy with the place and its community. Converted from the old library, she collected water from twenty-four glaciers and placed it in clear glass pillars [fig. 12]. On the rubber floor are words for weather in English and Icelandic, which she has called a kind of bilingual drawing. Words such as "calm," "rough," and "sultry" double as descriptions of temperament. Horn has likened it to a lighthouse in which the viewer is the light. But it also acts as a kind of gigantic optical instrument, the distorting lenses of the columns picking up, like so much residue or sediment, the fractured view that looks both inward, inside ourselves, and outward, to water.

Although *VATNASAFN/LIBRARY OF WATER* is an installation that gives way to a panoramic view beyond the huge bay window, the experience of being in it is a bit like being in one of her drawings. The precise points where it seems to split apart—a cut in the paper or the field of vision—are also what join it together and hold us to it both tenuously and tenaciously. It is hardly incidental that so many of the titles for Horn's drawings are short words like "too," "was," and "were"—the kinds of words that are the small joins in a sentence. They are often the smallest units of language that can define a whole change of tense and potentially a massive temporal shift. These words are, needless to say, as much a part of the work as any other element and symptomatic of the cuts and joins—the logic of contiguity not continuity—that hold the work together. The lack of fit is how it fits, perfectly.

coda

It's only after the title frames in French, Russian and English, that *Sans Soleil* can be said to begin: not in Iceland, now, but in Japan. This beginning takes place on a ferry boat from Hokkaido, the country's northernmost island, to the mainland. The day is dull and cloudy; the land in the distance shrouded in mist; you can feel the moisture in the air. The three sunlit children of the film's prelude have disappeared, a fleeting memory. Now, three older Japanese women are outside on the ship's deck, talking to each other and looking into the distance. What they are looking at and whether they are looking into empty space or the sea or both, doesn't really matter. There's just something mesmeric about looking at them looking out, over water. A sea-crossing like this passage between islands is suspended in time and as these women stare out

fig. 13: Chris Marker, *Sans Soleil*, 1983.
35mm, color and black and white, sound; 100 minutes.
Distributed by Argos Films, Neuilly-sur-Seine, France

of frame, they occupy a passage in time that remains detached: another missing part, you could say.

Looking at Roni Horn's work is a bit like watching water. Not because watching water is blank but on the contrary because it forces you to hone your observational skills. It constantly changes and evolves. The artist has written: "One paradox about water that I return to again and again is how something so intimate and familiar constantly presents itself as unfamiliar...Water is very elusive, it's more a state of perpetual relation"[17]. This resonates with the work of English poet Alice Oswald who describes "the simple mineral monologue of / water".[18] For Horn, water is a constant presence in its many states in her work, from the steam of Icelandic hot pools, through the taxonomies of fluids and flows to the liquidity of her watercolor drawings. But as she adds in a parenthesis, "(When you look at water you never know what you are actually looking at)".[19] Adjusting to the patterns, to the drift of it, is to be alert to its movements: the small squall, the choppy troughs, the hollowing out, the swirling, the undertow. Watching it can be bracing, as the weather can, but it can also allow us to glimpse what she has called "My Oz" and its potential freedoms.[20]

Horn allows time to enter the artwork undercover. There's no Time with a capital "T" but it's there, having arrived by a few circuitous or covert routes. One of these is her method of cutting up and reassembling a drawing or print that already exists and transforming it through its own undoing. This is both a straight description of how she makes many of her drawings but also of the complex temporalities involved in that long drawn-out process. It's comparable with – and even perhaps an extension of? – the habit Horn always had to return to the same places in Iceland. She has written that "the necessity of it was part of me."[21] She returned in all weathers, so that the island revealed different parts of itself through fog or mist – so, when we return to her work, it is susceptible, let's say exposed, to changing conditions and contexts; and both vulnerable and resilient to the "infirmities of time"[22].

In the series *Volcanic Phenomenon* (1990/2014), a group of earlier map drawings and prints from *To Place: Bluff Life* (1990) are intricately cut into one another (pp.78–83)[23]. This is a method she has been using for the large-scale drawings like *Else* (4: 2009; 9: 2010, pp.148–149) over many years. She also used it in her extensive series of works on paper, *Hack Wit,* which involves splicing together two found colloquial phrases or proverbs or quotations to destroy familiar meanings and create new couplings. "Happy as a clam" and "walking on air", spliced together, read "happy as walking a clam on air"; "cool as a cucumber" and "absence makes the heart grow fonder" makes "cool as absence" and "cucumber makes the heart grow fonder"; others, cut in the thinnest of slivers across and down, disintegrate at times to the point of illegibility.[24] In *Arctic Confidence, v. 1* (pp.82–83), and *v. 2,* (1990/2016), it's as if drawing is the site of its own geological plate movements (pp.78–83). These are collages not because of the glue involved, but because of the way aspects and entities adhere to one another in unpredictable ways. But also, and more importantly perhaps, they are "adhesive" in the sense that Horn writes about Iceland as adhesive: not just because it joins you to a place but also because it sticks to you.[25]

Series breed more series. And each – not only of works on paper but also sculptures – interconnect with others, all the while the cross references multiplying. The titles that appear to be caught in the cross-fire and then get left as sediment to be re-activated elsewhere. Words, the material units of language, have always provided Horn the means to dig around in the colloquial for accidental concordance. With typical irony, *Hack Wit* gives a clue to a mock job description combining senses of "a hack" as bad journalist and "to hack" as to strike a cutting blow or to gain illegal access to computer systems; a "wit" can be amusing but also caustic and cutting.[26] The titles of the series, and of the individual works within them, don't offer verbal explanations, let alone point to iconographic content or subject matter. Rather, these small bits of language are a material part of the work. The use of quotes and sayings as found materials – often in parenthesis – is entirely in keeping with the logic of the work. Colloquial phrases or cliches can be over-familiar to the point of being hackneyed. Over-use has emptied them of meaning. Repetition makes mincemeat of them, mashing up old pieties and trite homey proverbs. The supposedly benign often reveals an unnerving, at times even sinister, lining in the process. None of it is comfortable, but nor is it didactic.

An economy of multiple series and groups grounded in repetition, in both its generative and degenerative forms, constantly drives the ever-shifting parts in relation to ever-shifting wholes and motivates the entire body of work that Horn has produced over the last four decades. Repetition of the same leads to maximum variation, as each series polymorphously transforms into so many different versions of itself. Nowhere is this more apparent than in the glass sculptures shown at the Pola Museum of Art (pp.50–58). They are all the same size at 11 inches by 48 inches and solid cast glass but they differ in colour – one black, one clear, the others pale colours of remarkable limpidity: pink yellow green. It's an informal group, made up of single units that exist as individual works. The complex casting process of the glass will never reproduce the same effect twice, whether in the minuscule air bubbles or variations in patina and surface. The pale colours are reminiscent of the palette of Agnes Martin's later paintings, that push the limits of perceptual nuance as we take time to re-adjust to the most minor differences.

Cast in solid glass, Horn's sculptures occupy the visual field very differently from the way Martin's paintings do and are even more dependent on their environmental surroundings. Depending on the lighting and weather conditions, they can be more or less absent or present. The same sculpture can be almost not there or a trap for the light that attracts like a beacon of light. Lying low on the ground, it's the opposite of the kind of sculpture that asserts itself. Instead, there's a reticence in the way the glass works spread out across our field of vision. We come upon them. They infiltrate us. The sense of looking down into them is in turn reminiscent of looking into a luminous pool. Like watching water, reflections get caught in them; attention alternates between a kind of blankness and more fleeting observations; and between seeing a surface and seeing a depth.

Each glass sculpture is titled *Untitled* followed by a snippet of a quotation in parenthesis, like an add-on. The colour of the glass is delicate: differing by degree, one very slightly more limpid than the other, one a little lighter, or darker than the other. In one (pp.50–51), the words in scare quotes cut against the grain of the sheer sensual beauty of a perfect circle of translucent glass, frosted on all its surfaces. Instead, it is a description of the landscape around Chernobyl, the site of the explosion of a nuclear power plant in Ukraine (then part of the Soviet Union) in 1986. "... a cow all wrapped in cellophane...": the words stick. Something deathly has been brought onto the scene of desire. The palest yellow – full of the promise of early morning light - is suddenly less luminous and more sickly, tinged with the yellow of a radiation map. It's hard to forget the cow and the cellophane once it has been lodged however removed it is from the physical entity that is the work. Radiation can also be a hazard, thwarting expectations. Celan's "black milk" has turned to the sallow yellow of Chernobyl's nuclear frost, heralding the environmental and planetary disaster that we are now in the grip of.

The contingent parts of a sculpture are inherently unstable if not outright paradoxical. The titles – just one of the parts – are a bit like asides that inflect or insinuate, typically going off at tangents rather than holding things together. A frosted pink glass sculpture becomes a touchpaper, for example, to the ambience of the place, to the words of a song, to the contingencies of circumstance (pp.50–51). The fragment in parenthesis "I get all the news I need from the weather report" is extracted from a well-known and well-covered Simon and Garfunkel song called "The Only Living Boy in New York"[27] but also references her own earlier works such as *Weather Reports You* (2007). In her original series of photographs from 1994–1995, *You are the Weather*, a young Icelandic woman's face appears and disappears in a mist of rising steam from a volcanic hot pool, her visibility entirely subject to the levels of moisture, as the heat of the water meets the cold of the air. A giant pink glass lens that absorbs and emanates light is obviously a very different entity from a photographic series that stretches around the walls of a room – but arguably both works dramatize exposure to their surrounding environmental and atmospheric conditions.

Air Burial (Hakone) (2017–2018, pp.182–184), a five-ton single unit of glass with a frosted white exterior that stands in the museum's forested park, is entirely at the mercy of the elements and the weather. Horn has been making this group of works since 2013 and several exist in various locations, all referring to the Tibetan funerary ritual of leaving the body of the dead on a mountaintop eventually to decay and so return to the earth. The solid block of cast glass will eventually disintegrate over time, exposed to fluctuations in temperature and the slow ravages of rain and snow. That it will entropically decay is certain, but the actual time the process will take depends on the local ecology and the impact of the climate on the materials and is much less predictable. But already *Air Burial* acts like a barometer, acutely sensitized to pressure, moisture and temperature, as well as reflecting sky and trees in the liquid shine of the upper surface of glass. As it stands there in a dark woodland, it collects light, like a hidden beacon at ground level, responsive to even the lowest light levels in dull weather but dramatically illuminated when it catches the sun. As a point of light and of orientation, the *Air Burials* return us uncannily to the lighthouse at Dyrhólaey and to the mosses and lichens of Horn's drawings for *Bluff Life* from 1982. The time in between, it feels like, has somehow gone missing.

Ambitious art makes demands on us to think and feel differently rather than confirm what we already know. In Horn's work, changes in thought-pattern – like tiny shifts in a field of vision – are subtle and incremental. It needs room to build, not in order to deliver its meaning all-figured out and neatly packaged for us, but because it turns out that in the body of work that the artist has produced over the last forty years, time has proven to be Horn's great medium. Marguerite Duras, if you remember, had asked what it was that she saw when she saw a film only the previous evening. But what if instead of a single night, we think of months or years or decades later? The temporal returns, delays and uncertainties that Roni Horn has made integral to her work allow us to think of it as a vast composite of parts spread out over and through time. The breaking down and reassembling of parts never flows continuously onward, but is always uneven, likely to double back on itself and full of interruptions.

Just as the work is constantly evolving, the whens and wheres of it are constantly being thrown into question – the very ground of uncertainty, we could say, upon which an ethics of the missing part is built.

[Professor of the History of Art at University College London]

The first part of this essay was published on the occasion of *Roni Horn aka Roni Horn* Exhibition catalogue (Göttingen: Steidl; New York: Whitney Museum of American Art, 2009). The Coda was added on the occasion of the exhibition at the Pola Museum of Art, 2021.

1 Roni Horn in *Art and Architecture*, James Ackerman et al. (Marfa, Texas: Chinati Foundation, 2000), p. 70.
2 Claude Lévi-Strauss, *Tristes Tropiques* (1955; repr., London: Penguin, 1976), p. 437.
3 Robert Smithson in *Robert Smithson: The Collected Writings,* ed. Jack D. Flam (Berkeley: University of California Press, 1996), pp. 7–9, 100–113.
4 Vija Celmins, "Interview with Ann Seymour" in *Vija Celmins: Drawings of the Night Sky*, Anthony D'Offay (London: Phaidon, 2003).
5 Alex Potts, *The Sculptural Imagination: Figurative, Modernist, Minimalist* (New Haven: Yale University Press, 2000), p.209.
6 Lévi-Strauss, p. 68.
7 Joseph Conrad, *The Shadow-Line: A Confession* (New York: Vintage 2007), p.101.
8 Paul Celan, *Snow part/Schneepart* trans. Ian Fairley (Manchester, England: Carcanet Press, 2007), pp. 14–15.
9 Roni Horn, *To Place: Pooling Waters,* 2 Vols. (Cologne: Walther-König 1994), p.23.
10 John Ruskin, *The Elements of Drawing* (1857; repr., London: George Allen, 1902).
11 Roni Horn in *Art and Architecture* James Ackerman et al., p.64.
12 Roni Horn, *Another Water (The River Thames, for Example)* (London: Scalo, 2000), n.p.
13 Paul Celan, "Death Fugue", Poems of Paul Celan, trans. Michael Hamburger (New York: Persea, 2002), p.31. My thanks to Mark Godfrey for discussing these connections with me.
14 Ludwig Wittgenstein, *Remarks on Color* (Oxford: Basil Blackwell, 1977), p. 7.
15 Samuel Beckett and Georges Duthuit, *Three Dialogues* (1965; repr., London: John Calder, 1999), p. 101.
16 Hans Ulrich Obrist, *Interviews* (Florence: Charta/Fondazione Pitti Immagine Discovery, 2003).
17 Roni Horn, interview with James Lingwood *Some Thames,* Steidl, 2003 as cited under 'Water' in *Roni Horn aka Roni Horn* (Göttingen: Steidl; New York: Whitney Museum of American Art, 2009), p.165.
18 Alice Oswald, *Nobody* (Cape Poetry, Jonathan Cape, 2019), p.63.
19 Roni Horn, *Still Water,* 1999, as extracted in *Roni Horn aka Roni Horn*, op cit, p.165.
20 Roni Horn would think of Iceland for a long time as 'My Oz', invoking the chromatic utopia 'over the rainbow' of the Judy Garland film (1939). She gave a talk at the Reykjavik Academy where she talked about the role weather played in her work and how she had discovered in Iceland – and certainly long before it was the big news it is today now that 'weather is an important thing in our lives…no longer simply an occasion for small talk.' Roni Horn, *Island Zombie Iceland Writings* (Princeton and Oxford: Princeton University Press, 2020), p.127.
21 Roni Horn, *ibid*, p.1.
22 Chris Marker, *Sans Soleil,* 1983. The film is narrated by Florence Delay.
23 The double dating makes this temporal doubling clear. The *Bluff Life* special edition prints are used as the 'substrate' throughout.
24 I have written on Roni Horn's approach to drawing in 'More War: The Disaster Series' in Roni Horn, *Dogs' Chorus* (Göttingen: Steidl, 2019), and in 'Words in the Wild'.
25 Roni Horn, 'An Adhesive Feeling', *Island Zombie*, op cit, p.89.
26 The poet Anne Carson offers a brilliant response to this series in 'Hack Gloss', Roni Horn, *Hack Wit* (Göttingen: Steidl, 2015).
27 Simon and Garfunkel 'The Only Living Boy in New York', written by Paul Simon and released 1970, from the album *Bridge Over Troubled Water,* also covered by Everything But the Girl in 1993. The Tennors' reggae adaptation of the song, 'Weather Report' (1973) changed the words to 'the only little girl in my hometown'.

図版 ｜ Plates

Roni Horn

水の中にあなたを見るとき、あなたの中に水を感じる？

When You See Your Reflection in Water, Do You Recognize the Water in You?

水による疑い（どうやって）
2003–2004年

Doubt by Water (How)
2003–2004

死せるフクロウ
1997年

Dead Owl
1997

無限の瞬き
1991/1997年

Brink of Infinity
1991 / 1997

［前頁］
左から右

無題（「…最新の新聞記事より：地方に暮らす女性が病院で手術を受け男性になった。彼女の名前は『ヴェロニカ』であったが、手術後に彼女、いや彼は『ジュリアス・シーザー』という名前を選んだ。」）

無題（「必要なニュースはすべて天気予報から手に入れる。」）

無題（「事故の最中にしか、速度は生じない。」）

無題（「魔女は山雨の中で想像していたよりもずっと素敵だ。」）

無題（「…どの家でも、土間の上、敷物の上、板寝床の上で、村人たちは動かず、黙って横になっていた。その顔は汗だらけ。村全体がさながら深海の底の潜水艦であった―確かに存在はしているのに、声も、動きもなく、生きているしるしがない。」）

無題（「車で［チェルノブイリの］郊外にでると、道路沿いにかかしのようなものが見えます。ビニールですっぽりおおわれた雌牛が放されているのです。となりには、これまた全身をビニールにくるまれたおばあさん。」）

無題（「私の社会的な意識は、ほんの数十年前までは未開拓だった土地で形成された。寂寥感、なにもない土地、広々とした空、どこまでも続く地平線、そして、ほんのわずかな人々。これらが私の最初の事実であり、長い間、支配的なものであった。」）

無題（「実際には、巧みな恩恵がある。」）

2018-2020年

［Previous page］
From left to right

Untitled ("...the latest newspaper item: a woman in a remote state went to the hospital and turned into a man. Her name was 'Veronica,' but after the transformation she, or he, chose the name of 'Julius Caesar.'")

Untitled ("I get all the news I need from the weather report.")

Untitled ("Speed only happens when you're having an accident.")

Untitled ("A witch is more lovely than thought in the mountain rain.")

Untitled ("... In all the dwellings, on the earthen floors, on mats, on bunks, lay silent, inert people. Their faces were bathed in sweat. The village was like a submarine at the bottom of the ocean: it was there, but it emitted no signals, soundless, motionless.")

Untitled ("If you drove out of town [Chernobyl] you'd see these scarecrows: a cow all wrapped in cellophane and then an old farmer woman next to her, also wrapped in cellophane.")

Untitled ("My social awareness was formed in a place that had been virgin land only a few decades earlier. Emptiness, space, vast skies, long horizons, and few people were my first facts, and for long, the dominant facts.")

Untitled ("The actual is a deft beneficence.")

2018-2020

無題（「私の社会的な意識は、ほんの数十年前までは未開拓だった土地で形成された。寂寥感、なにもない土地、広々とした空、どこまでも続く地平線、そして、ほんのわずかな人々。これらが私の最初の事実であり、長い間、支配的なものであった。」）

2018-2020年

Untitled ("My social awareness was formed in a place that had been virgin land only a few decades earlier. Emptiness, space, vast skies, long horizons, and few people were my first facts, and for long, the dominant facts.")

2018-2020

無題（「…最新の新聞記事より：地方に暮らす女性が病院で手術を受け男性になった。彼女の名前は『ヴェロニカ』であったが、手術後に彼女、いや彼は『ジュリアス・シーザー』という名前を選んだ。」）
2018-2020年

Untitled ("...the latest newspaper item: a woman in a remote state went to the hospital and turned into a man. Her name was 'Veronica,' but after the transformation she, or he, chose the name of 'Julius Caesar.'")
2018-2020

無題（「魔女は山雨の中で想像していたよりもずっと素敵だ。」）
2018-2020年

Untitled ("A witch is more lovely than thought in the mountain rain.")
2018-2020

無題（「…どの家でも、土間の上、敷物の上、板寝床の上で、村人たちは動かず、黙って横になっていた。その顔は汗だらけ。村全体がさながら深海の底の潜水艦であった―確かに存在はしているのに、声も、動きもなく、生きているしるしがない。」）

2018–2020年

Untitled ("... In all the dwellings, on the earthen floors, on mats, on bunks, lay silent, inert people. Their faces were bathed in sweat. The village was like a submarine at the bottom of the ocean: it was there, but it emitted no signals, soundless, motionless.")

2018–2020

A BLOSSOM PERHAPS IS AN INTRODUCTION TO WHOM NONE CAN INTIM

エミリのブーケ
2006–2007年
6点組

Bouquet of Emily
2006–2007
Set of 6 parts

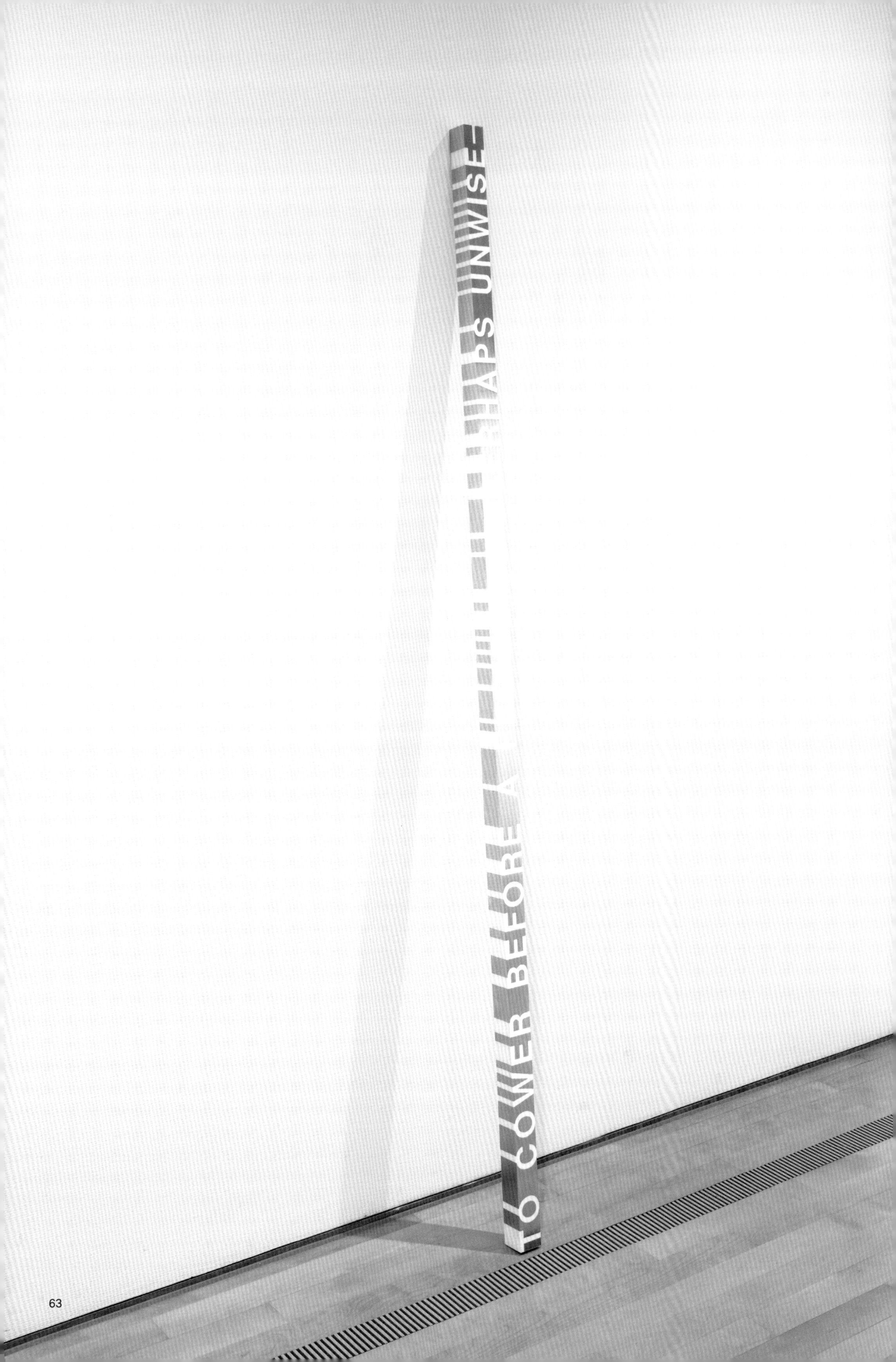
TO COWER BEFORE A
APS UNWISE

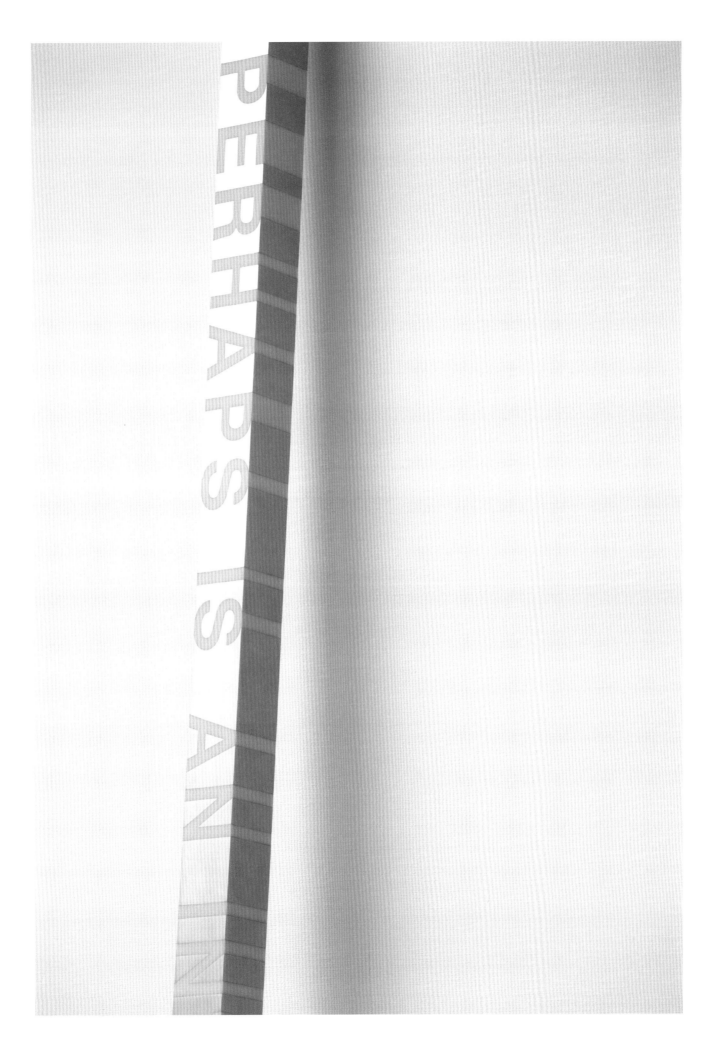

A BLOSSOM PERHAPS IS AN INTRODUCTION. TO WHOM—NONE CAN INFER—

ゴールド・フィールド
1980／1994年

Gold Field
1980 / 1994

トゥー・プレイス
1989年 –

To Place
1989 – ongoing

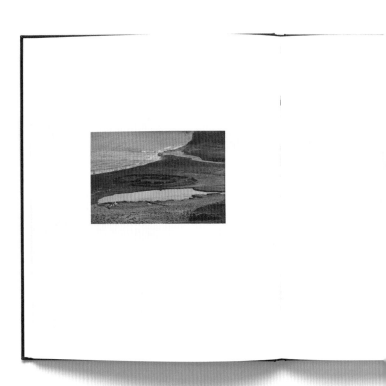

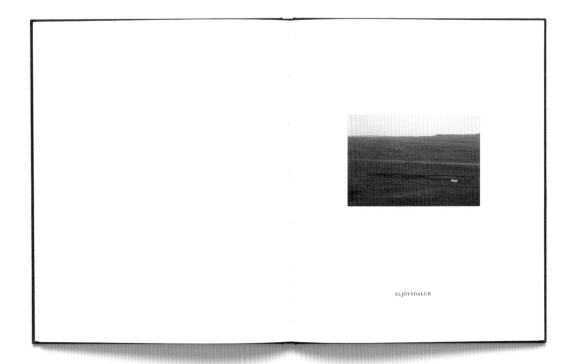

FLJÓTSDALUR

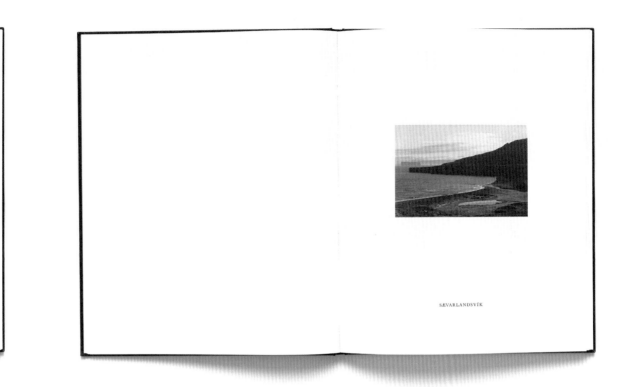

SÆVARLANDSVÍK

VÍDIDALSTUNGA

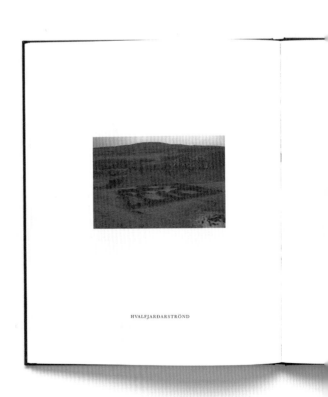

HVALFJARDARSTRÖND

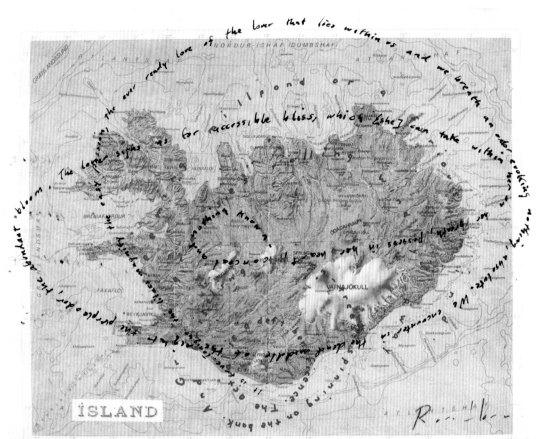

人生について考える…　　　島、島 v.1
1990年　　　　　　　　　1990／2012年

I Think About Life ...　　*Island, Island, v. 1*
1990　　　　　　　　　　1990 / 2012

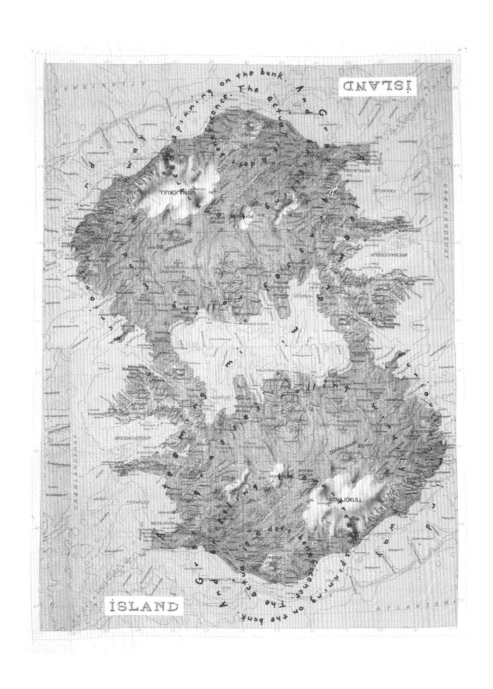

溶岩島 v. 2
1990年／2012年

Lavaland, v. 2
1990 / 2012

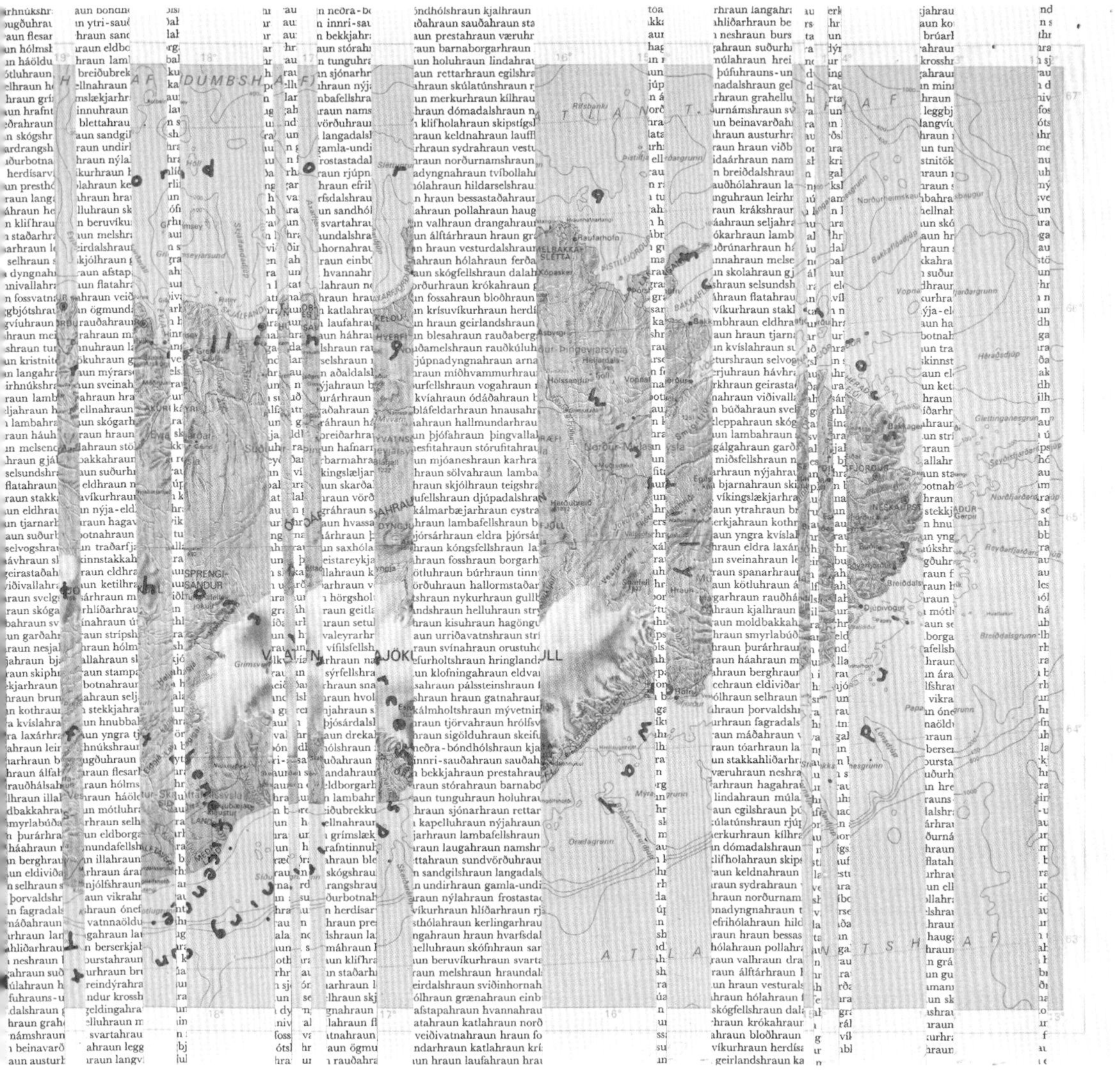

kötluhraun álfaraun

valhraun seljahraun hellnahraun kálfat

bóndhólshraun kjalhraun tóarhraun langahraun lanahr aun nýjahraun burfi

aun máðahraun vatnnaöldurarselshraun aðaldalshraun sandahraun bekkjahraun prestahraun

sauðahraun innri-sauðahraun sauðahraun stakkah liðarhraun berser hraun suðurárhraun kvíahr

drekahraun sigölduhraun skeifuh valhraun drangahraun háahraun seljahraun hellnahraun

confidence

forcehraun

北極の自信 v. 1
1990／2016年

Arctic Confidence, v. 1
1990 / 2016

円周率
1997/2004年

Pi
1997/2004

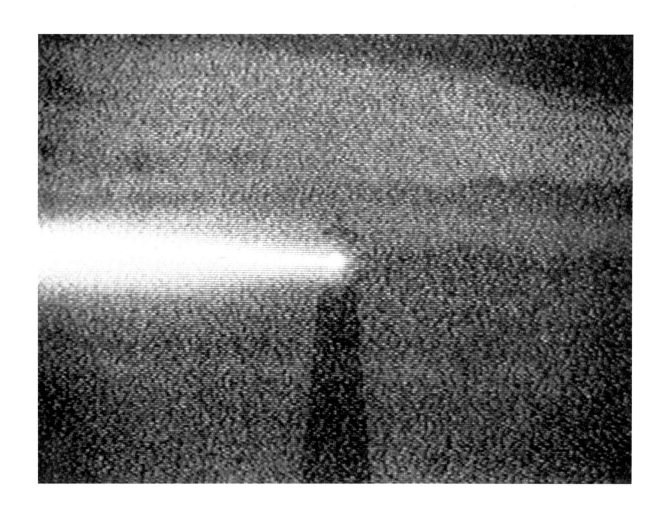

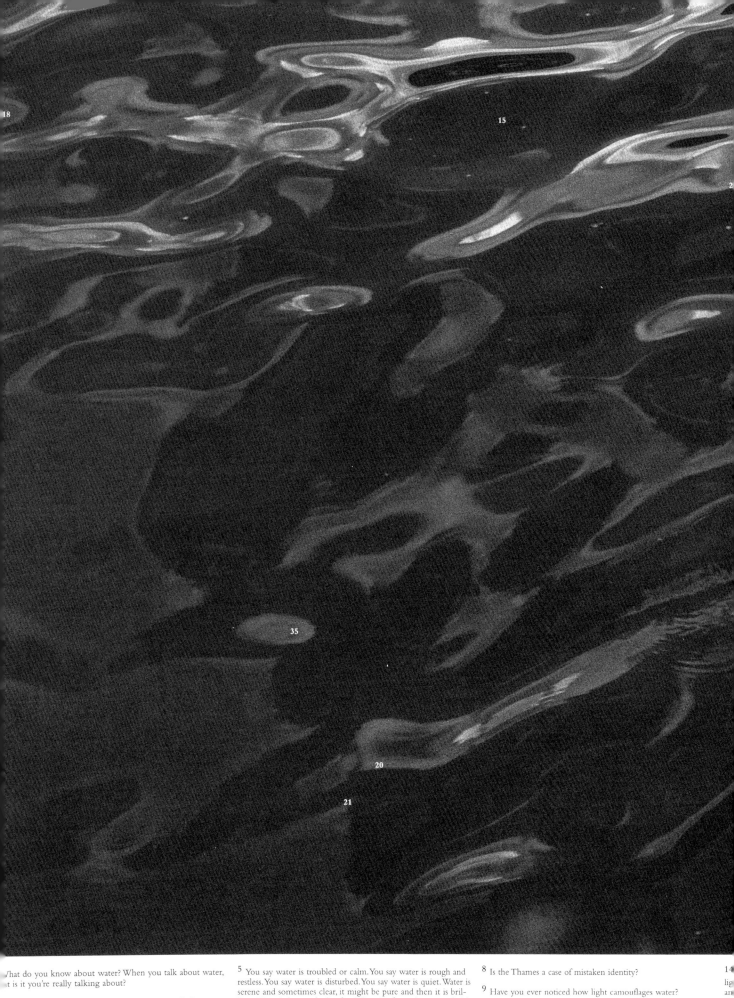

What do you know about water? When you talk about water, what is it you're really talking about?

What do you know about water? Isn't that part of what water that you never really know what it is?

What do you know about water? That it's everywhere, so familiar-seeming and yet so elusive (a kind of everything with-definition), never quite graspable, even as an ice cube?

What do you know about water? Only that it's everywhere differently?

5 You say water is troubled or calm. You say water is rough and restless. You say water is disturbed. You say water is quiet. Water is serene and sometimes clear, it might be pure and then it is brilliant. Water is heavy; that's a fact. Water is often calm, even placid. Water is still and then it might be deep as well. Water is cold or hot, chilly or tepid. You say water is brash or brisk, sometimes crisp. You say water is soft and hard. You say water irritates and lubricates. You say water is foul. You say water is fresh. You say water is tranquil and languorous. You say water is sweet.

6 What is water?

7 You say it's a river. I can believe that. But when you say it's water, I get suspicious. [8]

8 Is the Thames a case of mistaken identity?

9 Have you ever noticed how light camouflages water?

10 Have you ever noticed how rarely water looks like water?

11 What does water look like? [12]

12 See military camouflage. For example: "Polish Presidential," "Italian Woodland," "San Marco Mediterranean," "Indonesian Spot," and "Belgian Jigsaw" patterns.

13 Have you ever noticed how reflections on the water at night make water look more watery?

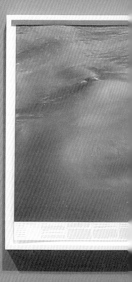

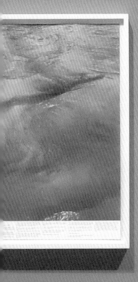

静かな水（テムズ川、例として）
1999年

Still Water (The River Thames, for Example)
1999

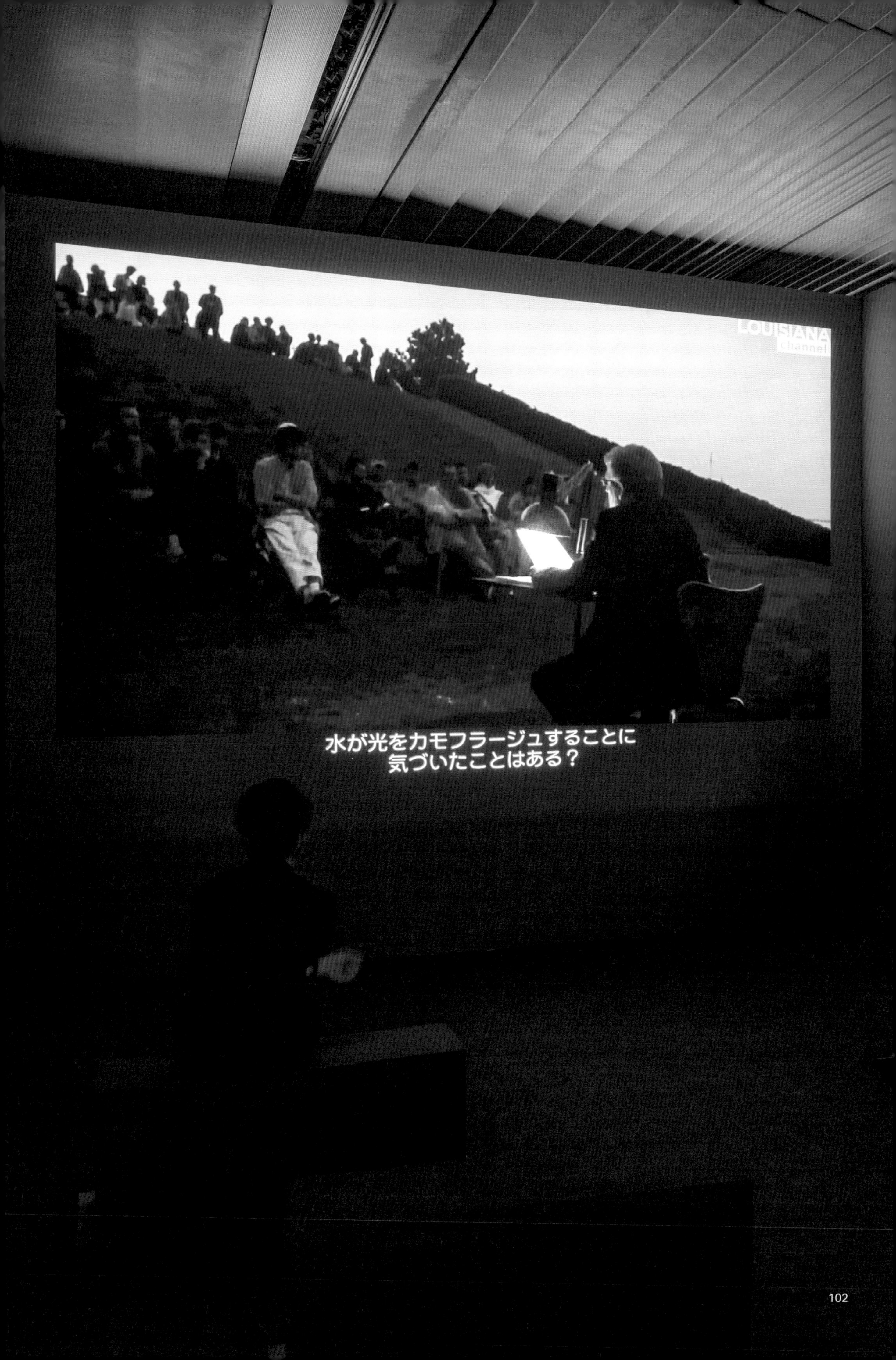
LOUISIANA
channel
水が光をカモフラージュすることに
気づいたことはある？

水と言う
2012年5月、ルイジアナ近代美術館（フムレベック、デンマーク）でのパフォーマンス

Saying Water
Performance at the Louisiana Museum of Modern Art (Humlebæk, Denmark), May 2012

水の中にあなたを見るとき
あなたの中に水を感じる？

どの川でニール・ヤングは
恋人を撃ったのか？

ウォレス・スティーヴンズの詩
「黒の支配」を参照

ちょっと急がなければいけませんね。日が沈んできたので。
少し大きめの声でいきましょう。

これは一種のモノローグです。本来は美術作品に関連するものとして書いたテキストですが、
その視覚的要素をすべて取り除いて、モノローグにまとめました。タイトルは

《水と言う》

数年前、ある医院の待合室で、子どもたちがそれを怖がるのだという母親の声が聞こえてきた。中が見えなければ、子どもがそこに入ることはないだろう。ばらばらにされたような気分だ。この黒い流体、養分なきミルクのようなものの中へと歩みをすすめ、あなたの姿は消えてゆく。

消えてしまうこと。ゆえに自殺者はそれに惹かれ、子どもはそれを怖がるのだ。ただここからいなくなることへのやわらかい入り口。その川を想像するとき、それはわたしが入れるもの、わたしを包み込むもの、ここからわたしを連れ去るものだ。しかしまた、その痛みは想像しがたい。暴力や化学よりも。

水について考えることは、その未来について考えること、あるいはただ未来を。わたしの未来、あなたの未来。それは個人的なこと、特に今は。中が見えない水を子どもたちが恐れるのは当然のことだ。だとすれば、未来を想像できないものが、未来に惹かれるなんて理解することができるだろうか。この水のようなものや、別の水に惹かれるなんて。

夜。その水の暗さは空の暗さを映し出す。しかし、やがて夜が明けても、その水は暗いまま、その内にあるすべてのものをその外にあるすべてのものから切り離す。

その水は不透明だ。一度その中に入れば、あなたの姿はもはや見えず、あなたも何も見えなくなる。そう思うと心が落ち着く。純然たる視覚の絶え間ざる要求からの解放。

闇に紛れて。夜が明ければ、やがて流れ去る。しかし、その水の黒さは消えないだろう。その黒さやその水は流れ去っても、決して消え去ることはない。

その水の色は、どんな色であれ、変化しつづける。その半分は空だ。

その水の色は変化しつづける。その半分はカーキ色だ。すべての色彩がその中にあるのに、いずれも目には見えず、全体は漠然としている。どのみち一度潜ってしまえば、何も見えなくなるだろう。その水の色はわたしにふさわしい、ベージュ。わたしにふさわしい、それは色ではなく、その意味では白に似ている、だが区別はない。ベージュは凡庸のひとつ。白は卓越。もしかしたら迷宮のようなもの、命がけのものになる。

あなたがそれを川と言う。わたしはそれを信じる。でもあなたがそれを水と言うなら、わたしはそれを疑う。

テムズ川は誤認されたアイデンティティの一事例なのか？

あなたが水と言うとき、それは何を意味しているの？

あなたが水と言うとき、それは天気について話しているの？それともあなた自身？
水の中にあなたを見るとき、あなたの中に水を感じる？

わたしたちの未来の砂漠は水の砂漠になるだろう。

水はどのように見えるのか？

砂を参照。（特に砂丘を。）

砂漠を参照。たとえば、ゴビやサハラを。

みなさん、聞こえていますか？ よかった。ここからが良いところだから。

ある男が椅子に手錠で繋がれたままウェストミンスター橋まで地下鉄で移動したという話がある。彼は椅子とともにその川に身を投げた。数日後、下流で発見された遺体には木の切れ端とビニールレザー（アーモンド色）が付着していた。

水はあなたを受け入れ、あなたを肯定し、あなたが何者かを明らかにする。そして、水というほとんど知覚できない性質のすべてがあなたを翻弄する。その曖昧さを以て。あなたを翻弄し、世界へと拡張していく。

テムズ川は都市を流れる川の中で最も自殺率が高い。一番ではないかもしれないけど、ほとんどそれに近いものだろう。たとえそうでなくてもそれほど問題はない。どうせそう見えるのだから。

最近、パリの若い女性がロンドンにやってきて、その川で溺死した。なぜテムズ川が遠くの人々を惹きつけるのかは興味深い。このような川は他に聞いたことがない。いや、わざわざカナダからやってきてハドソン川で自殺する人なんていない。オハイオ州からでさえも。

黒い水は不透明な水だ、毒があろうがなかろうが。黒い水は常に暴力的だ、ゆっくりと動くときでさえも。黒い水は支配し、魔法をかけ、服従させる。黒い水は魅力的だ、その不穏と不調和ゆえに。黒い水は暴力的だ、その魅惑ゆえに。そして、それが水であるために。

闇は太陽を映し出す。黒は無を映し出す。

闇は太陽を映し出す。黒は無を映し出す。（「悲しみと無の間にあって、おれは悲しみを選ぼう。」）

ウィリアム・フォークナーの小説『野性の棕櫚』より。

黒と水は対の要素だ。黒が形容詞にすぎないという考えは間違っている。

あなたは水の何を知っているのか？ あなたが水の話をするとき、本当は何について話しているのか？

あなたは水の何を知っているのか？ あなたが水の話をするとき、本当に話しているのはあなた自身なのでは？ その点で、水は天気みたいではないだろうか？

あなたは水の何を知っているのか？ その正体を決して知ることができないこと、それが水の一部ではないだろうか？

あなたは水の何を知っているのか？ それはどこにでもあり、親しみやすいようでいながら、あまりにも捉えどころがなく（いわば定義なきすべてのもの）、たとえ氷の形をしていても決して摑むことができない。

あなたは水の何を知っているのか？ それがいろんな場所でいろんな形をしているということを除けば。

あなたは水の概念にしがみつく。それはあなたが育った環境の水で、透明で性的な水。ともかくこれはあなたの個人的なアイデンティティの一部で、たとえ見知らぬ人であれ、あらゆる人々と共有するもの。アプリオリな交わり。

水はセクシーか？

ここからが良いところ。

水はセクシーだ。それは水のパワーであり傷つきやすさ、それは水のエネルギーであり壊れやすさ。

水はセクシーだ。近づくとその官能性がわたしをじらす。

水はセクシーだ。液体が肌の上を滑っているのを感じたい。液体がわたしの体中を洗い、わたしのすべてを洗い尽くすのを感じたい。その流動性の塊がわたしの身体の各部を駆けめぐるのを感じたい。髪を、手を、足を、目を、耳を。わたしはそのそばにいたい。浸りたい。奥深くに入っていきたい。もっと深くに

入っていきたい。その重みがわたしを軽くし、楽にし、解放してくれるのを感じたい。

黒い水は黒いミルクだ。

ミルクは黒いときもミルクなのか？

水の透明感はミルクの白さのようなものなのか？

水は常に神聖な存在だ。（水と一緒にいると、わたしの中に自分を超越した存在を感じる。）

水は常に神秘的な存在だ。（水を見ているとき、あなたは自分が実際に何を見ているのか知らない。）

そして、もうひとつの水についての漠然とした詩的観察はどうだろう？ それを詩にする可能性。それは人間の条件の一部だろうか？ 畏怖を抱くもの、生命を脅かすもの、延々と続く陰湿で危険なもの、それらを改善するために。だからといって、あなたがその全体を見えなくなってしまわないように。

ありふれているが壮観だ。陽の光がその川を照らし、光の粒がきらきらと水面を揺れ動く時間。それは星のように驚きを与え、魅了する。それを取り巻く暗闇、未知の宇宙、そして、もう少しで手の届きそうなところを想像してみる。

わたしはいかに水は鏡であるのかについて語らない。

あなたはいかに湖が鏡になりうるのかを知っている。浴室にあるような鏡。太陽が対になって沈む田園の風景。そして、あなたは静かな湖面に静止した完璧なる姿を見る。だが、あの種の鏡はいずれにせよいかなる川の言語でもない。よろしい、水面が凪ぎ、物がまだらに増殖する夜があるのかもしれない。けれども、物の姿が川で二重になることなどほとんどない。それ故に川の近くにはさまざまな種類の孤独があるのかもしれない。

あなたは自分がどんな風に川沿いを歩いているのかを知っている？ あなたは湖畔を同じようには歩かない。同じように腰を下ろすかもしれないけど、同じようには歩かない。あなたは歩き、川は流れる。あなたは川の流れとか反射とか、なにかしらを見ている。水の中に何かを見るのではないかと考えながら。あなたはじっと見る。何かが現れてくるのを待ちながら。たいていは何も現れないけど、あなたは待ちながら、引き込まれている。思考はあてもなくさまよう。何かが別の何かを呼び、また別の何かを呼ぶ。

あなたは自分がどんな風に川沿いを歩いているのかを知っている？ あなたは歩き、川は流れる。あなたは川の流れとか反射とか、なにかしらを見ている。水の中に何かを見るのではないかと考えながら。あなたはじっと見る。何かが現れてくるのを待ちながら。ただ、もしそこが湖ならば、あなたは腰を下ろしただろう。もしそこが湖ならば、こうした予感は生まれないだろう。今にも何かを見つけるのではないかという予感。おそらくは何か気分の悪くなるようなもの、あるいは価値のあるもの。

テムズ川にはたくさんの橋が架かっている。仮想の森のようだ。こんな河川は他にない。そして、橋はすべて魅力的な大きさで、個性に満ちあふれている。決してフーバーダムなんてものではないが、いったい誰がそれらを結びつけようとするだろう。いや、個人的な見解だけど。フーバーダムやその他の50万トン級のコンクリートの塊に近づくと、あなたとその塊の間にはただ距離しかない。たとえその上に立っていようが、そのダムはまだ遠くに見える。コロラド川のことは忘れていた。どこにある？ はるか下方。（726フィート下方だ。）ダムがなかったら、そこに川があることにすら気づくことはなかっただろう。

テムズ川にはたくさんの橋が架かっている。仮想の森のようだ。こんな河川は他にない。そして、橋はすべて魅力的な大きさで、個性に満ちあふれている。どうやらわたしも含まれているようだ。どの橋の上にいるときも、川自体も魅力的な大きさで、個性に満ちあふれているように見える。その川に近づくたびにこんな声が聞こえてくる。「こんにちは、どうぞ入って」とか「いらっしゃい」とか。

先週、その川で中年の男が見つかった。3,000ポンドの札束が彼自身の葬儀の指示書とともに腹部にテープで留められていた。

黒は完全だ。他のものが入り込む余地はなく、比類なき純粋さを備えている。黒はあらゆるものを排除する。あなたも含めて。そこにあなたが加わることも、何かを加えることも、影響を及ぼすこともできない。飛び込み、この黒さの中に入って、絶えず形を変えゆくものに包み込まれ、無視されることでしかあなたの存在が認められることはない。

あなたは水は波立つか凪ぐかだと言う。あなたは水は荒れ狂い静まることがないと言う。あなたは水はかき乱されていると言う。あなたは水は静まりかえっていると言う。水はのどかで時に澄んでいて、純粋かもしれないし、きらきらと輝いている。水は重い。それは事実だ。水はしばしば平穏で、落ち着いてさえいる。水はじっとして動かず、奥深くもあるだろう。水は冷たかったり温かかったり、ひえびえとしていたりぬるかったりする。あなたは水はせかせか、きびきび、時にてきぱきしていると言う。あなたは水はやわらかく、かたいと言う。あなたは水はちくちくしているし、つるつるしていると言う。あなたは水は腐敗していると言う。あなたは水は新鮮だと言う。あなたは水は静穏で物憂げだと言う。あなたは水はやさしいと言う。

黒い水は決してやさしくない。黒い水は冷たく、たいていは冷ややかで、時にひんやりしているが決してなまぬるくはない。黒い水はかたく、やわらかくない。けばけば、ざらざらしている。ちくちくするかもしれないけど、つるつるしている。それはよく騒めいていて、穏やかではない。少なくともただ穏やかなことはない。新鮮かもしれないけど、あなたは知る由もないし、決して信じることもない。しきりに動揺している。たいてい騒然としている。黒い水は決してのどかでもなく、輝いても、澄みきってもいない。止まっているときですら落ち着きがない。深く、それがどこまで続くのかわからない。この黒い水でさえ濡れてはいるがほとんど乾いた状態にある。

あなたはこの水が汚れていることを知っている。けれども今なおその周辺を歩いているのは奇妙なことじゃないだろうか? 水が澄んだ場所よりもそうではない場所に行ってしまうのはわかるけど、そうした場所は牧歌的な変化に富んでいて、魅力にあふれている。そう思わない? それともこれは倒錯者の見方なのだろうか?

あなたはこの水が汚れていることをよく知っている。けれどもあなたが今なおその水に惹きつけられていたり、それを見てまわっていたりするのは奇妙なことじゃないだろうか?

わたしはこの水が汚れていることをよく知っている。その方がより説得力もあるし、より謎めいてもいる。

若い女が黄色のフォード・フィエスタを運転し、車ごとその川に落ちた。警察が車を引き揚げると、窓はすべて閉まっていて、ドアには鍵がかかっていた。警察は運転席にその女を見つけ、後部座席には彼女の愛犬（アイリッシュセッター）サミュエルの姿、彼女の手にそのリードが巻きついていた。

この世界の不透明性は水の中で霧散する。

黒い水は世界の不透明性を霧散できない。

混乱している? 迷っている? 広大な水面は砂漠のようだ。目印もなければ、こことそこを見分けるための違いもない。（どこにいるのかわからずに、自分が誰なのかわかるだろうか?）ただ騒動が至る所で絶え間なく。騒動はまた別の騒動へとあちこちで果てしなく転調しつづける。その変化は絶えず繰り返され、どこまでも行き渡り、まったく容赦のないものなので、アイデンティティや場所、階級といったあらゆる尺度は薄れ、弱まり、遂には消えてしまう。この水のまわりで過ごす時間が長くなるほど、尺度の記憶は薄れていく。

水は神秘的なものと物質的なものの謎めいた結合だ。想像して。あらゆるものと接触するあらゆるものの影響を受けながらも、少量を手に取ってみれば、今日に至るまでほとんどは透明のまま。それどころか水晶のように澄みきっている。

水はあらゆるものの存在から得られる透明性だ。水はあらゆるものの存在から得られる透明性だ。

すなわち水は地球を通してふるいにかけられ濾過される。地球、帯水層は不純物を取り除き、純粋性を獲得する。このフィルターが絶妙な平衡を維持し、結果として、いかなるものとも似ても似つかない物質が得られる。あらゆるものがひとつのアイデンティティに収束する。水というアイデンティティに。

水はユートピア的な物質だ。水の間とは? 水は複数形? たとえ一本の川でも、単数形だなんてことがあ

りえるだろうか? その水はどこから来たのか?

どの川でニール・ヤングは恋人を撃ったのか?

「ダウン・バイ・ザ・リバー」を参照。(「川のほとりで、俺はあいつを撃った…あいつを撃ち殺しちまった…」)。彼はこの曲の中でその川の名前を特定していない。

2日前、その川で中年男性の遺体が引き揚げられた。警察は男性の外套のポケットに収まった辞書を見つけた。ズボンや上着のポケットの中、腰にベルトで留められたポーチの中には細々とした金属類が、ナット、ワッシャー、ネジ、そして、168ポンド52ペンス分のコインが入っていて、その重さは32ポンドにも及んだ。

この水はあらゆる他の水と一枚岩のように分割できない連続性をもって存在する。いかなる水も他のいかなる水と分かつことはできない。

テムズ川、北極の氷山、あなたのグラス、雨粒、結霜した窓ガラスの表面、あなたの目、そして、あらゆる極小の小宇宙的な、あなたの(そしてわたしの)細部の中に、すべての水が収束する。

不可分の連続性は水に内在するものだ。この連続性はわたしたちの内の最大を占めるものでありながら、わたしたちを超越している。この連続性こそが、わたしたちが水に及ぼす影響というものをわたしたち自身に及ぼす影響に変える。すなわち「わたしはテムズ川だ!」あるいは「テムズ川はわたしだ!」というように。

その川を訪れることは一石二鳥だ。あなたはそこに立ち、同時にいろいろな場所に行く。

アンハイドロニー。

アンハイドロニーは水なき水、水とは正反対にあるものだ。形態は液体のまま、その物質が変わる。もうひとつのアイデンティティに置き換えられる。アンハイドロニーは乾いた水だ。

アンハイドロニーはまだ認知されていない言葉だ。存在しないということが、その意味を受け入れることの難しさを指摘している。

水の中にあなた自身を見るとき、あなたの中に水を感じる?

「テムズの河口湾は、ここから果てしない水路が始まるというように、私たちの眼の前に延びていた。…鷗が漂っている岸辺の低地は海に向かって薄平たく消え入っていた。上流のほうを振り返れば、グレイヴゼンドの町の上は空気が薄黒く、さらにその向こうでは薄黒い空気が凝って陰鬱な闇となり、じっと動くことなく、地上最大の最も素晴らしい都市の上にのしかかっているように見えた。」

『闇の奥』を参照。

イングランド人には殺人において死体をばらばらに切断する傾向がある。ロンドンの歴史において、テムズ川やその岸辺でばらばらになった頭や手足や臓器を目にしない時代などあるのだろうか。先週、警察は腸と足を発見した(右足か左足かという報告はない)。シルバータウンを越えたところに、腸と片方の足。

昨日、イブニングスタンダード紙にこうあった。「通行人が人間の頭部や手足が泥から突き出ているのを目撃した…」。11もの部位がその川から発見されたが「由々しきことに胴体は見つからなかった」と。

どこにその胴体はあるのか?

身体の一部(殺人事件の被害者)、死体(自殺、主に飛び降り自殺)、下水(人間の排泄物)、重金属(鉛、水銀、カドミウムなど)。鷺や鶴がその光景をやわらげてくれるけれども、わずかな気休めにすぎない。

少し前の新聞に橋から飛び降りた若い男性の記事が載っていた。彼はファントムという名の黒い自転車を胸に縛りつけて飛び込んだ。(身元判明に半年かかった。)

あなたはそれを期待しているのだろうか? あなたはそれを求めているのだろうか? アイデンティティを失う

ことを。テムズ川にはアイデンティティを溶かす力がある。

どの川でブルース・スプリングスティーンは恋人を妊娠させたのか?

「ザ・リバー」を参照。

(「俺たちは車であの川に向かい、飛び込んで泳いだものさ。俺たちが泳いだあの川。それから俺はメアリーを孕ませた。彼女はそれだけ書いてよこした。夜、俺たちはあの川に向かい、飛び込んで泳いだ。叶わぬ夢は嘘なのか、それともっと酷いのか。だから俺はあの川に向かう。そこに水がないのはわかっているが。」)

わたしの視線がその水に止まる、その川のどこかに。ここでその水はまわる。ここでその水は、その流れの力でいくつもの渦を巻く。(わたしはこの締め付けるように回転する円から逃れられない。)わたし自身がねじれるのを感じたい。わたしは見たい、時間のねじれを感じたい、螺旋が形成されていくのを見ながら。時間がねじれ、わたしが回転するのを感じたい、それらが消えていくのを見ながら。回転する水とともにねじれたい、渦巻きが消えてなくなるのを見ながら。それらが水面から見えない深みへとまわりながら沈んでいくのを見たい。それらと一緒に見えなくなりたい。それらと一緒にまわってみたい、見えなくなって、まわりつづけたい。

ウォレス・スティーヴンズの詩「黒の支配」を参照。

わたしの視線がその水に止まる、その川のどこかに。ここでその水はまわる。ここでその水は、その流れの力でいくつもの渦を巻く。わたし自身がねじれるのを感じたい。渦巻きがうねり、泡立ち、広がっていくのを見たい。平らになった水のまわりに泡立つ波紋が生まれるのを見たい。隆起し、平静する水に静寂が訪れるのを見たい。そして、その静寂の表面で、乾いたように見える水がその深みへと、このような水温と粘度と流出量の水が複雑な質感のまま流れ込むのを見たい。

わたしの視線がその水に止まる、その川のどこかに。そして、わたしの視線が止まるとき、かつて見たことがないものを見ているかのような気持ちになる。どうして水はこんなにもよそよそしいのだろうか。

あなたの姿は水の中で結びつかない。あなたからゆらゆらと離れていく。岸や橋の上に立って、どうすることともできないまま、自分の姿が漂い、そして消えゆくのをじっと目で追いながら、黒い水はいかなる力を呼び寄せるのだろうかと不思議に思うだろう。しかしあなたは本能的に、それが幾何学よりも魔法に近いものだと知っている。

「最高の魔法は幾何学。」

エミリ・ディキンスンの詩「1158番」を参照。

前述のパリから来た若い女性を覚えている? ホテルの部屋から姉妹に宛てた遺書が見つかった。(それはフランス語で書かれていた。)遺書には彼女の悩みが事細かに書き綴られ、歯並びの悪さにも触れられていた。(彼女は自分が出っ歯だと思い込んでいた。)

警察によれば、彼女は出っ歯ではなく、これには驚いたそうだ。

少年は汚れた川で洗礼を受ける(偽りの名の下に)。翌日、少年はその川に戻り、入水自殺する。

フラナリー・オコナーの短編「河」を参照。

水が光をカモフラージュすることに気づいたことはある?

最近、その川で若い男が溺死したという話を聞いた。彼は耳が聞こえず、口も利けなかった。両親が考案した手話を使っていた。(家族だけがそれを理解した。)

その川は自らに影を投げかけ、本来の姿になる。影や汚物は、暗闇やあらゆるものを貫く時の流れでその水を濃くする。アイデンティティ、場所、地質などを貫く時の流れによって。その水はイメージなき闇に満たされた底知れぬ深さに向かって流れ込む。

夜、その川は可能性の風景の音を奏でる。

夜、その川は可能性の風景の音を奏でる。耳をすまさなければ、それは聴こえてこない。急流が生み出すホワイトノイズ以上のものを聴くためにはということだが。そして、あなたが暗闇の中で耳にするのは繊細で捉えどころのない音。昼もそこにあるはずの音は、光に遮られ、聞こえない。

水がほっとため息を吐き。水がちゅうちゅうと吸い。水がぺろぺろと舐め。水がぴちゃぴちゃと飲み。水がびちゃん。水がびしゅう。水がぼちゃん。水がばちゃん。水がざぶん。水がざぶざぶ。水がじゃぶじゃぶ。水がさらさら。水がしんと静まりかえり。水がどっと流れ出し。水がぶしゅっと噴き出し。水がぶくぶく泡立ち。水がざわざわさんざめき、水がごぼごぼ流れゆき。水がちゅうちゅうと吸う。

この歌を知っている?
　　　「ブラー、ブラー、ブラー、あなたの髪
　　　ブラー、ブラー、ブラー、あなたの瞳
　　　ブラー、ブラー、ブラー、ブラー、愛する
　　　ブラー、ブラー、ブラー、ブラー、空に。」

アイラ・ガーシュウィンが作詞した「ブラー ブラー ブラー」より。

テムズ川が透き通っていたことなど一度もなかったのではないだろうか。しかし、今日、その透明性の欠落が意味するものは200年前や500年前のそれとは違う。

昨日、読んだ夕刊紙にこうあった。「7月8日夜、ロウアープールの川辺を歩いていた男性が偶然人間の頭部を見つけた」と。死亡者の身元は特定されておらず記事はこう続いていた。「顔の皮が剥がれていた。」その頭があるべき身体は数週間にわたって、足はここ、手はあそこといった具合にばらばらに発見された。ひと月かかったが、警察は胴体を含むすべての部位を見つけ出した。

(水は万能な動詞だ。恒久的関係の行為。)

光が水をカモフラージュすることに気づいたことはある?

水が水らしく見えることなんて滅多にないと気づいたことはある?

水はどのように見えるのか?

軍用迷彩を参照。ポーリッシュ・プレジデンシャル、イタリアン・ウッドランド、サンマルコ・メディテラニアン、インドネシアン・スポット、そして、ベルジャン・ジグソー。

どの川でジミ・ヘンドリックスは恋人を撃ったのか? それが川だったのか定かではないけど、おそらく川だったはずだ。

「ヘイ・ジョー」を参照。(「俺はあいつを撃ち殺す。いいか、俺はあいつが別の男といちゃついているのを見ちまったんだ…。」)

「わたしをその川に連れていって、その水の中に投げ込んで。」

(テムズ川なら殺人事件だろう。)

アル・グリーンの「テイク・ミー・トゥー・ザ・リバー」を参照。

無数の星のような、泡や無限小の虹、そして細密かつ迅速に仕上げられた反射の数々。儚きものの中の儚きものたちが、偶然にも、その無常と透明性をほんの一瞬輝かせる。

あなたがこのような経験をしたことがあるかわからないけど、わたしがその水をじっと見つめていると、川からいろいろな歌が断片的に聞こえてくることがある。(時にわたしはその声を聞くことさえある。)

昨夜、わたしがその水をじっと見ていると、川から「エイント・ノー・ウェイ」が聞こえてきて、ゆっくりと何度も、「ありえない…ただありえない、無理なの…そんなのありえない…絶対にありえない…ただもうありえない…ありえない…」と。

歌手じゃない理由がわかりますよね。

キャロリン・フランクリンの「エイント・ノー・ウェイ」より。わたしが歌おうとしたのはかつてアレサ・フランクリンが歌ったもの。

光の中で、水は単純に水である。

水がかがやき、水がゆらめき、水がぽっと、水がちらちら、水がぴかぴか、水がぽつぽつ、水がきらきら、水がきらり、水がきらっ、水がぴかっ、水がまたたき、水がまばたき、水が波打つ。

この水は未知なるものに溢れている。言葉に絶するような、発音できないものに。時にわたしはその水の中にあらゆるものを想像して自分自身を慰める。その恐怖によって。それはネズミやコンドームや下水のようなわかりやすいものだけではなく。これらはまだ序の口。わたしはウイルスやバクテリアなんかを思い浮かべようとする。肝炎や大腸菌、赤痢菌やコレラ、ワイル病と呼ばれているもの、そして、本当かどうかわからないけど、ペストの残滓と思われるもの、ほとんど水のようなものとして消えることなく残っているものたちを。

そして、金はどうだろう? あらゆる秘密の財宝は? 結婚指輪や金の詰め物は?

そして、近代の神話である次のような錬金術の類。たとえば、ポリフェノール、ポリ塩化ビフェニル、塩素化炭化水素、トリクロロエタン、そして、はっきりとした姿形もわからないまま、世界中からもたらされるこの種のものたち。

そして、すべての娼婦たちはどうだろう? それが全身であろうと身体の一部であろうと、その川で人生を終えた娼婦たち。

娼婦たちは? どうして娼婦たちが川の近く、時には川の中で見つかることが多いのか疑問に思ったことはある?

川の話。川沿いのシーンからはじまる(おそらくライン川)。夏の日の明け方、夜が明けようとしている。あたりはまだ薄暗い。男娼が河岸に立っている。ほどなくひとりの客が彼に声をかけ、ふたりはキスを始める。ところが男娼は、(男性のような服装をした)そいつが実は女だと気づき怒り狂う。エルヴィラという名前のその客が男娼仲間に打ちのめされる。物語の後半、あなたはエルヴィラは男として生まれたことを知る。親友を喜ばせるためにエルヴィラは性別を変えた。だが、アントンは彼が女であることを望んではいなかった。最後に、エルヴィラは自殺する。

ライナー・ヴェルナー・ファスビンダーの映画『13回の新月のある年に』を参照。

この歌を知っている?
　　　　「ブラー、ブラー、ブラー、ブラー、月
　　　　ブラー、ブラー、ブラー、の上
　　　　ブラー、ブラー、ブラー、ブラー、口ずさむ
　　　　ブラー、ブラー、ブラー、ブラー、愛を。」

『サイコ』は覚えている? フロントガラスにワイパーが擦れる音。(おそらくあれはバイオリン。)そこには一種の執拗さがあった。何かを予感させるような。川の水、とりわけ夜の川の水が持っているような。あの執拗さは止まることはない、川が流れつづけるように。事実、あのバイオリンは止まらない。わたしの頭の中で延々と鳴り響く。果たして川に終わりはあるのか?

果たして川に終わりはあるのか? たとえあなたがここからテムズ川が北海に流れ込むのを目で追っていったとしても、そこに終わりはあるのか?

果たして川に終わりはあるのか？ そう、川はただ流れつづけ、また別の名前となって流れていく。

その水をじっと見つめながら、わたしは意味のめまいに襲われる。

その水をじっと見つめながら、わたしは意味のめまいに襲われる。水は究極の結合だ。無限の形態、関係性、内容。

数年前、若い役者がその川に身を投げた。エドガー・アラン・ポーの生涯を描いた舞台で、彼はちょうどポーの役に抜擢されたところだった。その後すぐに、彼は演出家にその役を外し、彼が彼自身を演じる役に置き換えるよう進言していた。

雨降りや曇り空の下、わずかな光しか届かない天気の中で、水は単純に水であるわけではない。

雨が降ると、虫のように小さな斑点がその川の水面に一時的に集まる。雨粒のひとつひとつはほんの小さな闇、飛んでは消えていくような点。

あなたは何を考えている？ 水面を打つ雨はそこに映るものを破壊し、景色を鎮める。

あなたは何を考えている？ 水面を打つ雨は魅力的で心地よく、軽やかだ。その川は干潟、寝そべるのにちょうどよいやわらかな場所となる。

雨が降ると、虫のように小さな斑点がその川の水面に一時的に集まる。雨粒ひとつひとつがその水に触れることで、とても小さな円がいくつも形成される。接触による束の間の幾何学。

どの川でハンク・ウィリアムズは自殺しようとしたのか？

「魚を見るためにその川に向かった。なのに、そこに着いたら孤独で死にたくなったんだ。そして俺は飛び込んだ。だが、その忌まわしい川に水はなかった…。」

アルバム『ロー・ダウン・ブルース』より。

夜、あなたはその黒さを見ることができない。そこにはただ闇のみ。あなたがその黒さを見ることができるのは昼だけ。そこで、あなたはそれが反射ではないと知る。

黒は場所だ。それがどのようなものかもわからないし、見ることもできないけれど、そこにあることはわかる。そこに行くことはできるが、どこにあるのかは決まっていない。黒は傷むことがなく、不活性で腐敗することもない。金のように。そして、それがどこであろうとも常に変わることがない。あなたはそれについてそれほど知らないし、その正体が明らかになることもない（それが黒の概念）。ただそこに行くしかない。黒はあなたの信仰を宙吊りにできる場所だ。

あなたが水を見つめるとき、あなたは自分が思い描いているのは水面に映るあなたの姿だと理解している。でも、それはあなたの姿ではない。（あなたは水の反射した姿である。）

　　ありがとうございました。

翻訳：石井麻希・良知 暁

訳註：
《水と言う》に引用・参照された文献のうち、ジョセフ・コンラッドの『闇の奥』、ウィリアム・フォークナーの「野生の棕櫚」、エミリ・ディキンスンの詩に関しては、以下の既訳を使用した。
・コンラッド『闇の奥』黒原敏行訳、光文社、2009年。
・ウィリアム・フォークナー「野生の棕櫚」『フォークナー全集14』井上謙治訳、冨山房、1968年。
・『完訳エミリ・ディキンスン詩集（フランクリン版）』新倉俊一監訳、東雄一郎、小泉由美子、江田孝臣、朝比奈緑翻訳、金星堂、2019年。
※ただし、《水と言う》内ではジョンスン版の作品番号が使用されている。

I feel like I have a little bit of competition here, with this setting sun. So I'll speak a little louder.

What I'd like to do is a kind of monologue, which actually comes from a text I wrote in conjunction with visual art, but I decided to get rid of the visual part of it entirely and just go with the monologue. It's called

Saying Water

In the waiting room of a doctor's office some years ago I overheard a mother talking about how her kids were afraid of it. If they couldn't see into it, they wouldn't go into it. It's like being dismembered. When you wade into this dark fluid, a kind of milk without nurture, you disappear.

Disappearance: that's why suicides are attracted to it. It's also why children fear it. It's a soft entrance to simply not being here. When I imagine the river, it's something I can enter, something that will surround me, take me away from here. But then the pain of it is less imaginable, too. Less than violence or chemistry.

Thinking about water is thinking about the future—or just a future. My future— yours. It's a personal thing—especially now. It makes sense that children fear water they can't see into. And then, too, doesn't it make sense for someone who can't imagine a future to be attracted to it, to this semblance of water, to this other water?

It is night. The darkness of the water reflects the darkness of the sky. But when daylight comes again the water will remain dark, cutting everything in it off from everything beyond it.

The water is opaque. It is comforting to imagine that once you are in it, you won't be visible any longer and you won't see anything, either—relief from the unending demands of simple sight.

Hidden by the dark. It's only night and that will pass. But the blackness of the water won't pass. The blackness and the water pass by but they never go away.

The color of the water (whatever it is) changes constantly. Half of it is the sky.

The color of the water (whatever it is) changes constantly. Half of it is khaki: with all the colors in it, though none are visible, and the whole of it nondescript. And anyway, you wouldn't really see it once you were under. It suits me—beige; it suits me—it isn't a color; it's like white that way—but without distinction. Beige is a form of mediocrity. White is important, maybe a labyrinth of sorts—that makes it a wager for life.

You say it's a river. I can believe that. But when you say it's water, I get suspicious.

Is the Thames a case of mistaken identity?

When you say water, what do you mean?

When you say water, are you talking about the weather or yourself?

When you see your reflection in water, do you recognize the water in you?

The deserts of our future will be deserts of water.

What does water look like?

See sand. (Especially sand dunes.)

See deserts, for example the Gobi or the Sahara.

Can you all hear me? Just checking. I'm getting to the good part now.

A man travelled by tube to Westminster Bridge handcuffed to a chair. He threw himself in the river with the chair. He was found some days later downstream, attached to a stick of wood and a section of naugahyde (almond colored).

Water receives you, affirms you, shows you who you are. And all the near-imperceptible qualities that are water tease you with their ambiguity. Tease you and extend you out into the world.

The Thames has the highest rate of suicides of any urban river. Well, maybe it's not the highest but it's close. And it doesn't really matter because even if it doesn't, it looks like it does.

A young Parisian woman came to London recently to drown herself in the river. It's curious how the Thames attracts people from far away. I've never heard of any other river doing this. I mean people don't travel from Canada to kill themselves in the Hudson—or even from Ohio.

Black water is opaque water, toxic or not. Black water is always violent, even when slow moving. Black water dominates, bewitches, subdues. Black water is alluring because it is disturbing and irreconcilable. Black water is violent because it is alluring, and because it is water.

Darkness reflects the sun. Blackness reflects nothing.

Darkness reflects the sun. Blackness reflects nothing. ("Between grief and nothing, I will take grief.")

From the novel *The Wild Palms* by William Faulkner.

Black and water are twin elements. It's a mistake to believe black is merely an adjective.

What do you know about water? When you talk about water, what is it you're really talking about?

What do you know about water? When you talk about water, aren't you really talking about yourself? Isn't water like the weather that way?

What do you know about water? Isn't that part of what water is, that you never really know what it is?

Oh, what do you know about water? That it's everywhere, so familiar-seeming, and yet so elusive (a kind of everything without definition), never quite graspable, even as an ice cube?

What do you know about water? Only that it's everywhere differently?

You hold onto the idea of water, which is the water you grew up with, clear and sexual. Somehow this is part of your personal identity. You share it with everyone, even strangers. It is an *a priori* communion.

Is water sexy?

This is the good part.

Water is sexy. It's the power and the vulnerability of it; It's the energy and the fragility of it.

Water is sexy. (The sensuality of it teases me when I'm near it.)

Water is sexy. (I want to feel its liquid form slipping over my skin. I want to feel its liquidness washing me all over, washing all over me. I want to feel the fluid mass of it rushing among the parts of me: my hairs, my fingers, my toes, my eyes, my ears. I want to be near it. I want to immerse myself in it. I want to go deep into it. I want to go deeper still into it. I want to feel the weight of it lighten me, ease me, release me.)

Black water is black milk.

Is milk milk when it's black?

Isn't transparency to water as whiteness is to milk?

Water's always a spiritual presence. (In the company of water, I feel in me the presence of things that exceed me.)

Water is always a mysterious presence. (When you look at water you never know what you're actually looking at.)

And what about these vaguely poetic observations about another water? The possibility of poeticizing it—is that part of the human condition? To ameliorate something awful, something life-threatening, something so insidious and protracted in its danger, because not to prevent you from seeing it altogether?

It's so familiar and so spectacular: the times when sunlight strikes the river and sparks twinkle and flit on the water. They surprise and mesmerize the way stars do. I imagine the darkness that surrounds them, an unknown universe and just a few feet from my grasp.

I won't talk about how water is a mirror.

You know how a lake can be a mirror? A mirror as in a bathroom. A country scene where the sun sets in pairs and you see on the still lake water a still and perfect reflection. That kind of mirror isn't a part of river language anyway. Okay, there might be an occasional evening when the water is calm and things multiply in a mottled way, but mostly things don't double in rivers, and maybe there's a different kind of solitude near them because of it.

You know the way you walk along a river? Well, you don't walk around a lake the same way. You might sit in front of it in the same way, but you don't walk. You walk and the river runs, you watch the currents or the reflections or whatever. You think maybe you'll see something in the water. You watch—waiting for something to appear. Usually nothing does, but while you're waiting, you're drawn in, your thoughts meander, one thing leads to another and so on.

You know the way you walk along a river? You walk and the river runs, you watch the currents or the reflections or whatever. You think maybe you'll see something in the water. You watch—waiting for something to appear. But you know if it was a lake, you'd be sitting down. If it was a lake, there wouldn't be this feeling of anticipation, of imminent discovery, of something perhaps awful—or valuable.

There are so many bridges over the Thames—it's a virtual forest. It's not like any other river that way. And they're all so invitingly scaled and full of character. They're not exactly the Hoover Dam, but who can relate to the Hoover Dam?—I mean, personally speaking. When you approach the Hoover, or any other five-hundred-thousand-ton mass of concrete, there's nothing but distance between you and it. Even when you're standing on it, the dam is still a distant view. And forget about the Colorado River, I mean where is it? Way the hell down there. (Seven hundred and twenty-six feet down there.) You wouldn't even know there was a river if it wasn't a dam.

There are so many bridges over the Thames—it's a virtual forest. It's not like any other river that way. And they're all so invitingly scaled and full of character. They seem to include me somehow. And when I'm on one of them, the river itself seems so invitingly scaled and full of character. Whenever I approach the river, I hear it saying, "Hello there. Come on in." Or, "Welcome."

A middle-aged man was found in the river last week. £3,000 in notes was taped to his chest along with instructions for his funeral.

Blackness is complete. No room for anything else. Complete with an untouchable purity. Blackness excludes everything—including you. You can't participate in it; you can't add anything to it or affect it. Jumping in, entering this blackness, being surrounded by something that reforms endlessly, that can only admit you by disregarding you.

You say water is troubled or calm. You say water is rough and restless. You say water is disturbed. You say water is quiet. Water is serene and sometimes clear; it might be pure and then it's brilliant. Water is heavy; that's a fact. Water is often tranquil, even placid. Water is still and then it might be deep as well. Water is cold or hot, chilly or tepid. You say water is brash or brisk, sometimes crisp. You say water is soft and hard. You say water irritates and lubricates. You say water is foul. You say water is fresh. You say water is limpid and languorous. You say water is sweet.

Black water is never sweet. Black water is cold, often frigid; sometimes cool, but never tepid. Black water is hard, not soft. It's brash and rough; it might irritate. It still lubricates. It's often disturbed, but it's never calm; at least, not simply calm. It might be fresh but you'd never know it, and I'm sure you'd never believe it. It's frequently agitated, it's often troubled. I don't think you can question that, even when it appears quiet. Black water is never serene or brilliant or clear. It's unsettled even when still. It can be deep, but it's hard to know where. Even black water is wet but mostly in a parching way.

You know this water is filthy.

But isn't it strange the way you still go places around it? It's true you go different places than if it was clear. But those places are as alluring as the pastoral variety, don't you think? Or is this the view of a pervert?

You know very well this water is filthy. But it's strange the way you're still drawn to it? The way you still hang around, watching it.

I know very well this water is filthy. It's more compelling that way, more unknown.

A young woman drove her yellow Ford Fiesta down a ramp into the river. When police pulled the car out, all the windows were closed, and the doors were locked. They found the woman in the front seat and in the back—Samuel, her dog (an Irish Setter), his leash wrapped around her hand.

The opacity of the world dissipates in water.

Black water cannot dissipate the opacity of the world.

Confused? Lost? Large expanses of water are like deserts; no landmarks, no differ-ences. (If you don't know where you are, can you know who you are?) Just tumult everywhere, endlessly. Tumult modulating into another tumult, all over and without end. The change is so constant, so pervasive, so relentless that identity, place, scale— all measures lessen, weaken—eventually disappear. The more time you spend around this water—the more faint your memories of measure become.

Water is a mysterious combination of the mysterious and the material. Imagine something that, impinged on by everything, in contact with everything, remains to this day mostly transparent—even crystal clear, when taken in small enough quantities.

Water is transparence derived from the presence of everything. Water is transparence derived from the presence of everything.

That is, water is sifted down, filtered out through the planet, earth. Earth: aquifer that clarifies and realizes purity. This filter of everything modulates to exquisite balance. A substance is obtained that bears no likeness. All things converge in a single identity: water.

Water is utopic substance. Among water? Isn't water a plural form? How could it ever be singular, even in one river? Where did that water come from?

Which river did Neil Young shoot his baby down by?

See the song "Down by the River:" ("Down by the river, I shot my baby . . . . I shot her dead . . . .") He doesn't identify the river in the song.

A body of a middle-aged man was taken from the river two days ago. In a pocket of his overcoat, police found a large dictionary. In his trousers and coat pockets, and in a pouch buckled to his waist, they found various bits of hardware—nuts, washers, and screws, and £168 and 52p. in coins—weighing thirty-two pounds.

This water exists in monolithic, indivisible continuity with all other waters. No water is separate from any other water.

In the River Thames, in an Arctic iceberg, in your drinking glass, in that drop of rain, on that frosty windowpane, in your eyes and in every other microscopic, microcosmic part of you (and me), all waters converge.

Indivisible continuity is intrinsic to water. This continuity exceeds us even while being the biggest part of us. It's this continuity that makes our effect on water an effect on us. That is to say: "I am the Thames!" or "The Thames is me!"

When you go down to the river you're killing two birds with one stone: you stand there and you go places.

Anhydrony.

Anhydrony is waterless water. The opposite of water. The form remains liquid, but the substance is altered—replaced with another identity. Anhydrony is dry water.

Anhydrony is not a recognized word. Its nonexistence points to the difficulty of accepting its meaning.

When you see yourself reflected in water, do you recognize the water in you?

"The sea-reach of the Thames stretched out before us like the beginning of an interminable waterway. . . . A haze rested on the low shores that ran out to sea in vanishing flatness. The air was dark above Gravesend, and farther back still seemed condensed into a mournful gloom, brooding motionless over the biggest, and the greatest, town on earth."

See *Heart of Darkness*.

The English have a penchant for dismembering their murder victims. I doubt there's a period of London history free from the heads, limbs, and vital organs found in the Thames, or washed up on its banks. Last week police found intestines and a leg (they didn't say if it was right or left). Over near Silvertown—intestines and one leg.

Yesterday I read in the *Evening Standard*: "A passer-by spotted a man's head and limbs sticking out of the mud. . . ." Eleven body parts were found in the river but, "significantly, not the torso."

Where is the torso?

Body parts (victims of murder), corpses (suicides—mostly jumpers), sewage (human waste), heavy metals (lead, mercury, cadmium, for example). Herons and cormorants lighten up the look, but not much—only briefly.

There was an article in the newspaper some time ago about a young man jumping off a bridge. He strapped his bicycle, a black Phantom, to his chest, and jumped in. (It took six months to identify the body.)

Isn't that what you'd expect? Isn't that what you'd be after—to lose your identity? The Thames looks like a solvent for identity.

Which river did Bruce Springsteen get his baby pregnant down by?

See the song, "The River:"

("...We'd go down to the river and into the river we dived, oh...down to the river we'd ride. Then I got Mary pregnant, and man, that was all she wrote...That night we went down to the river and into the river we'd dive...Is a dream alive if it don't come true, oh is it something worse—that sends me down to the river, though I know the river is dry...")

My gaze alights on the water—on some spot on the river: here where the water is turning around, where the currents turn the water in tightening circles. (I can't turn away from these tightening, turning circles.) I want to feel myself twisted around. And I want to watch, I want to feel time twist as I watch these spirals forming. I want to feel time twist and myself turning as I watch them disappear. I want to twist with the turning water. I want to watch these spirals turn themselves invisible. I want to watch them turning from the surface, turning down into the depths, where I cannot see them. I want to turn invisible with them. I want to turn with them: invisible— and keep turning.

See the poem "Domination of Black," Wallace Stevens.

My gaze alights on the water—on some spot on the river: here, where the water is turning around, where the currents turn the water in tightening circles. I want to feel myself twisted around, I want to watch these spirals swelling and bubbling and expanding. I want to watch the flattened water as frothing ripples form around it. I want to watch as the stillness of the swollen and smooth water comes. And on the surface of that stillness, I want to watch as dry-looking water rushes over its depths, rushing with the intricate texture that water has at this temperature and viscosity and flow.

My gaze alights on the water—on some spot on the river. And as my gaze alights it feels as though I'm seeing something I've never seen before. How does water remain so unfamiliar?

Your reflection uncouples in this water. It drifts away from you. As you stand there on the bank or bridge, helpless, watching your reflection float downstream and disappear, you may wonder what forces black water gathers. But instinctively you already know they must be closer to witchcraft than geometry.

"Best witchcraft is geometry."

See poem No. 1158 by Emily Dickinson.

Do you remember the young Parisian woman I mentioned earlier? They found a suicide note in her hotel room addressed to her sister. (It was written in French.) The note referred in detail to her problems, including her bad teeth. (She thought she had buck teeth.)

Police said this surprised them since, in their judgment, she did not have buck teeth.

A boy is baptized in a filthy river (under a false name). The next day he goes back and drowns himself in it.

See the short story "The River," by Flannery O'Connor.

Have you ever noticed how water camouflages light?

I heard an account recently of a young man drowning himself in the river. He was deaf and dumb. He used a sign language invented by his parents. (Only the family understood it.)

This river casts a shadow into itself, becoming itself. The shadows and dirt thicken the water with a darkness and distance that slices through everything: identity, place, geology. The water rushes along in its unseeable depths, full of a darkness that has no image.

The sound of the river at night is a landscape of possibilities.

The sound of the river at night is a landscape of possibilities. You have to get fairly close before you can really hear it. I mean, hear something more than the white noise of its rush. And what you hear in the dark are delicate, elusive sounds. Sounds that must be there in the day as well, but are unheard, muted by the light.

Water sighs. Water sucks. Water licks. Water laps. Water splishes. Water swishes. Water sploshes. Water splashes. Water washes. Water swashes. Water sloshes. Water murmurs. Water hushes. Water rushes. Water gushes. Water burbles. Water babbles. Water gurgles. Water sucks.

Do you know this ditty?
> "Blah, blah, blah, your hair,
> Blah, blah, blah, your eyes;
> Blah, blah, blah, blah, care,
> Blah, blah, blah, blah, skies."

From the song "Blah, Blah, Blah," written by Ira Gershwin.

Probably the Thames was never clear, but its lack of transparence means something different today than it did two hundred or five hundred years ago.

Yesterday I read in the evening paper: "On the night of July 8th a man walking on the foreshore at Lower Pool stumbled on a human head." To obscure the identity of the dead person, the article went on to note: The face had been skinned. The body it belonged to was found in pieces over the following weeks, a leg here, a hand there. It took one month but police found all the parts including the torso.

(Water is the master verb: an act of perpetual relation.)

Have you ever noticed how light camouflages water?

Have you ever noticed how rarely water looks like water?

What does water look like?

See military camouflage. For example: "Polish Presidential," "Italian Woodland," "San Marco Mediterranean," "Indonesian Spot," and "Belgian Jigsaw" patterns.

Which river did Jimi Hendrix shoot his baby down by? Well, I'm not certain it was a river, but it probably should have been.

See the song "Hey Joe:" ("I'm going down to shoot my old lady, you know I caught her messin' round with another man . . . .")

"Take me to the river, drop me in the water."

(In the Thames that would be murder.)

See the song "Take Me to the River," by Al Green.

A congress of star-like specks, bubbles, infinitesimal rainbows, and finely though quickly wrought reflections. Ephemerals among other ephemerals of coincidence, giving momentary visibility to the transient and transparent.

I don't know if you've had this experience but occasionally when I'm watching the water I hear snippets from various songs drifting up from the river. (Sometimes I even recognize the voice.)

Last night when I was watching the water "Ain't No Way" came wafting up, slow and endless: "Ain't no way... just ain't no way, no... ain't no way, baby... sure ain't no way... just ain't no way... ain't no way, baby..."

   Well, you can tell why I'm not a singer.

From "Ain't No Way," by Carolyn Franklin. The version I'm trying to sing was once sung by Aretha Franklin.

In the light, water is water more simply.

Water shines. Water shimmers. Water glows. Water glimmers. Water glitters. Water gleans. Water glistens. Water glints. Water twinkles. Water sparkles. Water blinks. Water winks. Water waves.

This water is full of unknown things—unspeakable, unpronounceable things. Sometimes I console myself by imagining all the things in the water. I console myself with the horror of it. It's not just the obvious stuff like rats and condoms and sewage. That's easy to imagine. But I try to visualize the viruses and bacteria as well, like hepatitis and E. coli and the little bacteria of dysentery and cholera, and that disease called Weils and, who knows, maybe a remnant of the plague, just lingering the way things tend to do near water.

And what about the gold? All the hidden treasures? The wedding rings, for example— or the gold fillings?

And what about all those Greek chemistries that are modern mythology: polyphenols, polychlorinated biphenyls, chlorinated hydrocarbons, trichloroethane and those kinds of things that don't have much of an image but come from all over the world?

And what about all those prostitutes, whole or in pieces, that wind up in the river?

And what about prostitutes? Have you ever wondered why it's so common to find prostitutes down by the river, or even in the river?

River story: begin with a scene that takes place along a river, possibly the Rhine. It's summertime, early in the morning, the sun is rising. The view is murky and dark. A male prostitute is working the waterfront. Soon he's picked up by a john and you see them kissing. But the prostitute is upset when he realizes that the john (who is dressed as a man) is really a woman. The john, whose name is Elvira, is beaten up by the prostitute's cohorts. Later in the story you learn that Elvira was born a man. To please his boyfriend, he had his sex changed. But Anton didn't want him as a woman. In the end Elvira kills herself.

See the film *In the Year of 13 Moons*, by Rainer Werner Fassbinder.

Do you know this ditty?
    "Blah, blah, blah, the moon.
    Blah, blah, blah, above.
    Blah, blah, blah, blah, croon.
    Blah, blah, blah, blah, love."

Remember *Psycho?* —remember the sound of the windshield wipers? (Maybe it was the violins.) It had this kind of insistence—this prophetic insistence—river water's got it, too, especially at night. And that insistence doesn't have to stop, the way rivers don't. In fact, those violins don't stop, they keep going, on and on, in my head. Do rivers ever really end?

Do rivers ever really end? Even while you stand here and watch the Thames flow itself into the North Sea, does it end there?

Do rivers ever really end? You know they just keep going, keep going with another name.

Watching the water, I am stricken with vertigo of meaning.

Watching the water, I am stricken with vertigo of meaning. Water is the final conjugation: an infinity of form, relation, and content.

A young actor drowned himself in the river a few years back. He had just been chosen for the part of Edgar Allan Poe in a play based on the life of the writer. Recently he had spoken to the author of the play about dropping the part of Poe and replacing it with a role in which he would play himself.

In the rain, or under a grey sky, in a weather that imparts little light, water is water less simply.

When it rains, fly-like specks mass briefly on the surface of the river. Each raindrop is a pin-sized bit of darkness, a dot seeming to flit and disappear.

What are you thinking about? Rain falling on water flattens the reflections and tranquilizes the view.

What are you thinking about? Rain falling on water is so alluring, so soothing and tender. The river becomes a meadow, a soft place to lie down in.

When it rains, fly-like specks mass briefly on the surface of the river. As each raindrop touches the water, miniscule circles form, ephemeral geometries of contact.

Which river did Hank Williams attempt suicide in?

"I went down to the river to watch the fish swim by. But I got to the river so lonesome I wanted to die. Then I jumped in the river but the doggone river was dry...." From the album *Low Down Blues.*

You can't see the blackness at night—only the darkness. It's only during the day that you can see the blackness. That's when you know it's not a reflection.

Black is a place. I don't know what it's like, can't see it, but I know it's there. You can go there—though it's not fixed in location. Black travels well, it's inert, incorruptible— like gold. And no matter where it is, it's always the same. You never know much about it, it doesn't give much away (that's the idea of black); you just have to go there. Black is where you can suspend your faith.

When you look at water, you see what you think is your reflection. But it's not yours. (You are a reflection of water.)

Thank you.

遍在多様

アンドリュー・マークルによるインタビュー

683　水はセクシーか？

あなたは以前、アイスランドを「エロティックな体験」と表現しました。

自分が倒錯者だったら、そこにあるものでやりくりしますよね。あの頃はいたるところにエロティックなものを感じていたので、ひとたびアイスランドに深く魅了されたら、そのような体験を見出すのは難しいことではありませんでした。私は概念的なものを重視する人間で、そういう側面はずっと変わっていません。ただ、アイスランドを旅する上で、エロティックな要素は鍵となるものでした。つまり、官能的な体験です。望もうが望むまいが、そこには身体的なものが溢れていました。天気は容赦なく干渉してくるので、どうしたって逃れられません。風であれ雨であれ極端な気温の変化であれ、あなたがどう感じるか、何をするか、どのようにするのかについて、天気は必ず影響します。昔はテントで旅していたので、いまよりずっと悪天候に左右されました。でも、太陽が姿を現したときには、まわりを冷たいものに囲まれながらも一条の光の暖かさを一身に浴びるのです。こうしたことはすべて、私のアイスランドの経験において、はっきりと目には見えなくとも極めて強烈な―肌身に感じる―官能性の一部なのです。

あなたの作品にはほぼ一貫してエロティックな構造が見受けられます。「対のオブジェ[pair object]」や「対のイメージ[paired image]」という概念にさえ、欲望と疑念が交差する「二度見」のメカニズムを通じたエロティックな緊張状態が示されています。

なるほど。最も重要な対のイメージだと思われる《死せるフクロウ》（1997年、pp.44-47）について考えてみましょう。「これは同じイメージですか？ それとも異なるイメージ、2羽のフクロウですか？」と必ず聞かれるのですが、これは私たちが疑念から決して逃れることはできないことを物語っています。ガラス彫刻についても言えることですが、完全に透明であるがゆえに「なかには何が入っているの？」とよく尋ねられます。最も透明な状態であればなおさら疑念や懐疑心を抱く。私はこのわからないことによる悪循環に魅力を感じました。これにより鑑賞者は経験に対して能動的に関わり続けることになります。
　いやむしろ、この「対のオブジェ」シリーズにはもともと、文字通り鑑賞者を作品に組み込もうという動機がありました。もちろん意識の上でのことですが。このシリーズの最初のものが《再来するもの》（1986年）で、機械で仕上げた瓜二つのオブジェをそれぞれ異なる部屋に配置しました。技術的な面では同じものですが、ふたつは常に違う場所にあるので同じではない。ということは、「同じ」は矛盾した言い方になりますよね。私はあるオブジェを片方の部屋に置き、それと瓜二つのオブジェをもう片方の部屋に置くことで、鑑賞者に反復が引き起こす独特な経験をもたらそうとしました。このふたつの体験はまったく異なります。1度目は新鮮な初めての体験。2度目には1度目の歴史が付きまといます。

それは意図的な重複[redundancy]でしょうか。

「重複[redundant]」は適切な言葉ではありませんね。より正確には「反復[repetition]」でしょうか。反復は差異。反復する形式。この方が歴史や、韻律、音楽や時間といった要素との繋がりを引き寄せることができます。

570 （水の中にあなたを見るとき、あなたの中に水を感じる？）

二重化や反復は、両性具有に対する意思表示なのでしょうか。

両性具有は本質的に二重化というよりも複数化だと考えています。私には子どもの頃に与えられたふたつのジェンダーに対して確固とした自己認識がまったくありませんでした。ジェンダーにおけるグラデーション、男らしさと女らしさとの度合い、そして、その間にあるあらゆるものについて考えてみると、私はどちらになるともなく、両方における最良のものを得たように感じていました。私にとって、両性具有とは差異を統合したものです。そう理解することで、これまでのような生き方ができたのだろうし、このような作品を制作することができたのだと思っています。

「両性具有は、ひとつのものの中に複数のものが含まれている可能性である（中略）あなたはあれであり、これでもある」と書いていますね。

その通りです。私はそう確信していて、両性具有はセクシュアリティとは関係ないと感じています。私は1955年に生まれたのですが、まったく啓蒙されていない時代に育った女性にとっては、国際的に活躍したいと願っても本当に不利な状況でした。いまもそれほど改善されていませんが……。建築に対する強い関心を持ち続けていたので、建築の道に進もうと考えたこともあったのですが、実のところ、当時は第一線で活躍する女性の建築家の名前をひとりも知りませんでした。最終的には美術にたどり着き、そこが良い状況だったというわけではありませんが、ただ、その概念的な幅の広さに興味を持ちました。

どうして美術の道に進むことになったのでしょうか。

孤独でしょうか……。自分がやりたいことならどんなことでもやれる、そう自分自身を信じられたら、あとはもうやるだけです。理想的な世界においては、美術は自然に対し何かをもたらすことができます。より大きな調和のために欠かせないものです。それが魅力的でした。社会的な役割ではなく、ただ私にとって必然性があり、それに従うだけでした。

487 黒い水は解毒薬（あなたの、そしてわたしの）。

エロスから死へと話題を移しましょう。もしくは、死が私たちを魅了することについて。本展に出品している《静かな水（テムズ川、例として）》（1999年、pp.94–101）を見ながら、こんにちこれほどあからさまに自殺を語る作品はなかなか制作できないのではないかという考えが頭に浮かんできました。例えば、現在、自殺やメンタルヘルスの問題を伝える新聞記事には、たいてい助けを必要とする読者向けのホットラインの情報が記載されています。

私は自殺を誤ったものとして捉えていません。この作品を制作していたとき、私には確かに自殺願望がありました。自殺を考えながら、その背後に、激しい痛みや絶望を感じていました。その願望はしばらく離れず、私生活において要因となる事情もありました。しかし、私は自分には自殺などできないだろうと直感的にわかっていました。制作が進む中で、この制作は自殺に対するある種の代替行為なのだと感じました。制作を通じて、実際に痛みもやわらいでいきました。

あの作品の写真やテキストからテムズ川の持つ魅惑がはっきりと伝わってきます。

あのような形の自殺を選ぶ人々は、ただ死ぬことを選択しているのではなく、消え去ることを選んでいるのではないかと思います。そして、それがテムズ川のエネルギーの大部分を成しているのではないでしょうか。テムズ川は感潮河川〔潮の満ち引きの影響を受ける河川〕で、1日に6、7メートルも水

位が上がったり下がったりし、また流れを圧迫する重厚な堤防もあるので、本来より気性の激しいものになっています。これらふたつの要因がテムズ川の致死率を高めています。テムズ川を見下ろしたとき、「なるほど。飛び込んだら、たぶん出てこられないな」と思いました。それはまだリサーチを始める前のことです。いたるところで渦を巻く様子や水の力を目の当たりにする。それは魅惑的なものでした。自分の感覚が麻痺し、ほだされ、まさに誘惑されているかのようでした。

こうした観察により、私はテムズ川を徹底的に泳げるようになりました。その歴史、物理的な性質、専門的に知りうるあらゆることの間を。とはいえ、この観察の大部分を占めるのは経験に基づくもので、水の観察には終わりがありません。私は水を「究極の結合 [ultimate conjugation]」と呼んでいます。目に見えるものであれ見えないものであれ、水はあらゆるものをひとつに結びつけます。数ある水のパラドックスのひとつは、それが常にほかのものと直に交わり、不潔で不健全なものとの交わりも少なくないにもかかわらず、それでもなお透明だということです。私はそこに根源的なものを見ています。

汚染、マイクロプラスチック、下水、ごみ、死体。

ここでもうひとつの論点が浮かんできます。水について話すとき、私たちは自分自身について話しています。外にあるものが内にある。私の身体のなかに。水は生命を与えるもので、だから純粋に違いないと思われています。しかし、水とその純粋さとの関係性は変わりつつあり、いまやその純粋さの定義には「永遠に残る化学物質」やマイクロプラスチックを含めざるを得ません。これはどういうことでしょうか。蒸発と凝縮の循環を経て、雨水には「永遠に残る化学物質」がたっぷりと含まれています。海に入れば、その水のなかにはメタンフェタミン（覚せい剤）からセルトラリン（抗うつ剤）まで、あらゆる薬が含まれています。人間は代謝したものを排出し、それらは水の中に流れていきます。

そして、とても受け入れがたい現実ですが、結局のところ、水はひとつしか存在しません。私たちは水の価値を十分に尊重していません。コカ・コーラ社、ネスレ社、ほかにも清涼飲料水を扱う大企業は、ひそかに動き回り、土地土地の水資源を買い占めています。中国もチベットで、その人口を維持するために世界最大の水資源を確保しようとしています。政治的観点から見て、これを認めてはいけません。それが国家のためだとしても。水の分配にいかなる障害や制限も設けるべきではありません。しかし、現在それは至る所で起きています。

395 繊細な肌理（テクスチャー）、その場限りの構造（ストラクチャー）。なんて捉えどころのない財宝（トレジャー）！

《静かな水（テムズ川、例として）》は、水をひとつのテキストとして提示していますが、読むことはあなたのほかの作品の多くにも見られる特徴です。なにか意識的にそこに立ち戻っているのでしょうか。

率直に言って、意識的に行っていることは制作のほんの一部に過ぎません。無意識で行っていることの方が多いです。ただ、「白のディキンスン」シリーズのように、確かに私は見るための形式として、頻繁に読むことに立ち戻っていますね。私は「白のディキンスン」を「眺めのいい部屋」[a room with a view]とは対照的に、「部屋の内在する眺め」[a view in a room]として考えています。それは物理的に理解できるものの向こうがわを知るための考え方です。私は「真昼に2匹の蝶が飛びたち」のような、一方では不条理なイメージとして、もう一方ではこれまでに数え切れないほど繰り返されながらも、正確に事実に即して観察され、記述された物事の精密な表現といえる簡潔な言い回しを好んでいます。そのようなテキストを「鍵 [key]」や「合図 [cue]」と呼んでいます。「鍵」は入り口で、「合図」はプロンプト、行き先を教えてくれるものです。私はこのように「白のディキンスン」の彫刻を捉えていて、テキストは目に見えるものの向こうへと視野をひろげる [a view beyond the visible] ための出発点になります。

同一性と差異性について考えるとき、読むという行為は、はじめは同じ形のようなものとして見えていたものが、よく見るとそれが示す微細な意味の違いが明らかになるという、ほとんど妄想に等しいプロセスです。漢

字における「大」と「太」と「犬」の違いや、日本語にはない英語のスペースの使用法（「a sphere［球体］」と「asphere［非球体的なもの］」）を考えてみてください。《静かな水（テムズ川、例として）》の写真にも似たようなことが起きていて、テムズ川の水面にあるさまざまな渦や光のきらめきに付された註釈が、水の意味を深く洞察するように観客を導きます。同様に、あなたのドローイングもある種のイメージとして、また、とても複雑な表面処理^{ファクトゥーラ}があらわれています。いわば、イメージに対して偶発的で不可欠な痕跡としてあらわれています。

ドローイングにあるものはすべて、そのドローイング自体が生み出したものです。そこには画面構成を調整したり、特定の形にするために描かれたものは一切ありません。イメージを作り出しているのではなく、これはコンポジションです。私のドローイングはすべて、2点以上のドローイングから成り立っています。2点、時に3点の類似したドローイングを切り刻み、それらを再びひとつに新しく組み立てます。表面にある言葉や線は、元に戻すために記入した印に過ぎません。ただ、これ以外の方法でさらなる痕跡を描き加えることはありません。これが私のやり方です。色は、そうですね。私はこの手法にかなう顔料を使っているだけです。チタニウムホワイトは不透明で、粘着性があるから良いけど、ウルトラマリンは透き通っていてもろいから駄目。偶然ですが、カドミウムのような最も毒性のある顔料が最適でした。カドミウムは粘着性も強く、透過もしません。このように物理的な条件で使う顔料を決めています。言ってみれば、私はこれらのドローイングをパリンプセスト〔重ね書きされた羊皮紙の写本〕だと考えています。それは存在の軌跡を自ら重ねていくのです。

ということは、何枚かのドローイングが先にあって、それらを切り刻み、そこからひとつのコンポジションに結合するというわけですね。

はい。壁面を使って作業し、ドローイングの切れ端を動かしたりして試しています。それは雲を眺めることにも似ています。そこに何かを発見する。ある発見はほかのものよりも面白く、そうしたものを選んでいきます。それは常に完成に至るプロセスの中にいるようなものです。ほとんど立ち止まることなく、最終的なところに到達するまで動き続けます。いきなり到達するようなことはなく、少しずつ近づいていくのです。

ドローイングの表面にある言葉や線は記入された印に過ぎないとおっしゃいましたが、そうした要素同士、また、それ以外の部分との共鳴も起きていますね。

その通りです。大抵のものは近くに置くと、単なる近さ［proximity］を超えた意味合いを帯びていきます。それが人間というものです。関係を読み取り、ああ、この色彩はあの色彩には合わないなどと考えます。ふたつのものを結びつけることで、個々に存在するときよりも大きなことが起こり得ます。ドローイングのサイズが大きく、より複雑になっていくと、その痕跡もまた非常に複雑なものになっていきます。私は数ヵ月にわたってそれに向き合います。あるとき、自分がラジオから時事や名前を引っ張ってきていることに気づきました。ポーラ美術館で発表しているドローイングのほとんどすべて、それを制作していたときに誰が亡くなったのかを答えることができます。ネルソン・マンデラが亡くなったときに制作していたもの、ジェシー・ノーマンが亡くなったときに制作していたもの、パリでシャルリー・エブド襲撃事件が起きたときに制作していたものがあります。ほかにも、そのときに読んでいた本に出てくる主人公が記入された印になっていたりもします。それはまさに偶然の成り行きですが、間違いなく私の人生から生まれたものです。

362（水は万能な動詞だ。恒久的関係の行為。）

それはロゴスに抗う行為（神は言われた…神は言われた…）、あるいは、言葉は字義通りであるべきだという期待に抗う行為でもあるのでしょうか。私たちは、言葉は不変だと考えたがります。「島」という言葉を辞書で調べて、普遍的な定義を知ることで安心する。しかし、言葉は絶えず新しい意味を手に入れ、古い意味を手放し、意味をなさないものにしてしまいます。言葉を世に差し出したとき、その意味はあなたのドローイングの制作のようにほぐされて、ばらばらになります。

まったくその通りです。言語は固定されたものではなく、確定した事実でもありません。「島」は「島」ではない。もしもあなたが島を孤立し隔離されたものだと定義するならば、この世界のどこにそんな事実が存在しているでしょう。もはやそんなものはありません。なくなってしまいました。私がかつてアイスランドを訪れていたのは、アイスランドが島だったからです。しかし、いまや経済的、科学的、物理的理由から、アイスランドはその周囲のあらゆるものと完全に繋がっています。現在、あらゆるものがあらゆる場所にあります。水の中にあるものはいたるところに、植物や動物、昆虫、そして当然、病もいたるところにあります。おそらく私たちは島性［islandhood］というものについて話す必要があるのではないでしょうか。

　もともとアイスランドの何が良かったのかと言うと、地図上のあらゆるものからはるか遠く離れて見えていたことでした。実際にはスコットランドの海岸から500から600マイル〔約804−965キロメートル〕の距離なので、それほど離れていません。アイスランドは1960年代から大きく変わっていきました。それ以前は控えめな土着の建物に住み、地産のものを食べていました。まず鮭や鱒があって、それは悪くないし、ジャガイモを手に入れるのは難しいけれどあるところにはあるし、ニンジンもあって、たまに羊肉なんかも食べていました。それは基本的な生活［rudimentary］。消費主義やブランド品といった資本主義など微塵もありませんでした。時は金なりなどと言うことはなく、アメリカ式の社会から遠く離れた美しい休息のようなものがありました。アイスランドで誰か雇おうとするとき、どんな条件を提示しようとも、ほとんどの場合はほかにすべきことがあるからと引き受けてくれません。これは生活の質に関することなのです。アイスランドでは生活の質とお金はあまり関係がありません。私はそれを本当に尊敬しています。

アイスランドのスティッキスホールムルの旧公営図書館に設置された《ヴァトナサフン（水の図書館）》(2007年)は、保存や共同体の諸問題に触れていますが、私にはこのプロジェクトが新自由主義や民営化の進む社会へと移り変わっていくアイスランドへの応答ではないかと思われました。少なくともプロジェクトが公開された翌年の2008年に起きたアイスランドの金融システム崩壊を予想していました。

あのプロジェクトにはそういう側面もありますね。1995年頃まではアイスランドに百万長者なんてひとりもいなかったのではないでしょうか。その後、格安フライトがどんどん行き来しはじめて、誰もが莫大な資金を手にしたみたいですが、そのほとんどが盗まれたり、不正に生み出されたりしました。どんなグループやカルチャーに属しているかにかかわらず、どこにでも必ず一定の割合で愚か者がいるということです。どちらかと言えば牧歌的であるアイスランドですら、文字通り20数名がただただ狂ったような巨額のローンを銀行で組み、債務不履行を起こしました。そして、それらの銀行が国営だったために国民は負債で首が回らなくなってしまいました。大きな代償を払うことになりました。

《ヴァトナサフン（水の図書館）》には、アイスランド各地に流れる氷河の水を保存する24本の円柱のインスタレーション《水、選ばれた》(2007年)が設置されています。プロジェクト公開後、少なくともそのうち1本の氷河が死んでしまったと公表されました。

氷河は死にません。ですが、そう、いくつか消えてしまったものもあり、私の知る限りでは、それらの氷河から採取した水はこの円柱のなかにしか残っていません。とはいえ、こうした事態はこの作品を制作する動機ではありませんでした。むしろ、これまで話し合ってきた問題、特に水の透明性をめぐるパラドックスや、水を目に見える実体として提示することの不条理に関心がありました。

289 幼い少女たち、姉妹は互いをハンカチで結びつけ、その川に身を投げた。

対のイメージに話を戻しましょう。《死せるフクロウ》以外にも、《これはわたし、これはあなた》(1998−2000年)や《あなたは天気》(1994−1996年)などがありますね。2003年にヴィンタートゥール写真美術館で開かれたあなたの個展『もし、ある冬の夜に…ロニ・ホーン…[If on a Winter's Night... Roni Horn...]』のカタログで、ティエリー・ド・デューヴは、鑑賞者が複数のイメージがまったく同じものなのか違うものなのかを知

るために、それらの間を行ったり来たりする動きを「時間が空間になる」と記しています。このような要素は、あなた自身がニューヨークとアイスランドを行き来する動きとなんらかの関係はありますか。

あなたが挙げたすべての作品はアイデンティティを主題にしています。先に制作した《あなたは天気》の場合は、すべての個人を多数［multitude］とみなす可能性について考えていました。ある特定の顔を通じて、ひとつの文化の似姿を生み出すことができるのかを試してみたかったのです。写真はもともと『ハラルズドッティル［Haraldsdóttir］』という題名の書籍を意図したもので、この題名の意味は「ハラルドの娘」、匿名のようなものですね。ただ、その素材を使って制作を始めたところ、私は群衆としての彼女のすべて、あるいはその大半が、天気によって引き出されていることに気がつきました。そのとき、これはインスタレーションになると思いました。

　攻撃的なイメージ、両性具有のイメージ、男らしさのイメージ、そこにあなたが見るものはすべて彼女がまわりの物理的な現実との関わりの中から生み出したものです。そして、鑑賞者はそれぞれの感性、気づき、好奇心をインスタレーションに持ち込みます。すべて同じイメージだと考える人。各イメージを識別する独特なものや微妙な差異を認識する人。こうした幅があります。私の仕掛けはその体験を引き延ばし、そこに留まらせるためのものです。

《円周率》（1997／2004年、pp.84-93）にも、シンプルな介入によって、鑑賞者が空間を動き回るようになる仕掛けがありますね。

ええ、壁面の少し高めの位置に展示することで、鑑賞者はイメージに近づいて極端に顔を上げて見ようとしない限り、展示室の中央まで下がることになります。後ろに下がって距離を取ることで、イメージ同士の関係性が見えてくる。そうすることで、鑑賞者にどのイメージが最も重要なイメージかなどと考えさせないようにします。結果的に全体がひとつの視野に収まる、つまり、イメージや関係性の集合体をひとつのものとして見ることができるようになります。《あなたは天気》の場合は、各イメージがもっと小さく、その差異も繊細なものなので、鑑賞者はより近づいて見ることになります。

「白のディキンスン」の場合はどうでしょうか。このシリーズも鑑賞者を作品との動的な関係に巻き込む形になっています。ある位置に立つと判読しやすくなりますが、その判読可能性は束の間のものです。これは鑑賞者と作品の遭遇に認識論的な境界を定めるものです。なぜなら、この作品に関する知識や真実を得るために、私たちは作品にある構造を課さなければなりませんが、立ち位置を変えた瞬間にその構造は崩れてしまいます。私たちが思うよりも、事物は多孔的［porous］〔さまざまな侵入を受けやすい構造をもつもの〕です。

構造や枠組み、文脈というものは、世界を身近なものとして扱うために、その一部を取り出すというスケールの問題なのではないでしょうか。それはほぼすべての芸術作品や実験的な演出の際に起きることです。好むと好まざるとにかかわらず、文脈は必ず存在します。その文脈の重要性や限界はまた別の問題です。私の作品は主に形而上学的な領域に軸を置いていると思っていますし、素材自体にはそれほど関心がありません。《ゴールド・フィールド》（1980／1994年、pp.60-61; pp.68-71）において、金は単なる出発点に過ぎません。最終的に私は素材について語りたいのではなく、私たちと金との関係について、いかに金という物質がそのアイデンティティを奪われ、それがイメージそのものになるところまで貶められているか、という誤解や劣化［degrading］について語りたいのです。

272 このイメージを見るとき、あなたはこの紙の滑らかさを考えている？
　　　どれほどやわらかく官能的か？（でも、あなたは飛び込めない。）

　　鑑賞者が自分自身を作品に投影するための空間として、空虚［emptiness］をどのように取り入れていますか。壁に何気なく立てかけられた「白のディキンスン」も空虚を意識させますし、非常に重たく硬い物体であ

るにもかかわらず透明なガラス彫刻も空虚を感じさせます。展示室に入ると、まるでそれらが現れたり消えたりしているかのように思えてくるのです。

空虚に結びつくかどうかはわかりませんが、ガラス彫刻は静かで、鑑賞者は思い思いの時間を過ごすことができるでしょう。私は鑑賞者との関わりにおいて、繊細さや微細な違いを重視しています。それでも、《ゴールド・フィールド》が俗っぽい煽情主義[sensationalism]だと批評されたことがありました。煽情主義とはある種のインパクトを生み出すために何かを選ぶことですが、《ゴールド・フィールド》はそうではありません。あるがままのものとして金を選んだわけで、それ以上の効果を生み出すためではありません。ただそのリアリティを示したかっただけです。同じように、鑑賞者はガラス彫刻を見ているとき、自分が何を見ているのかわかっていないかもしれませんが、そこで起きていることがわかったとき、まるで頬を叩かれたような気分になるでしょう。ある意味、建築がそうであるように、それはそこにあるのです[It's there]。私はこれらの作品が経験を引き起こすものであって欲しいですし、その経験はオブジェのアイデンティティと分かちがたく結びついたものなのです。

464 水は究極の結合だ。無限の形態、関係性、内容。

もし水が動詞であり、アイスランドも動詞であるならば、動詞になることはあなたにとって何を意味しているのでしょうか。

そうですね、私自身を動詞だとは考えられないので、その観点から答えることはできないのですが、水に関して言えば、それは単に物体－物質にとどまらない、関係性についての問題となるでしょう。いかなる水のイメージも単なる水ではありません。それは光であり、まわりの世界を何度も映し出します。そして、そのまわりの世界はその色彩、質感、見え方、内容に影響を及ぼします。その意味で、水はとても能動的な形態です。アイスランドについて言えば、その島が私に与えた影響や、この島がいかに私に軸と安定をもたらしたかを理解したとき、私は能動的な形態としてのアイスランドの真のアイデンティティを発見しました。ただし、この理解はアイスランドに対するものであると同じように、私自身に対するものでもあります。いかなる場所であれ重要なのは見る人です。量子力学やほかの科学分野では、現実を規定する際に、観察者の果たす役割が長く認められてきました。そして、私はこのことにずっと関心を寄せてきました。なぜなら、それは「アイデンティティが唯一のものである」という考えの矛盾を明らかにするものだからです。あなたはまわりにあるものと積極的に関係を結び、それらはあなたに深く、元に戻ることができないほどの影響を与えます。不可逆的な、それはその瞬間だけかもしれないけど、それでもその瞬間、あなたは何かになります。別の何かに。

168 水はユートピア的な物質である。

註：このテキストは、2021年9月21日に東京で行われたロニ・ホーンへのインタビューをもとに構成した。数字を冠した文言は、ロニ・ホーン『Another Water: The River Thames, for Example』(スカロ、チューリッヒ、2000年)からの引用。

訳註：「真昼に2匹の蝶が飛びたち」はエミリ・ディキンスンの詩の一部。翻訳は以下を引用。『完訳エミリ・ディキンスン詩集(フランクリン版)』新倉俊一監訳、東雄一郎、小泉由美子、江田孝臣、朝比奈緑翻訳、金星堂、2019年、204頁。

EVERYWHERE DIFFERENTLY

Interview by Andrew Maerkle

683 Is water sexy?

You once described Iceland as an "erotic adventure."

Well, when you're a pervert, you've really got to make do with the options available. In those days you found your erotic adventures wherever you could, and it was not a difficult thing to do once I recognized the depth of my attraction to Iceland. Since I'm a conceptually oriented person, that side will always be there. But the erotic aspect was key to my travels in Iceland. It's a sensual experience. There's a lot of physicality, whether you want it or not. The weather is intrusive. You're never without it. Whether it's the wind or the rain or extreme temperature shifts, the weather is there, and it's affecting how you're feeling and what you're doing and how you're doing it. I used to travel with a tent, so add that in and you're really at the mercy of the elements. But then the sun would come out and you'd be standing in a little ray of warmth while everything around you was cold. All of that is part of a sensuality that's not terribly visible but absolutely powerful—*palpable*—in my experience of Iceland.

I find an erotic structure in many of your works. Even your idea of the "pair object" or "paired image" presents an erotically charged situation through the mechanism of the double take, which is where desire and doubt intersect.

Sure. Think about *Dead Owl* (1997, pp.44–47), which is probably the most important paired image. People are always asking whether it's the same image or two images, two owls. That tells me you can never get away from doubt. It also comes up with the glass pieces. Here is this perfectly transparent form, but I'm often asked "What's inside?" Even the most transparent situation inspires doubt and incredulity. I find that vicious circle of not knowing very compelling. I cultivate it in my work. It keeps the viewer engaged or active in the experience.

  In fact, the original motivation for the *Pair Object* series—and of course this is only what I'm conscious of—was to literally incorporate the viewer in the work. The first work of this kind, *Things That Happen Again: For Two Rooms* (1986), features two identical machined objects placed in different rooms. They are technically identical, but "identical" is an oxymoron, as two things are always in different places, and therefore not identical. My idea in putting one object in one room and a duplicate object in a second room was to give the viewer a unique experience followed by a repetition of it. The two experiences are completely different. The first is a fresh first time. The second is shadowed in the history of that first time.

A willful redundancy?

Redundant isn't the right word. It's more a repetition. Repetition is difference. It is repeated form. And that allows for more engagement with history, with cadence, with musical or temporal elements.

⁵⁷⁰ (When you see your reflection in water, do you recognize the water in you?)

Is doubling or repetition a gesture toward androgyny?

I think of androgyny more as a multiplying than a doubling, per se. I never had a strong identification with the two genders I was offered when I was growing up. I see shades of gender, degrees toward the masculine and degrees toward the feminine and everything in between. And I was somewhere in between, feeling like I had the best of both sides without being either. To me androgyny is the integration of difference, and that understanding has allowed me to live the life I've lived and do the kind of work I do.

You write that "Androgyny is the possibility of a thing containing multiple things. . . . You are this and that."

Absolutely. I feel very strongly about it, and feel it has nothing to do with sexuality. I was born in 1955, so for a woman growing up in a not very enlightened world—one that is still pretty dim as we speak—you were really at a disadvantage if you wanted to play on a world scale. I once considered pursuing architecture, because I'd always been interested in and connected strongly with it, but the truth is I don't think I could have named a single world-class female architect at the time. I ended up in art, which was not much better, although I think the conceptual range interested me more.

What convinced you to pursue art?

Solitude, I think. Imagine if you could believe in yourself enough to do whatever you wanted—why wouldn't you? In the best of all worlds, art adds to nature in some way. It's something necessary that fits into a larger balance. That really appealed to me. It had no social function, only the sense of necessity behind it—the one I gave it. The one that compelled me.

⁴⁸⁷ Black water is antidote (to you—and me).

Let's jump from Eros to death, or rather our attraction to death. Looking at Still Water (The River Thames, for Example) *(1999, pp.94–101) here at the Pola Museum of Art, it occurred to me that it might be difficult to make a work that speaks so openly about suicide today. For example, newspaper reports on cases of suicide or mental health issues now often include information on hotlines readers can call if they need help.*

I don't see suicide as being wrong. When I did that piece I definitely was suicidal. I felt the acute pain and despair behind the thought of suicide. It stayed with me for a long time, and there were circumstances in my life contributing to that. But I knew intuitively that I could never pull it off. As the work developed, I realized it was a kind of vicarious suicide. Making the work actually alleviated my pain.

The seductiveness of the river certainly comes across in the images and texts.

I think people who choose that form of suicide are not just choosing death, they're choosing disappearance, and that's a big part of the energy of the Thames. It's a tidal river, so it's going up and down six or seven meters a day, and it has heavy embankments that have constricted the flow, so it's much more aggressive than it originally was.

These two factors make it highly lethal. When I looked at the river, I thought OK, if you go in, chances are you're not coming out. That was before I had done any research. You could see all the eddies and the power of the water. It was mesmerizing. It was like you were being drugged or subdued or, indeed, seduced.

That observation allowed me to swim in the Thames quite thoroughly—its history, its physical qualities, all that one could know about it technically. But the biggest part of my observations was based in the experiential, and with water it's endless. I call water the "ultimate conjugation." It brings everything together, whether visibly or not. One of the many paradoxes of water is how it's always in direct communication with other things—often filthy or not very savory things—yet still is transparent. There's something radical to me about that.

Pollution, microplastics, sewage, trash, dead bodies.

That brings up another point: When you talk about water, you're talking about yourself. What's out there is in here. In my body. Water is life giving and one would think that it therefore needs to have a certain degree of purity. But water and its association with purity are changing, and now the definition of purity has to include "forever chemicals" and microplastics. What does that mean? You have rainwater full of "forever chemicals" through the cycle of evaporation and condensation. If you wade into the ocean, you have whatever pharmaceutical you could possibly want right there in the water with you, from methamphetamines to Zoloft. People are pissing out everything they metabolize and it goes into the water.

And there's only one water, ultimately, which I think is a pretty tough reality for us to accept. We don't really respect the value of water. I think Coca-Cola does, or Nestlé, or any of the other big bottling companies going around quietly buying up local water sources. You also have China going into Tibet and securing the world's largest fresh water sources for its population. From a political point of view this should not be an option, not even for a country. There should be no impediment or restriction to the distribution of water, but it's very much happening in our time.

395 Delicate textures, fugitive structures: more elusive treasure!

Still Water (The River Thames, for Example) *broaches the idea of water as a text, and reading informs many of your other works too. Is that something you consciously return to?*

Such a tiny part of what I do is conscious, to be honest. There's some other level of operation I'm subsumed in. But I do see that I frequently come back to reading as a form of viewing, as in the *White Dickinson* works. I regard the *White Dickinsons* as a view in a room, as opposed to a room with a view. It's the idea of seeing beyond what one can physically apprehend. I love that a simple statement like "Two butterflies went out at noon" can read as an absurd image while also being a precise articulation of something that has happened millions of times in the past but was observed so precisely, so factually and put down in writing. I call such texts "keys" and "cues." A "key" is a way in, and a "cue" is a prompt, it gives you direction. That's how I think of those objects. Text is a launching pad for a view beyond the visible.

Thinking of sameness and difference, reading is an almost psychotic process whereby we look at something that initially appears uniform and zoom in to its details to discover minute differences that signify things to us. Consider the difference between the Chinese characters for "big" (大), "fat" (太), and "dog" (犬), or the use of the space in English script ("a sphere" versus "asphere"), which doesn't really exist in Japanese. Something similar occurs in the Still Water

(The River Thames, for Example) photos, where the annotations to different eddies or glints of light on the surface of the river guide viewers into a deep examination of the significance of water. Your drawings likewise present viewers with both an image of a sort and a highly intricate faktura, say, or mark making that is both incidental to the image and integral to it.

Everything in those drawings is generated by the drawing itself. Nothing is laid to achieve a graphic balance or make it look a certain way. It's not image making; it's composition. All the drawings start from more than one. There are two, sometimes three very similar drawings that are cut and reassembled into one thing. The texts and the lines on the surface are simply registration marks so I know where to go back to. But there's no additional mark making beyond that. And that's how I wanted to do it. Even the color is ho-hum. I simply use pigments that work with the technique. Not all pigments do. Titanium white is opaque and adhesive, good, but ultramarine pigments are translucent and crumbly, bad. Coincidentally the most toxic colors work best, like cadmium. Cadmium has strong adhesive qualities and opacity. So your choices are determined by that set of physical limitations. I think of the drawings as palimpsests of themselves, if that's possible. They are building up traces in their path to existence.

So you start with several drawings that you cut up and then combine into a single composition?

Yes. You work it on the wall, move things around. It's a bit like cloud watching. You discover things. Some of your discoveries are more interesting than others. You go with those. It's like you're always in a process of arrival. You're barely descending, you just keep moving, until eventually you arrive. No real point of being over, just a gradual coming to.

You say the texts and lines are just registration marks, but they also take on resonance through their relations with each other and the other parts of the composition.

Totally. But I think most things when put in proximity will take on significance beyond mere proximity. It's human nature. You see a relation and think, oh, this color doesn't go with that one. Bringing two things together can make something happen that is bigger than either part. As the drawings got bigger and more elaborate, the markings also became extremely complex. It would take several months. At one point I noticed I was pulling things out of the radio, current events, names. With almost every drawing on view at Pola Museum of Art, I can tell you who died when I was making it. There's one where Nelson Mandela passed away, another where Jessye Norman passed away, and one when the Charlie Hebdo attack occurred in Paris. In other cases, I'm reading something interesting and the protagonist winds up as a registration mark. It's random, but very much out of my life.

362 Water is the master verb: an act of perpetual relation.

Could it also be an act of resistance against logos (And God said ... And God said ...), or the expectation that a word should be what it says? We like to think of words as being a constant thing. It reassures us to know that we could look up island *in the dictionary and get a universal definition. But words are constantly picking up new meanings and shedding old meanings, or dropping into meaninglessness. When we put words out into the world their definitions start to fray and fragment in a way that is similar to the construction of your drawings.*

Absolutely. Language is not fixed, it's not facts. *Island* is not *island*. If you define an island as an isolated, separate thing, where does that exist in the world as fact?

It doesn't anymore. It's gone. I used to go to Iceland because it was an island. But now, for economic, chemical, and physical reasons, Iceland has complete continuity with everything around it. Everything is everywhere now. Not just in the water, but plants, animals, insects, and of course diseases too. Maybe we need to talk about degrees of islandhood.

What was originally powerful about Iceland was that it looked far from everything else on the map. In fact, it's only five or six hundred miles off the coast of Scotland. Iceland has changed a lot since the 1960s. Until then people were living in modest, vernacular architecture and eating local: salmon, trout, not bad; potatoes, difficult, but yes; carrots; and occasionally lamb. It was rudimentary. You didn't really have capitalism in the form of consumerism or commercial brands. Time was never money there, which was a beautiful respite from the American way. You try to hire somebody in Iceland and it doesn't make a difference what you offer, they mostly have something better to do. It's about quality of life. Quality of life had very little to do with money in Iceland. I have a lot of respect for that.

I get the sense that your Vatnasafn / Library of Water (Iceland) *(2003–07) project, which is housed in a former library building in Stykkishólmur, Iceland, and touches on issues of preservation and community, is a response to Iceland's transition into a more neoliberal, privatized society. Or at least it anticipates the collapse of Iceland's financial system in 2008, a year after the project opened.*

There is an aspect of that. I would say up to about the year 1995 or so you might not have had any millionaires in Iceland. Then you started getting all these cheap flights in and out and everybody seemed to have lots of money to spend, and a lot of it was stolen or falsely generated. It doesn't make a difference what subgroup or culture you're in, there's always the same percentage of assholes. Even though Iceland was kind of idyllic, there were literally two dozen guys who just went crazy taking large loans from the banks and defaulting. And since those banks were owned by the people of Iceland, the people were stuck with the debt. It was a real reckoning.

The Library of Water *features an installation of 24 columns preserving water taken from glaciers around Iceland,* Water, Selected *(2003–07). At least one of the glaciers has since been declared dead.*

Well, glaciers don't die. But, yes, some of those glaciers have disappeared, and to my knowledge the only water from them that still exists is in those columns. That was not my motive for doing that work. I was also getting at the issues we already discussed, especially the paradox of transparency, and the absurdity of presenting water as a visual entity.

289 Two young girls—sisters—tied themselves together and jumped in the river.

I'd like to return to the paired images—works like This is Me, This is You *(1998–2000) and* You are the Weather *(1994–96), as well as* Dead Owl. *In the catalogue for your exhibition at Fotomuseum Winterhur in 2003,* If on a Winter's Night . . . Roni Horn . . ., *Thierry de Duve writes about the viewer's movement back and forth between images to see how they are the same or different as "time becoming space." Does that aspect of the work have anything to do with your own movement back and forth between New York and Iceland?*

All of the works you mention focus on identity. In the case of *You are the Weather,* which came first, I was imagining the possibility of every individual as a multitude.

I wanted to see whether I could create a likeness of a culture through a specific face. The photographs were originally intended for a book that I titled *Haraldsdóttir*, meaning "daughter of Harald"—anonymous in a sense. But once I started working with the material I realized that all of her multitude, or so much of it, is drawn out by the weather. That's when it became an installation. The image of aggression, of androgyny, of masculinity, anything you see there comes from her dealing with the physical reality around her. And people bring different degrees of sensitivity, awareness, and curiosity to the installation. Some think it's all the same image. Others recognize the uniqueness and nuance that distinguishes each of the images. That's the range. My game is to draw out that experience, to dwell in it.

The installation Pi *(1997/2004, pp.84–93) also prompts viewers to move through the space through a simple intervention.*

Well, when you put something up high on the wall, you push people into the center of the room—unless they prefer to crane their neck awkwardly to see each image up close. Moving back, taking more distance allows you to see the relationships between the images. It discourages the viewer from giving any one image more importance than any other. You wind up with a horizon, where things are leveled into one—that is, you can see the collection of images and relationships as one thing. With *You are the Weather*, you view it up close because the images are much smaller and the nuances are more subtle.

And the White Dickinsons*? This is yet another work that draws viewers into a dynamic relation. The work becomes legible from a certain position, but that legibility is fleeting. That sets an epistemological edge to the encounter, since in order to have knowledge or a sense of truth about the work, we have to impose a structure on it, but as soon as we change position and that structure collapses, things are much more porous than we assumed.*

I think the idea of a structure or framing or context is partly a matter of scale, where you're breaking off a chunk of the world in order to manage it more closely. That happens in pretty much all art works or any directed experiential moment. There is always a context, whether you like it or not. How important or limiting that context will be is another question. I do think that my work pivots mainly in the metaphysical realm. I'm not really interested in materials as such. In *Gold Field* (1980/1994, pp.60–61; pp.68–71), gold is only the starting point. I'm not talking about the material in the end, and more about how our relationship to gold is predicated on either misunderstandings or degrading the material to the point where it is stripped of its identity and becomes an image of itself.

272 When you look at this image, do you see how smooth the paper is? How soft and sensual? (But you can't jump in.)

To what extent do you employ emptiness as a space for people to project themselves into your works? The White Dickinsons *nod to emptiness because they are propped innocuously against the wall. Despite being extremely heavy, solid objects, the glass pieces seem empty because they are transparent. When you're in a room with them, it's like they come and go.*

I'm not sure I connect it with emptiness, but the glass pieces are quiet and allow the viewer their own time. I heavily depend on nuance in my engagement with my audience. But I've had people criticize *Gold Field* as crass sensationalism. I don't think it is, because sensationalism is about choosing something for the sake of making a certain impact. I chose gold to be what it is, not to make an impact beyond itself. I was just exposing its reality. Similarly, people don't know what they're looking at when they look at the glass pieces, but those things are like a smack in the face if you know what's going on. It's there, sort of in the same way the architecture is. I like to think these works are instigators of experience, where the experience is integral to the object's identity.

464 Water is the final conjugation: an infinity of form, relation, and content.

If water is a verb and Iceland is a verb, then what does being a verb mean for you?

Well, I'm not thinking of myself as a verb, so I can't really speak from that point of view, but with water, it's more than an object-substance, it's a state of relation. No image of water is merely water. It's light, often reflecting the world around it. And the world around it is affecting the color, the texture, or less visibly, the content. In that sense it's a strongly active form. With Iceland, when I understood the influence the island was having on me, how it was centering and balancing me, that was also my discovery of Iceland's true identity as an active form. And yet I know there's as much of me in this understanding as there is Iceland. A significant portion of any place is the viewer; quantum physics and other fields of science have long recognized the role of the observer in defining reality. And that's always fascinated me because of the paradox it presents: the idea that identity is unique. You are in an active engagement with things around you and those things deeply and irreversibly affect you. Irreversibly, though it may only be in that moment; still you become something in that moment, something other.

168 Water is utopic substance.

This text is based on an interview conducted with Roni Horn in Tokyo on September 21, 2021. Numbered passages are taken from Roni Horn, *Another Water: The River Thames, for Example,* Zurich: Scalo, 2000.

または 7
2013／2015年

Or 7
2013 / 2015

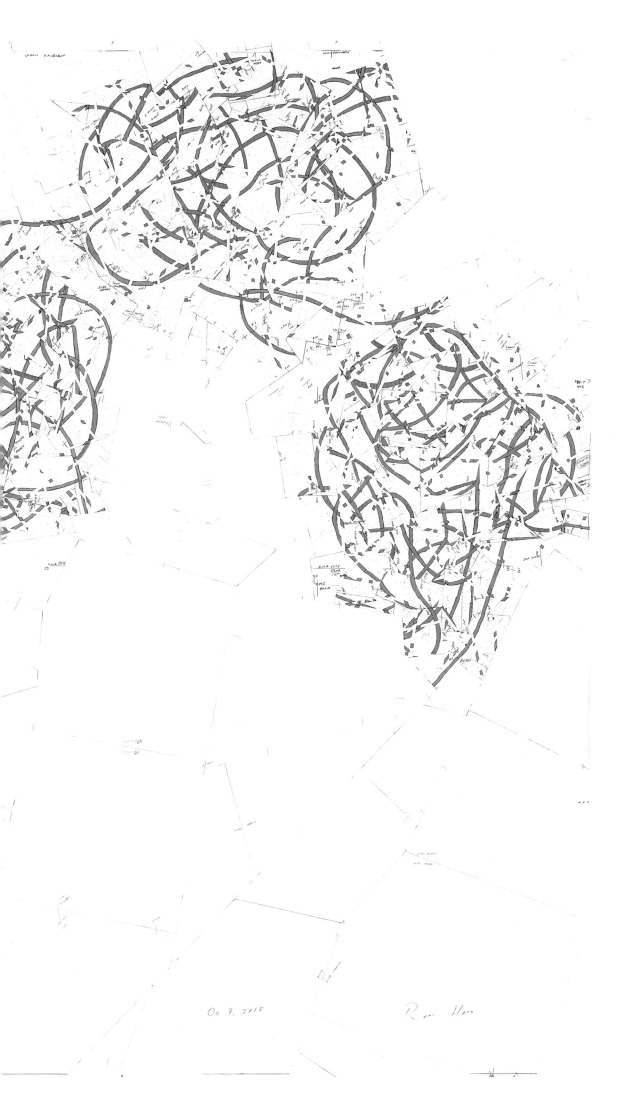

Or 7, 2015   Roni Horn

141

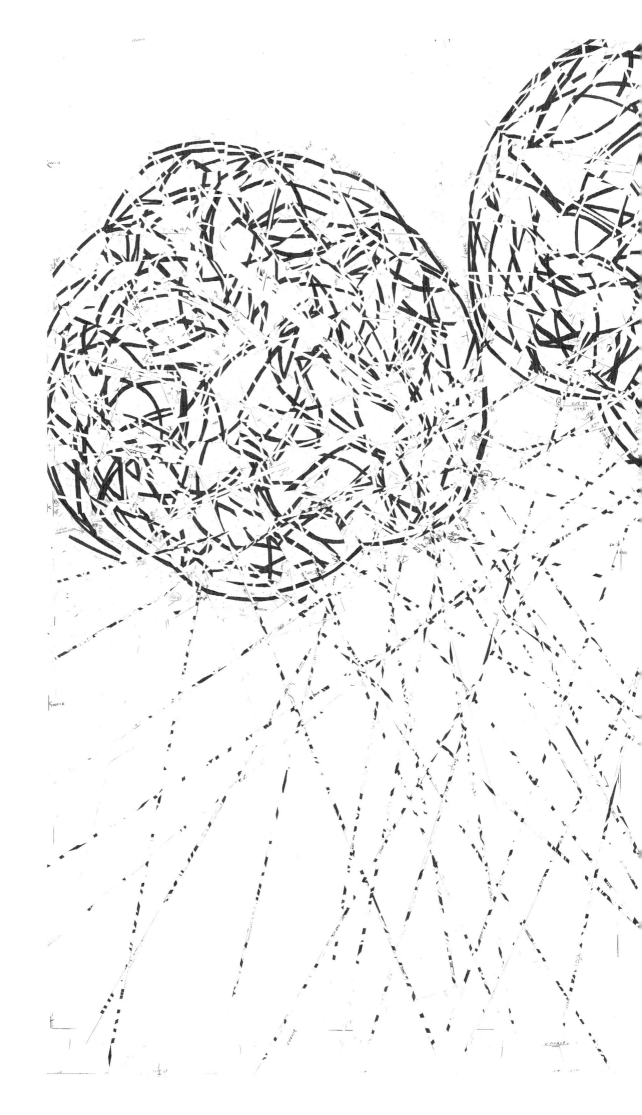

または 6
2013–2014年

Or 6
2013–2014

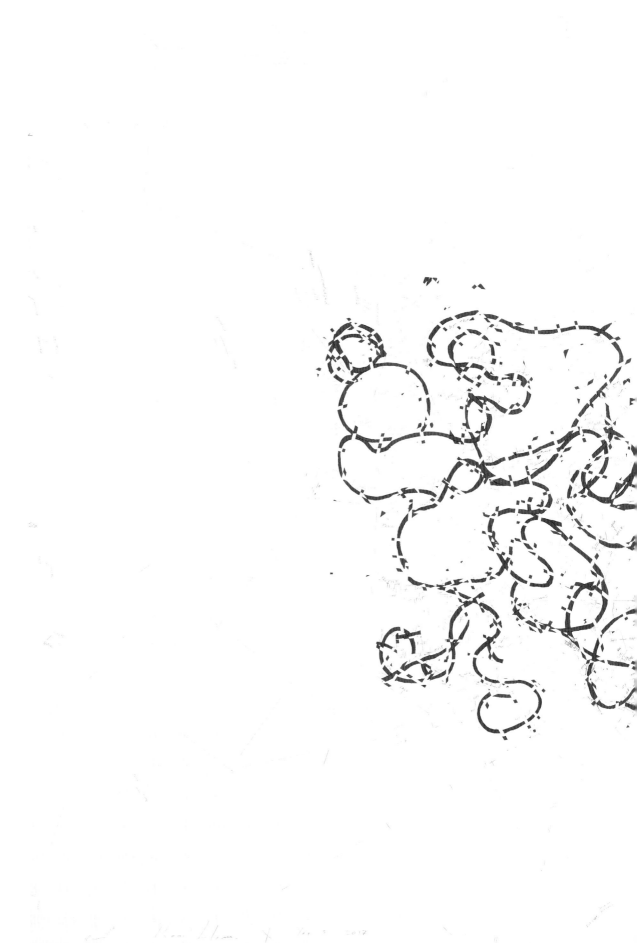

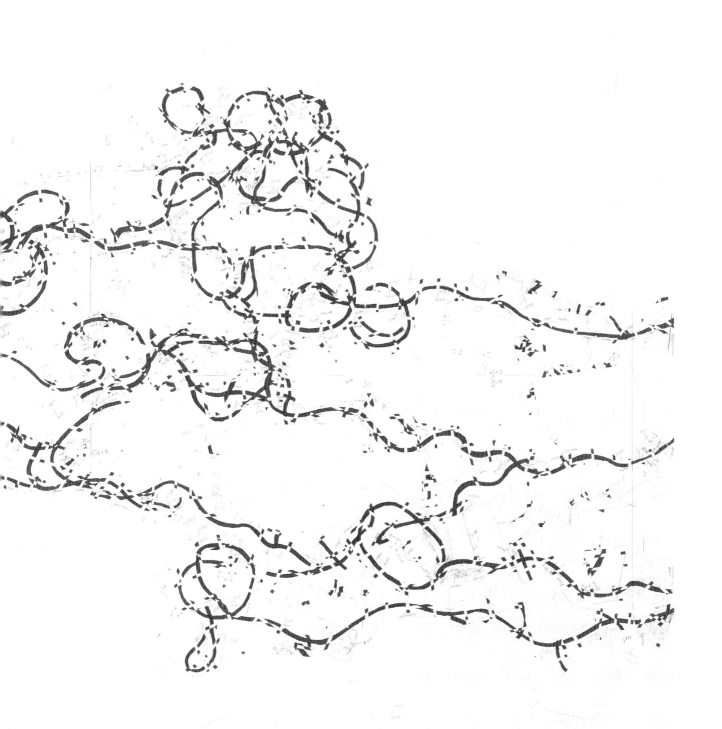

おく 3
2012–2013年

Put 3
2012–2013

ハック・ウィット—アサリを歩く v. 2
2014年

ハック・ウィット—鳥の言葉 v. 2
2014年

Hack Wit—walking a clam, v. 2
2014

Hack Wit—bird words, v. 2
2014

in my mouth
a little bird
put words
told me

cool as
absence

a cucumber

makes the

heart grow fonder

ハック・ウィット―キュウリのハート
2014年

Hack Wit—cucumber heart
2014

ハック・ウィット―安い痛み
2014年

Hack Wit—aching cheap
2014

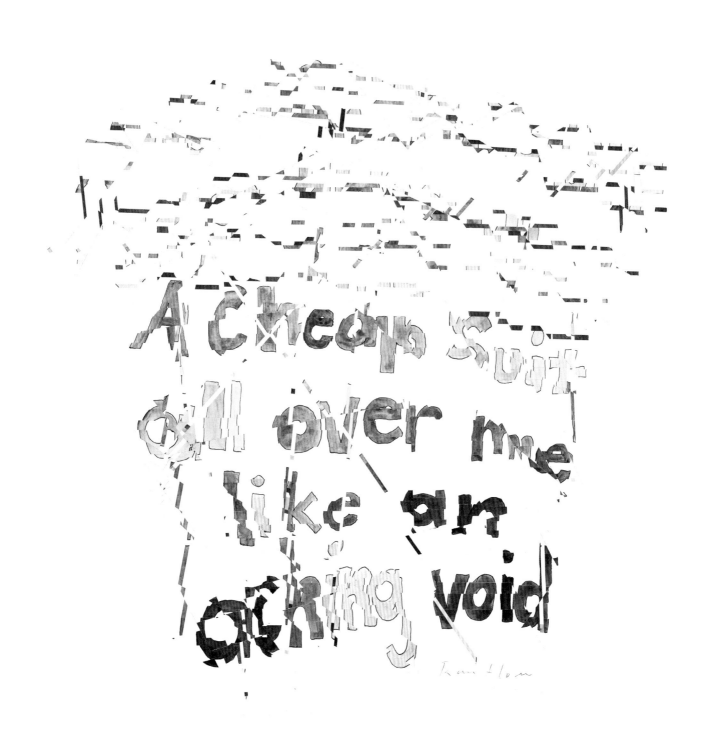

A cheap suit all over me like an aching void

ハック・ウィット—蝶の忘却
2014–2015年

ハック・ウィット—青を追いかける
2014年

Hack Wit—butterfly oblivion
2014–2015

Hack Wit—chasing blue
2014

Chasing
Blue out

of

rainbows

犬のコーラス—嘘のかたまりを放り出せ
2016年

Dogs' Chorus—Let Slip a Tissue of Lies
2016

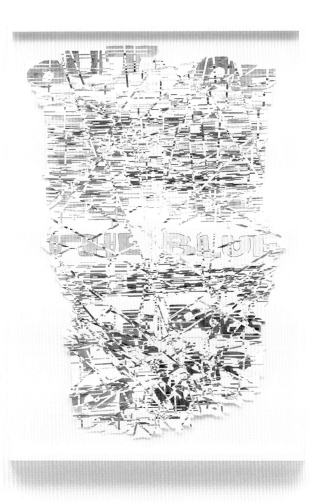

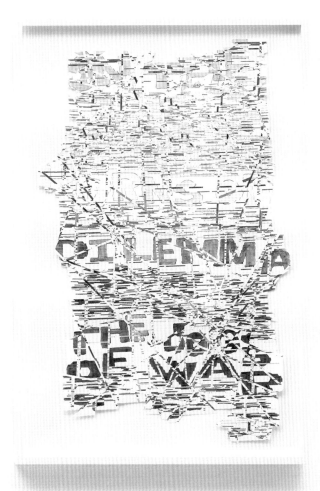

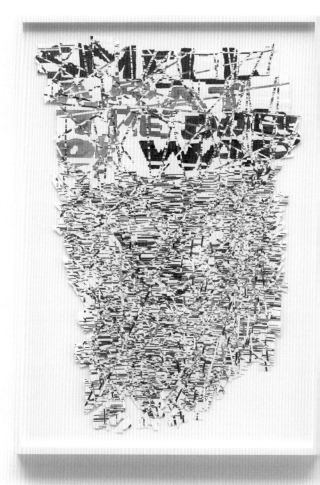

犬のコーラス―地球の果てまで滑り出せ
2016年

Dogs' Chorus—Let Slip to the Ends of the Earth
2016

犬のコーラス—フライパンから解き放ち、火の中に放り込め
2016／2018年

Dogs' Chorus—Let Slip From the Frying Pan into the Fire
2016 / 2018

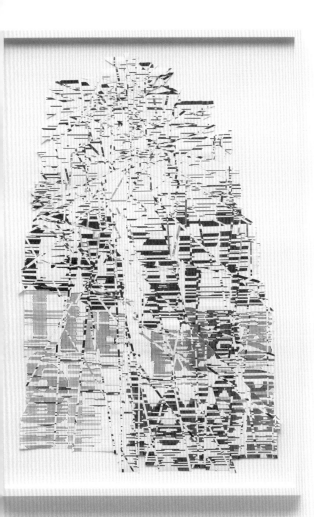

あなたは天気 パート2
2010−2011年

You are the Weather, Part 2
2010−2011

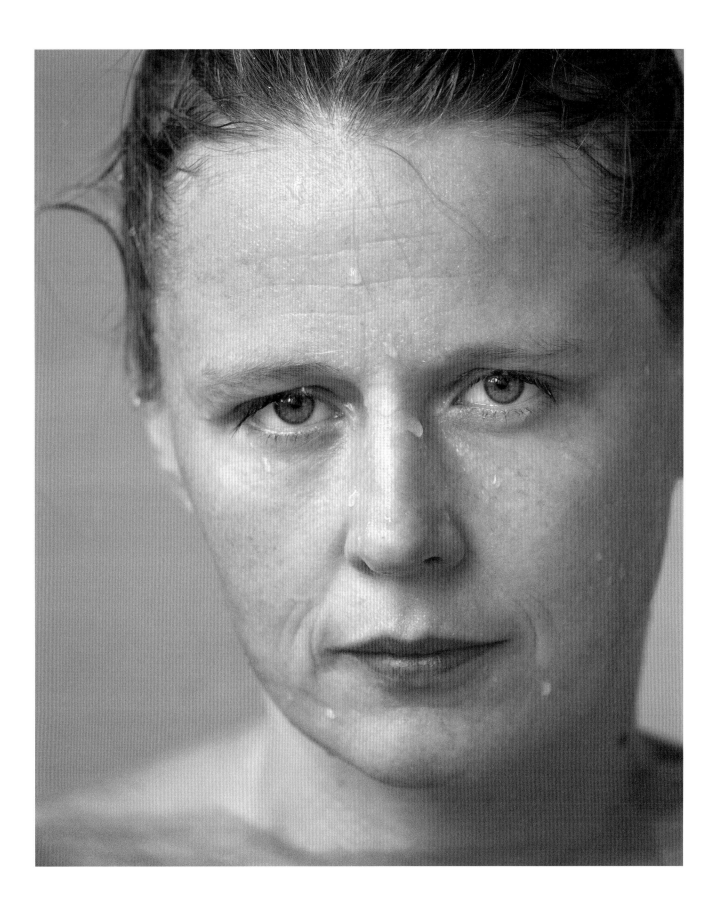

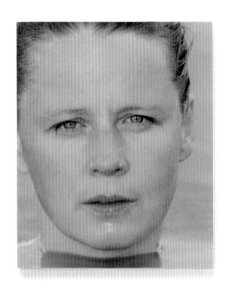

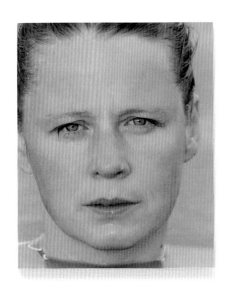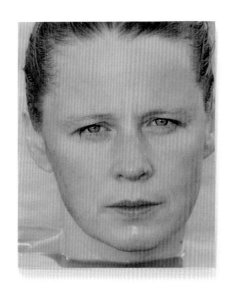

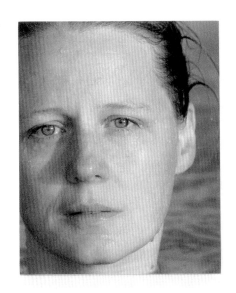 

鳥葬（箱根）
2017–2018年

Air Burial (Hakone)
2017–2018

泉の下に —— ロニ・ホーン展に寄せて[1]

鈴木幸太

1.

「水を妙なる花と見るものがある。…鬼は水をもって、猛火となし、血うみと見るという。龍魚は水を宮殿と見、楼台と見るという。あるいは水をもって七宝・珠玉と見、あるいは樹林・牆壁と見、あるいは清浄なる法性と見、あるいは人間の真実体と見、あるいは身のすがた・心の本性と見るものもある。それを人間は水と見るのである。」[2]

—— 道元「山水経」

2.

「したがって、感覚のうちの、もっとも官能的ではないもの、つまり視覚から始めて、それがどのようにして官能的なものになるかを見てみよう。」[3]

—— ガストン・バシュラール『水と夢』

3.

　視覚。ロニ・ホーンの《水と言う》(pp.102-104)は、写真とテキストを組み合わせた過去の作品から、視覚的な要素を消し去ることで生まれたモノローグだ。[4] 2012年にルイジアナ美術館の屋外で行われたこのパフォーマンスは、日頃私たちがいかに視覚を信じ、視覚に囚われているか、そして視覚以外の感覚が、いかに人間の感情を複雑に引き起こしうるかを改めて教えてくれる。

　このパフォーマンスにおいて最も重要な要素は、観客でも語りそのものでもなく、「時間」である。40分間のパフォーマンスを開始するにあたり、ロニ・ホーンは日没直前の時間を正確に選んだ。暮れかかった空が、語りの進行とともに次第に暗くなり、パフォーマンスの終盤にさしかかると作家の手元を照らす灯りのみが暗闇に浮かぶ。「水面に映る自分の姿だと思っているものをあなたは見ている／でもそれはあなたの姿ではない／あなたは水の反射した姿」という最後の一節が読み上げられ、作家の手によって灯りが消された瞬間、周囲は闇に包まれる。「見えなくなること」が私たちの心理・身体にいかに作用するか、それがいかに私たちの感覚を鋭く、あるいは脆くするかを知る作家による見事な演出だ。1982年、アイスランド南部海岸の灯台に6週間暮らしていたというホーンの手記を見てみよう。

　　　「恐ろしいイメージの数々——頭部のない女性、テムズ川に流れついた身体の一部、内臓を取り除かれた上半身——が、この断崖に宿ってしまった。灯台の中が狭く感じられ、閉所恐怖的なエネルギーが入り込んできた。私はじっと、身動き一つせず、深夜の静寂に耳を澄ませながら部屋の中に座っていた。恐ろしいイメージは執拗に、私を疲弊させた。体中を満たす恐怖のなか

1　本稿は、引用とテキストからなるロニ・ホーンの《水と言う》および《静かな水（テムズ川、例として）》(pp.94-101) の形式に倣っている。
2　増谷文雄『正法眼蔵（二）』講談社、2004年、35-36頁。
3　ガストン・バシュラール『水と夢 物質的想像力試論』及川馥訳、法政大学出版局、2008年、33頁。
4　《Another Water》(2000年刊行) は写真と脚註からなる本の形式の作品で、112頁におよぶ長編である。テムズ川の水面を写した52枚の写真と、832個の脚註が一連になっている。《水と言う》は、その脚註部分をモノローグとして読み上げるパフォーマンス。《Another Water》から、イメージがなければ機能しない、視覚的にしか意味を持たない脚註を削除し、順番を組み替えて制作されている。なお、本展出品作の《静かな水（テムズ川、例として）》も同じく《Another Water》から派生したヴァリエーションであり、ここでは15枚の写真が選ばれ、各写真ごとに完結するように脚註が付されている。

185

で、私は息つく暇を、逃げ道を、それが止むのを待った。急に停電が起こり、灯台の中が暗闇になったのはその時だった。数秒後、爆発するように発電機が稼働を始めた。私の恐怖と絶望の、歪んだパロディ。それは耐えられないほどにうるさく強烈だった。私は笑い、笑い、そして凍りついた。筋肉が引きつり硬直したのだ。」[5]

ロンドンのテムズ川を舞台とした本作《水と言う》は、私たちがふだん身近に感じている水についての別の側面、すなわちその複雑な純性と官能性、人々を死に引き寄せる魅惑、その暴力性についての散文詩だ。ジョルジュ・ペレックの詩的な内的独白を思わせるこのモノローグの中で、ポップ・ソングの歌詞や事件のニュースを参照しながら、作家の思索は自在にたゆたい連綿と続いてゆく。私たちは水の官能性に翻弄され、黒いミルクのような水は人を誘い、幾多もの人々が川に身を投げ、ニール・ヤングとジミ・ヘンドリックスが恋人を撃ち、時間がねじれ、消失する。

4.
　　「死がこの毒のこもる波にひそみ
　　入江に沿って墓が並んでいる
　　それは孤独な空想で
　　自分を慰めるひとにふさわしいところ―。」

　　　　　　　　　　　　　―― アントニー・アンド・ザ・ジョンソンズ「ザ・レイク」[6]

5.
　　死。「水」とともに、「死」のイメージはロニ・ホーンの作品に通底するもののひとつだ。《死せるフクロウ》（pp.44-47）と題された一対の白い梟、《円周率》（pp.84-93）に見られる動物たちの剝製や、渡り鳥の死骸、散る花の命を謳った《エミリのブーケ》（pp.60-69）、死者を弔うチベットの風習から名付けられた《鳥葬（箱根）》（pp.182-184）、無機質で荒涼とした無人の風景と、人を寄せ付けない氷河、切り刻まれたドローイング、分身、道化師、反復し続けるポートレイト。

　　本展に展示されたガラス彫刻作品のうちの一点《無題（「事故の最中にしか、速度は生じない。」）》（pp.50-51）のタイトルには、F1の天才ドライバーでありレーシングカーのエンジニア、デザイナーでもあったブルース・マクラーレンの言葉が引用されている。[7] 1970年、32歳のマクラーレンは、自ら開発していたマシンの試験走行中の事故で車外に投げ出されて亡くなった。「高みを目指した結果命を落とすことは、愚行ではない」[8]のか？ 死の危険に瀕しても止むことのない極限への憧れ、渇望は、どこからやってくるのか？

　　ドイツ人映画監督、ヴェルナー・ヘルツォークが自身の映画の中で扱うのは、地の果てで圧倒的なものに挑む人間 ―― 死の危険に瀕しても決意を鈍らせることなく、憑かれたように執念深く挑み続ける人間の姿だ。過酷な地平においては、狂気と恍惚の境界が曖昧になる。1984年の作品、『輝く峰　ガッシャーブルム』の舞台となるガッシャーブルム連峰は、中国とパキスタンの国境部・カラコルム山脈の高峰群であり、巨大な氷河を取り囲むように連なる6峰からなる。ともに8000m超えのI峰とII峰を縦走したラインホルト・メスナーに随行したヘルツォークは、この伝説の登山家から、自由と孤独への欲求、人間と死との関係についての哲学的な告白を引き出している。

5 Roni Horn, Bluff and Psycho, in *Island Zombie: Iceland Writings*, New Jersey: Princeton University Press, 2020, p.17.
6 歌詞はエドガー・アラン・ポーの詩「あのみずうみ、―― に」から引用されている。訳出は以下より。『対訳 ポー詩集』加島祥造編、岩波文庫、1997年。
7 別のガラス作品のタイトルは、スベトラーナ・アレクシエービッチ『チェルノブイリの祈り』（岩波書店、2011年）から引用されている。物理学的には液体でも固体でもないガラスの用途は極めて広く、原子力発電が生み出す放射性廃棄物をガラスの内部に閉じ込める「ガラス固化」の技術は多くの国々で採用されている。

「1970年に初めてヒマラヤに挑み、ナンガ・パルバットに2組が登頂した。その4人のうち、私以外の3人はもう故人だ。ショルツとクーエンは数年後に死亡。私の弟は下山途中に死亡した。1972年、世界で7番目に高いマナスルに登った時は2人の仲間が亡くなった。1人は凍死、もう1人は発狂してしまった。あの頃何人ものトップクライマーに会った。イギリス人が多かったね。彼らはその2〜3年後、命を落としたと聞いた。登山は退行の兆しなのかもしれない。」

「自分の内面がどうなってしまうか、孤立や孤独に耐えられるのか分からない。…でも数ヵ月後にはもう十分だという気持ちは消え、中毒のように再び登らずにはいられない。…登山は強迫観念的で、病的なものかもしれない。」

「人間が成しうることの限界に挑む行為は、死への願望だと思われがちだ。登山中に死にたいと思ったことはない。そういう気持ちを持つとしたらそれは山登り以外の時だ。」

「2人で制覇した山を眺めたりすると、まだ弟が生きてるような気がするんだ。一番の難所に弟と挑戦したことがあって厳しい状況を2人で耐え抜いた。どちらかが落ちた時には必ず支えると決めたんだ。あれ以来我々は非常に強い絆で結びつき、離れることはなかった。あの岩壁を見るたびに思い出すよ。指を失った足ではもう登れないけど。…弟が私の代わりに死んだとは思わない。むしろ私があの遠征で死んだと感じてる。…はぐれた弟を私は夜中捜し続けた。弟は現れず私は1人で下りたが、自分の命はどうでもよくなっていた。意思が働いて下山したのではない。「習慣」で下りたんだ。…この悲劇を経て感じたよ。自分はディアミール渓谷で一度死に、生まれ変わったのだと。」

6.

狂気と恍惚と孤独。「孤独とは井戸のように垂直的なものです。その中に、深く潜ってゆくのです。」とロニ・ホーンは言う。

1975年から今日まで、「孤独を求めて」アイスランドの地を踏み続ける作家の動機を、この地への愛着や好奇心といった言葉で片付けることは難しい。数十年間にわたり強い意思をもって、アイスランドにありとあらゆる言葉と、ありとあらゆるイメージを捧げる作家の姿はまさに「憑かれた」ようであり、あの登山家メスナーのように、彼女自身にもはっきりとはわからない動機に突き動かされ、荒涼とした大地へと導かれている。[9]「To Place」(pp.72-77)は作家が1989年からのライフワークとして、アイスランドの地をテーマに制作を続けている本のシリーズであり、アイスランドと彼女との関係を象徴する作品である。「新たな一冊を加えるごとに、より不完全になっていく」と彼女は言う。尽きることのない欲求は、枯渇しない井戸のようだ。孤独が垂直的なものであるならば、ラインホルト・メスナーとロニ・ホーンは同じ軸の上にいる。高く上昇する者と、深く下降する者。

奥深い山間の森の中に設置された《鳥葬(箱根)》や、ガラスの彫刻たちは、人々の孤独のための井戸、あるいは泉のように見える。日本語で「泉下」とは死後の世界のことをいうが、ガラスの中を覗き込む私たちは、死の向こう側を見つめているのか？ 山から生還した人間は、以前と同じ人間なのか？ あるいは、井戸に深く潜った人間は？「ある水(この水ではなく)に映るあなたの姿があなたに結びつく。それはあなたと同じ動きをする。

8 ロジャー・ドナルドソン監督『マクラーレン F1に魅せられた男』(2017年)。26歳で事故死したチームメイト、ティミー・メイヤーへの弔辞から。
9 「なぜアイスランドを選んだのか、初めて訪れたのはなぜだったか、なぜ今も行き続けるのか、自分にも分からないのです」。Roni Horn, *Island Zombie: Iceland Writings*, New Jersey: Princeton University Press, 2020, p.2.

あなたが川を離れるとあなたの姿は消える。…しかし、この水に映るあなたの姿はあなたに結びつかない。あなたからゆらゆらと離れていく。」[10]

7.

　　　「私は地球の中心への入り口を探していた。」[11]

　　　　　　　　　　　　　　　　　　　　　　　　　　—— ロニ・ホーン「ヴェルヌの旅」

8.

　　　「下へ、下へ、ずんずん落ちてゆくばかり。どこまで落ちてもきりがないのでしょうか?」[12]

　　　　　　　　　　　　　　　　　　　　　　　　　　—— ルイス・キャロル『ふしぎの国のアリス』

9.

　　　「『欲望』を見たことはある? 公園のシーンは覚えている? 風に吹かれて茂みが音を立てるのを。そしてあのカメラはただじっと見つめる、あのひらけた草地を歩きさまよう。茂みの音は不吉だ。その川はわたしにあの音を思い出させる。」[13]

　　欲望。ミケランジェロ・アントニオーニの『欲望』は、木々の揺れとざわめきが、控えめながらも実に効果的な印象を残す映画だ。昼下がりの木々は、逢い引きの官能性と解放感、あるいは人間の行為の虚しさと愚かしさ、そして謎めいた雰囲気を巧みに演出している。一方で夜の森は、不気味で危険な雰囲気を帯びる。ドラマティックに明暗を際立たせる照明効果によって、暴力的なものの影と、不穏な静けさが生み出される。騒々しい本編とは対照的に、ほぼセリフのない二つの森のシーンが、この映画を支えている。

　　自然の両義性は、奥深い山の中腹、豊かな森の中に佇むポーラ美術館においても顕著に感じられるものだ。陽光を浴びて、みずみずしい葉を揺らしながら生命力を輝かせる日中の森。緑と茶の豊かなグラデーションの中で、木々の合間に差し込む木漏れ日と、ヒメシャラの赤い木肌がアクセントとなり風景の中に明るいリズムを生んでいる。鳥がさえずり、まれに遭遇するリスや鹿といった動物たちも愛らしい。澄んだ小川の脇で深く息を吸えば、さわやかさに満たされる。

　　夜になれば森は一変する。深さのわからない闇に包まれた森の中で、先ほどまで親しみを感じたものたちは影にのまれ、黒く不穏に揺れ動くものに変わる。視界は狭く、静寂の中に正体のわからない音や鳴き声が響き、湿った空気と野生の獣の気配に包まれるのは恐ろしい。

　　両義的・多義的であることは、ロニ・ホーンというアーティスト、そして彼女の作品の核をなすものだ。写真、彫刻、ドローイング、パフォーマンス、本など、多岐にわたる作品はそれゆえ、時に対照的にさえ見える。その実践を少し乱暴に括ってみるなら、ガラスの彫刻や、アルミニウム・バーの作品群、《ゴールド・フィールド》(pp.60-61; 68-71)といった主に立体作品たち、そして写真作品は、作家の知性によって生み出された、統制されて構築的な、一種のリエナクトメントによる作品である。ロニ・ホーンによって演じられたロニ・ホーン(「Roni Horn aka Roni Horn」[14])と言えるかもしれない。対して、ドローイング作品や、《水と言う》のような詩作は、ロニ・ホーン自らの「手」を介して生み出される、内的な衝動・リビドーに突き動かされた作品である。前者のような一連のコンセプチュアルな作風を知る観者が、後者のようにより内省的・情動的で、過剰で、極端で、混沌をも含む別の作品たちを目にすると、戸惑いを覚えるのは当然かもしれない。

10 《静かな水》より
11 Roni Horn, Verne's Journey, in *Island Zombie: Iceland Writings*, New Jersey: Princeton University Press, 2020, p.33.
12 ルイス・キャロル『ふしぎの国のアリス』生野幸吉訳、福音館書店、1971年、15頁。
13 《静かな水》より

この分裂、対極性、あるいは二重性がしかしながら、作家の作品を一層味わい深いものにしている。澱のような混沌と複雑さを抱えながら、潔く、澄みわたっているのはなぜだろう？「あらゆるものと接触するあらゆるものの影響を受けながらも／今日に至るまでほとんどは透明のまま／それどころか水晶のように澄みきっている。」[15]

10.

　　　「豊かになるものは重くなる。こんなにも多くの反映と影で豊かになった水は、重い水である。…それはあらゆる種類の水のうちでもっとも重い水である。」[16]

　　　　　　　　　　　　　　　　　　　　　　　　　　　　　——バシュラール『水と夢』

11.

　澄んだ水。重い水。この展覧会を通してロニ・ホーンは、人間の魂の持つ対照的な二つの面を見せてくれる。重厚な闇の面と、軽やかで明るい面とを。光の角度によって浮かび上がる色が変化するフレスコ画の、淡く豊かな色彩を想起させるガラスの作品をあつめた一室には、中央に漆黒のガラスが据えられた。作家のユーモアに彩られた水彩による、物質的・言語的なコラージュ《ハック・ウィット》と《犬のコーラス》の部屋（pp.154-155）は（この狭い一角はしかしながら、最も彼女らしい部屋なのではないか？）、軽やかさと色彩に満ちている。水平線に貫かれた《円周率》の自然そのものの色彩と、人間を風景に見立てた《あなたは天気　パート2》（pp.170-181）がとらえる光と空気は、極北の生の美しさと官能性を捉えている。

12.

　　　「ずっと遠くの水平線の上にある黒い点が、私の方に向かってきている。一艇のカヤックが、前へ後ろへ、前へ後ろへ、パドルをリズミカルに切り替えている。その動きはゆっくりと滑らかで、私は目を離せなかった。まだ5月だというのに彼はウェットスーツを着ていた。彼の腕は太くたくましく、前後する動きは優雅で官能性に満ちていた。

　　　カヤックは私に向かってきた。岸に近づくと、漕ぎ手はカヤックから降りてそれを水面から陸に引きずり上げた。ウェットスーツを脱ぐと、彼の優美なプロポーションと美しい肌に私はくぎ付けになった。彼がキャップを脱ぐと長めの髪が落ち、私ははっとした。彼のふくよかな胸部のシルエットには、もはや疑いの余地がなかった。彼は女だった。

　　　一瞬にして、これまで私が見たものはゆったりとした愛撫、予期せぬ充足をもたらすエロティックな夢へと書き換えられた。海は官能的な出来事へと拡張され、クライマックスは過ぎ去らず、永遠に終わらないものとして、私が気づくまでの間影を潜めていた。」[17]

　　　　　　　　　　　　　　　　　　　　　　　　——ロニ・ホーン「代名詞に引き留められて」

13.

　　　「本物のポエジーとは目覚めさせる機能である。」[18]

　　　　　　　　　　　　　　　　　　　　　　　　　　　　——バシュラール『水と夢』

14　2009-2010年にテート・モダン、ホイットニー美術館ほか欧米4館を巡回した、ロニ・ホーンの展覧会のタイトル。ホーンはまた、同一人物とは思えないような30枚のセルフ・ポートレイトによって構成された《a.k.a.》（2008-2009年）という写真作品も制作している。

15　《水と言う》より

16　ガストン・バシュラール、前掲『水と夢 物質的想像力試論』91頁。

17　Roni Horn, Pronouns Detain Me, in *Island Zombie: Iceland Writings*, New Jersey: Princeton University Press, 2020, p.47.

14.

　官能と目覚め。水の記憶。筆者の最も古い水の記憶は、海の記憶だ。幼い私は広い海の中で伯父の肩に乗り、陸の丘陵と暮れかかった空を眺めている。もう少し視線を下げれば、浜辺には私の家族がいたはずだ。その光景と記憶が恐怖、そして安堵感とともにあるのは、その直前、溺れかけていた私を伯父がすくい上げたからだ。岸からそれほど遠かったわけではないと思う。穏やかな表情の伯父の肩の上で恐怖の余韻に身を竦（すく）めながら、私は緩慢に曲線を描きながら生きもののように波打つ水面を眺めていた。揺れる水が立てる小さな音は耳の奥に響くようで、自分の体を浸す水の音を聴くようだった。伯父はその後、私が海を恐れなくなった頃に若くしてこの世を去った。

　子供の頃、私が住んだ家から海までは歩いて10分ほどだった。早起きの父と、朝、海まで走ることもあった。足を踏み出すたびに砂が動くので、砂浜は走りにくい。足首から腰まで、一歩一歩さまざまな筋肉と関節を調整する必要があり、またやわらかい砂は着地時のバネを吸収してしまうので、体を前に運び続けることに注意とエネルギーが必要になる。この運動を永遠には続けられないことが分かっていたから、逆に私は力が尽きるまで必死に駆けまわった。私が住んでいたのは日本海側だったので、夕方になると空が燃えながら、水平線に太陽が溶けていった。父と私にとって夕日は雄大さと永続性の象徴であり、美しいものだったが、夕暮れの紫に染まる空を、不気味で恐ろしいという人たちもいた。

15.

　　「灯火をかざした腕がゆるやかにさらにさらに高く上げられると、ついには大きな火炎が見えはじめた。弧をなす炎は水平線の面上に燃えて、そのあたり一面、海は金色に燃え立った。」[19]

　　　　　　　　　　　　　　　　　　　　　　　　　　　── ヴァージニア・ウルフ『波』

16.

　　「僕たちは旅をしながら、数え切れない夕日を共に見てきた。でもこのオブジェは、一体どこから来たのだろう？ …それからは、どんな夕日も「ゴールド・フィールド」になった。」[20]

　　　　　　　　　　　　　　　　　　　　　　　　　　　── フェリックス・ゴンザレス＝トレス

17.

　夕日。《ゴールド・フィールド》は純粋な金のみからなる作品である。「純粋な」というのは異物がないということで、すなわち、作品に接着剤が使われていない。124.5×152.4cmという大判を作るためには、薄く引き延ばされた縦長の金のホイルを横方向に複数枚接ぎ合わせていく必要がある。横に並べて、重なった面を先の細い槌（つち）で叩く。熱処理（焼きなまし）を加えることで柔らかくなった金を槌で叩くと、素材同士が接着するのだ。作品の表面に、等間隔で小さな窪みの線が生じているのはこの制作工程による。

　無防備に床の上に横たわる、むきだしの金のオブジェは、その脆さゆえにさまざまな意味を引き込む。それは、単純な形態という点では先行するカール・アンドレやロバート・モリスといったミニマリストたちの彫刻とは明らかに異質の、豊かな叙情性を湛えている。「太陽とより親密な関係を持ちたかった」[21]と作家は言う。《ゴールド・フィールド》は夕日に輝く海原であり、「新たな風景、水平線になりうるもの、安息と絶対的な美の場」[22]

18　ガストン・バシュラール、前掲『水と夢 物質的想像力試論』26頁。
19　ヴァージニア・ウルフ『波』鈴木幸夫訳、角川書店、1954年、15頁。
20　Felix Gonzalez-Torres, 1990: L.A., "The Gold Field", in *Earths Grow Thick*, Ohio: Wexner Center for the Arts, 1996. フェリックス・ゴンザレス＝トレスと、そのパートナー、ロス・レイコックは1990年、ロサンゼルス現代美術館でロニ・ホーンの《ゴールド・フィールド》に出会う。エイズに侵されたパートナーとともに失意のうちにあったトレスは、この作品がいかに二人を死の絶望から救ったか、それがいかに必要なものだったかを記している。翌年レイコックは亡くなるが、トレスは2年後の1993年、《"Untitled" (Placebo – Landscape – for Roni)》という金色のキャンディーの作品を制作し《ゴールド・フィールド》に捧げた（彼らにとってホーンの作品は何ものにも代えがたい「Placebo（偽薬）」だった）。それに

である。本作をめぐるフェリックス・ゴンザレス＝トレスとの逸話（脚註20参照）や、窓の外の《鳥葬》との対比から、本作は死のイメージも帯びる。それはあるいは、ジョルジョーネによる《眠れるヴィーナス》（1510年）において、ヴィーナスの眠りに寄り添うシーツに近いもの。あるいはその黄金の襞は、ギベルティの《天国の門》（1452年）に綴られた、旧約聖書の物語だろうか？

エミリ・ディキンスンの詩句とともに、花の命の短さを謳う6本の《エミリのブーケ》に囲まれた《ゴールド・フィールド》は、やわらかな自然光に包まれた墓碑か、泉のようである。窓から森を望む位置に配されたその黄金の泉の前に立つと、森の中にいるかのような倒錯感がある。作品の周囲をゆっくりと廻れば、波打つ黄金の表面には光が乱反射してあそび、泡のような粒が瞬きながら、途切れることなく美しいことばを私たちに語ってくれる。泉の下には日の光に温められた安息があり、光の粒を静かに覗き込めばいつでも、私たちはそれを見つけられる。

18.

> われの吐く
> かそかなる吐息も
> 来たり奪はむ、
> 青くまた黄金なす水のうへにわれの讃へてありしものを、
> 空を、森を、
> また水の薔薇を……[23]

―― ポール・ヴァレリー「ナルシス交声曲」

19.

> 咲く花は、おそらく紹介状となりましょう―どなたに対してかは、誰も推し量ることはできません[24]

―― エミリ・ディキンスン

（すずき・こうた　ポーラ美術館　学芸員）

応える形で、ホーンは《ゴールド・フィールド》と同じ金のホイルを2枚重ねた作品《Paired Gold Mats, for Ross and Felix》（1994-1995年）を制作。重なり合う2つのものの間に、親密さと炎のような輝きが生まれている。1990年に《ゴールド・フィールド》を契機として始まった作家同士の深い親交は、6年後にトレスが亡くなるまで続いた。
21 Roni Horn, Production Notes, in *Artforum*, October 2007, p.310.
22 Felix Gonzalez-Torres, 1990: L.A., "The Gold Field", in *Earths Grow Thick*, Ohio: Wexner Center for the Arts, 1996.
23 ポール・ヴァレリー『ヴァレリー全集1 詩集』伊吹武彦訳、筑摩書房、1967年、312頁。
24 《エミリのブーケ》より。"A BLOSSOM PERHAPS IS AN INTRODUCTION, TO WHOM―NONE CAN INFER―"

Beneath the Fountain[1]

Suzuki Kota

1.

> "Some see water as miraculous flowers, though it does not follow that they use flowers as water. Hungry ghosts see water as raging flames or as pus and blood. Dragons and fish see it as a place or a tower, or as the seven treasures or the *mani* gem. Others see it as woods and walls, or as the Dharma nature of immaculate liberation, or as the true human body, or as the physical form and mental nature. Humans see these as water."[2]
>
> —Dogen, *The Mountains and Waters Sutra*

2.

> "So, let us start with the least sensual of the senses, the sense of sight, and see how it becomes sensual."[3]
>
> —Gaston Bachelard, *Water and Dreams*

3.

Vision. Roni Horn's *Saying Water* (pp.102–104) is a monologue created by removing visual elements from a past work that combines photographs and text.[4] In an outdoor performance at the Louisiana Museum of Modern Art in 2012, she shed new light on how we believe in vision, how vision entraps us, and the complex ways in which non-visual sensations can evoke human emotions.

The most important element of this performance is neither the audience nor the narrative itself, but *time*. Horn selected the moment precisely before sunset as the starting time of the 40-minute performance. As she speaks, the darkening sky gradually fades to black, and as the end of the performance approaches, only lights illuminating the artist's hands emerge from the darkness. The light is extinguished as she delivers the final lines of the monologue – "When you look at water, you see what you think is your reflection, but it's not yours. You are a reflection of water" – and the venue is shrouded in darkness. This is marvelous stagecraft by an artist deeply familiar with how things turning invisible affect us mentally and physically, and how this can make our senses both keener and more vulnerable. The following passage is from Horn's chronicle of living in a lighthouse on the southern coast of Iceland for six weeks in 1982.

---

[1] The format of this essay is based on those of Roni Horn's *Saying Water* and *Still Water (The River Thames, for Example)* (pp.94–101), which consist of quotations and texts.

[2] Written in 1240. Translation from Shohaku Okumura, *The Mountains and Waters Sutra*, p. 34.

[3] Gaston Bachelard, *Water and Dreams: An Essay on the Imagination of Matter*, Dallas: Pegasus Foundation, 1983, p. 33.

[4] *Another Water (The River Thames, for Example)* (published in 2000) is a work consisting of photographs and footnotes, in the form of a 112-page artist's book. It contains a series of 52 photographs of the surface of the Thames and 832 footnotes. *Saying Water* is a performance in which Horn delivers a monologue comprised of selections from these footnotes, removing the notes that require visual accompaniment and reordering the remainder. Another significant, related work is *Still Water (The Thames, for Example)*,

"These terrible images—headless women, body parts washed up on the Thames, disemboweled torsos—populated the bluff. The lighthouse diminished in size, a claustrophobic energy entered the building.

I sat still, very still, listening to the late-night silence of the room. It was loud and tiring. I waited for a break, a way out, a pause in the feeling of terror that filled me. It came quickly when the electricity shut down and the building went dark. Seconds later the electric generator exploded into action, a twisted parody of my fear and helplessness. It was unbearably loud and intense. I laughed and laughed and then I froze. My muscles strained with immobility."[5]

—Roni Horn, *Bluff and Psycho*

Focusing on the river Thames in London, *Saying Water* is a prose poem delving into different aspects of water, the substance so pervasive in our daily lives: the complexity of its purity and its sensuality, its enchantment that draws people to their deaths, its violence. In the monologue, reminiscent of the poetic inner monologues of Georges Perec, the artist's thoughts flow freely, referencing everything from pop song lyrics to news reports of incidents. We are at the mercy of water's sensuality: dark murky water beckons people, many throw themselves into the river, Neil Young and Jimi Hendrix shoot their lovers, time spirals away and disappears.

4.

"Death was in that poisoned wave
And in its gulf, a fitting grave
For him who thence could solace bring
To his dark imagining."

—Antony and the Johnsons, "The Lake"[6]

5.

Death. Along with water, images of death convey a recurring, underlying theme in Horn's work. Examples are seen in *Dead Owl* (pp.44–47), a pair of photographs of a white taxidermied owl; other taxidermied animals and migratory bird carcasses in *Pi* (pp.84–93); an elegy to the falling petals of flowers in *Bouquet of Emily* (pp.60–69); and *Air Burial (Hakone)* (pp.182–184), the title of which references a Tibetan funerary custom. She presents us with inorganic, desolate and unpopulated landscapes, the forbidding bulk of glaciers, cut-up drawings, alter egos, clowns, and endlessly repeated portraits.

The title of one of the glass sculptures featured in this exhibition, *Untitled ("Speed only happens when you're having an accident.")* (pp.50–51), quotes the legendary

featured in this exhibition, in which 15 images of the river are footnoted so that they form a self-contained unit within each photograph.

5 Roni Horn, "Bluff and Psycho," in *Island Zombie: Iceland Writings*, New Jersey: Princeton University Press, 2020, p. 17.

6 These lyrics are quoted from Edgar Allan Poe's poem "The Lake – To —" (1827).

7 The title of another of Horn's glass sculptures is quoted from Svetlana Alexievich's *Voices from Chernobyl* (1997, English translation by Keith Gessen, Dalkey Archive Press, 2005). Vitrification, a technology that traps radioactive waste from nuclear power plants inside glass (which is in physics terms neither liquid nor solid and extremely versatile) has been adopted in many countries.

F1 driver, racecar engineer and designer Bruce McLaren,[7] who died at age 32 in 1970 when he was thrown from the car while test-driving a vehicle he was developing. Is it true that "To die trying to do it better cannot be foolhardy"?[8] What is the source of our longing and hunger for the ultimate, which never subsides even on the verge of death?

In his films, the German director Werner Herzog has documented people who relentlessly take on staggering challenges at the ends of the earth, as if possessed, never losing determination even in the face of death. In the harshest of terrestrial environments, the line between ecstasy and madness is blurred. The Gasherbrum mountains, a group of six towering peaks surrounding a huge glacier, the highest in the Karakoram mountain range on the border between China and Pakistan, are the setting of his 1984 film *The Dark Glow of the Mountains.* Herzog accompanied Reinhold Messner, who scaled Gasherbrum I and Gasherbrum II, both of which are over 8,000 meters, and drew forth an introspective confession from the legendary mountaineer about his desire for freedom and solitude, and the relationship between humans and death.

"When I went to the Himalayas for the first time in 1970, we scaled Nanga Parbat in two groups. Three of us are already gone. Scholz and Kuen died a few years later, and my brother was lost descending the mountain.

In 1972, two of my friends died climbing Manaslu, one of the world's highest peaks. One must have frozen to death. The other lost his mind.

Around this time I met any number of the world's top climbers. Many were British. They were dead within two or three years. I believe mountaineering is a regressive behavior, human beings evolving backward."

"It's especially what happens to me internally—I don't know if I can endure the solitude and loneliness. But after a few months I can't help but climb again. …This desire of mine is morbid."

"If you push the limits of human capability, you will be told you have a death wish. But I have never wanted to die while climbing. If I ever have a desire to die, it is when I am not on a mountain."

"When I look at the mountain that the two of us climbed for the first time, I have the illusion that my brother is alive. The two of us were in the toughest spots together, and we made it through alive. We swore that once the ropes were in place, if one of us fell the other would support him. This strengthened our bond so that we were never apart. When I look at a cliff face, it reminds me of my brother. I can't climb any more after losing my toes, though. I don't think my brother died for my sake—I feel like I was the one who died on that expedition… I kept on searching for my lost brother. But I never found him,

8   From the film *McLaren* (2017) directed by Roger Donaldson. Excerpt of a eulogy for his teammate Tim Meyer, who died in an accident at the age of 26.
9   "I'm often asked but have no idea why I chose Iceland, why I first started going, why I still go." Roni Horn, *Island Zombie: Iceland Writings,* New Jersey: Princeton University Press, 2020, p. 2.

and I went down alone, my own life didn't matter to me anymore. I did not descend the mountain through force of will, but more out of 'habit'... After this tragedy, I felt I had died there in the Diamer Valley and had been reborn."

6.

Extremes, ecstasy, and solitude. Roni Horn has said, "Solitude is like a well going into the ground. It allows me to go vertical."

From 1975 until today, Horn has traveled again and again to Iceland "in search of solitude," and it is difficult to summarize what draws her there so powerfully with such simple words as fondness or curiosity. The figure of the artist, who has shown such strong will to explore Iceland in every possible way through words and images over the course of several decades, is like Messner, the mountaineer quoted above, magnetically attracted to that harsh northern land like one "possessed," for reasons even she cannot clearly explain.[9] *To Place* (pp.72–77) is a series of books that Horn has been producing on the theme of Iceland since 1989, as a lifelong endeavor that embodies her relationship with the island. She says that "with each new book, the series becomes more incomplete." An inexhaustible urge, like a well that never runs dry. If solitude is vertical, then Reinhold Messner and Roni Horn travel along the same axis, one climbing ever higher, the other descending ever deeper.

Her *Air Burial (Hakone)*, installed in a forest deep in the mountains, and glass sculptures appear to be wells or fountains of our solitude. The Japanese word *senka*, literally "beneath the fountain," refers to the afterlife, but when we look into the glass, are we seeing what lies beyond death? Is a person who survived a perilous mountain ascent, or who descended deep into a well, the same person as before? "In some water (not this water) your reflection is coupled to you. It goes where you go. When you walk away from the river your reflection disappears. ...But in this water your reflection uncouples. It drifts away from you."[10]

7.

"I was looking for the entrance to the center of the earth."[11]

—Roni Horn, *Verne's Journey*

8.

"Down, down, down. Would the fall *never* come to an end?"[12]

—Lewis Carroll, *Alice's Adventures in Wonderland*

9.

"Did you see *Blow-Up*? Do you remember the park scene?— and the rustling of the bushes in the wind? And the camera—just watching—wandering over the clearing? The sound of the bushes was dark. The river reminds me of that sound."[13]

10 Roni Horn, *Still Water (The River Thames, for Example)*, 1999.

11 Roni Horn, "Verne's Journey," in *Island Zombie: Iceland Writings*, New Jersey: Princeton University Press, 2020, p. 33.

12 Lewis Carroll, *Alice's Adventures in Wonderland*, 1865.

13 Roni Horn, *Still Water (The River Thames, for Example)*, 1999.

Bushes. In Michelangelo Antonioni's film *Blow-Up*, the swaying and murmuring of foliage makes a subtle yet compelling impression. Leaves in daylight are skillfully employed as devices that convey the sensuality and openness of encounters, the vacuity and stupidity of human behavior, and an enigmatic atmosphere. And then there is the eerie and perilous atmosphere to the forest at night. Dramatic lighting effects accentuate light and darkness, generating shadows that hint at violent acts, shrouded in disturbing tranquility. In contrast to the commotion of the main story, two forest scenes almost completely lacking dialogue are linchpins of the film.

The ambiguity of nature is also a distinctive feature of the Pola Museum of Art, which stands amid a verdant forest deep in the mountains. In the daytime, abundant leaves flutter in the sun, glowing with the energy of life. Dappled sunlight shining between the leaves and the reddish bark of camellias accent the scenery, creating a cheerful rhythm amid the gradated hues of green and brown. Birds twitter overhead, and we may see delightful creatures such as squirrels and deer that we rarely get to meet. Breathe deeply beside a clear mountain stream, and one is filled with refreshment and renewal.

At night, the forest changes completely. In the woods, plunged into darkness of unknown depth, what previously felt comfortingly familiar is swallowed up by shadows and turns into something black and unsettlingly writhing. With one's field of vision narrowed, amid the moist nocturnal air and the sensations of unseen beasts, unidentified sounds and cries in the silence chill the blood.

The ambiguous and multifaceted are at the core of Horn as an artist, and of her works. Her practice, in media ranging from photography, sculpture and drawing to performance and books, is so widely varied that it can at times seem to contradict itself. To sum up this practice somewhat simplistically, on the one hand there are largely three-dimensional works—glass sculptures, aluminum bars, pieces such as *Gold Field* (pp.60–61; 68–71)—and photographic works that are controlled and constructive, constituting a kind of reenactment governed by the penetrating intelligence of the artist, and could be called Roni Horn acted by Roni Horn ("Roni Horn aka Roni Horn").[14] On the other hand, there are drawings and poetic pieces such as *Saying Water* propelled by internal impulses and drives, and created by Horn's own "hands." It may be only natural for a viewer familiar with the conceptual style of the series in the former category to be perplexed when encountering works in the latter, which contain more introspection, emotion, extremes, and even chaos.

This splitting, opposition, or duality, however, gives her work even greater depth. With all the chaos and complexity of the sediment that lies beneath the water, how does it manage to be so clean and pure? "Imagine something that—impinged on by everything, in contact with everything—remains to this day mostly transparent, even crystal clear."[15]

14 *Roni Horn aka Roni Horn* was the title of Horn's 2009-2010 exhibition held at four museums in Europe and the US including the Tate Modern and the Whitney Museum of American Art. She has also produced a photographic work, *a.k.a.* (2008–2009), consisting of 15 paired images (30 photographs) taken throughout her life that do not appear to be the same person.
15 Roni Horn, *Saying Water*.

10.

"What is rich is also heavy. Water full of an abundance of reflections and shadows is heavy indeed. ... It is the heaviest of all the varieties of water."[16]

—*Water and Dreams*

11.

Pure water. Heavy water. Throughout this exhibition, Horn shows us two contrasting aspects of the human soul: the deep, dark side and the bright, light side. A jet-black glass piece is placed in the midst of a delicate gradation in a room of glass works in pale yet vivid hues, reminiscent of a fresco with colors that shift depending on the angle of light. The room containing *Hack Wit* and *Dogs' Chorus* (pp.154–155), water-color drawings with physical and linguistic presence tinged with the artist's humor (is this not the most Hornesque of rooms, despite being a small fraction of the show?) are brimming with light and color. The true colors of the natural world pierced by the horizon in *Pi*, and the light and air captured by *You are the Weather, Part 2* (pp.170–181), in which a person stands in for a landscape, present us with a paean to the beauty and sensuality of life in the far north.

12.

"Off in the distance a dark spot on the horizon moves toward me. A kayak, oar switching rhythmically over and back, over and back. The movement is smooth and slow, fixing my attention. He's wearing a wetsuit, it's still only May. His arms are large and muscular and the back-forth movement is full of grace and sensuality.

The kayak heads towards me. Approaching the shore, the oarsman gets out and lands the kayak, dragging it up from the water. As he pulls his wetsuit off, the delicacy of his proportions and fineness of his skin transfix me. When he takes his cap off the longish hair fails to enlighten me. The fullness of his chest in silhouette provokes no doubt. He is a woman.

Instantly this history of watching is recast as a slow caress, an erotic dream of unexpected fulfillment. The sea becomes an extended sexual event with a climax that attenuates until I am aware, not that it's over, but that it never ended."

—Roni Horn, *Pronouns Detain Me*[17]

13.

"The function of genuine poetry is to open our eyes."[18]

—*Water and Dreams*

14.

Senses and awakenings. Memories of water. My earliest memory of water is a memory of the sea. As a young child, I sit on my uncle's shoulders in the midst of the wide

16 Gaston Bachelard, op. cit., *Water and Dreams: An Essay on the Imagination of Matter*, p. 91.
17 Roni Horn, "Pronouns Detain Me," in *Island Zombie: Iceland Writings*, New Jersey: Princeton University Press, 2020, p. 47.
18 Gaston Bachelard, op. cit., *Water and Dreams: An Essay on the Imagination of Matter*, p. 26.

water, looking at the hills on shore and the dark sky above. Looking a little further down, I would have seen my family on the beach. The view and the memory are accompanied by both terror and relief, because my uncle had just swept me up as I was about to drown. It was probably not very far from shore. Scrunching up my shoulders, still shaking from the close call, on the shoulders of my uncle with his kind and gentle expression, I could not take my eyes off the dark surface of the water, describing a gradual curve and undulating like a living creature. The quiet splashes of the rippling waves echoed deep in my ears, something that could swallow me up and at the same time fascinated me. My uncle died young afterward, around the time I ceased to fear the sea.

It was about 10 minutes' walk from my childhood home to the seashore. My father was an early riser, and we sometimes ran down to the sea in the morning together. On the beach, it was hard to run because our feet sank into the sand. With each step one needed to fine-tune all the muscles and joints from ankles to hips, and the soft sand absorbed the bouncing energy of a step, so it was necessary to proceed with caution and took a lot of energy just to keep moving forward. I knew I couldn't keep this up indefinitely, so I ran like crazy until I wore myself out. We lived in the west near the Sea of Japan, so in the evenings the sky was on fire and the sun melted into the horizon. For my father and I, the setting sun embodied all that was majestic, persistent and beautiful, although some others found the violet sky at dusk eerie and frightening.

15.

"Slowly the arm that held the lamp raised it higher and then higher until a broad flame became visible; an arc of fire burnt on the rim of the horizon, and all round it the sea blazed gold."[19]

—Virginia Woolf, *The Waves*

16.

"We traveled together to countless sunsets. But where did this object come from? ...After that any sunset became 'The Gold Field.'"[20]

—Felix Gonzalez-Torres

17.

Sunset. *Gold Field* is a work consisting of 99.99% pure gold. Here "pure" means there are no foreign substances, i.e. no adhesives, used in the work. In order to make this large expanse of pure gold, 124.5 x 152.4 cm, it was necessary to horizontally connect multiple thinly elongated vertical strips of gold foil. They were arranged in rows and their overlapping surfaces struck with a fine-tipped mallet. When gold softened by heat treatment (annealing) is hit with a mallet, neighboring pieces of the material

---

[19] Virginia Woolf, *The Waves*, London: Hogarth Press, 1931, p. 3.

[20] Felix Gonzalez-Torres, "1990: LA, 'The Gold Field'" in *Earths Grow Thick*, Columbus, Ohio: Wexner Center for the Arts, 1996. Gonzalez-Torres and his partner, Ross Laycock, first saw Roni Horn's *Gold Field* at the Museum of Contemporary Art, Los Angeles in 1990. Gonzalez-Torres described how the work delivered him and his AIDS-afflicted partner from despair in the face of death, and how it provided the salvation they needed at the time. Laycock died the following year, but two years later, in 1993, Torres created a golden candy piece, *Untitled (Placebo – Landscape – for Roni)*, and dedicated it to *Gold Field*. (For the two men, Horn's work had been an irreplaceable "placebo.") In response Horn produced another work, titled *Gold Mats, Paired—for*

adhere to one another. It is because of this production process that small rows of dents occur at regular intervals on the work's surface.

This golden object, exposed and appearing far too vulnerable to lie right on the floor, draws in webs of meaning through its very fragility. Its rich lyricism clearly differentiates it from the sculptures of minimalists such as Carl Andre and Robert Morris, whose works were precedents in terms of employing the formal simplicity. Horn says, "I wanted a closer relationship to the sun."[21] *Gold Field* is the ocean gleaming in the setting sun, "A new landscape, a possible horizon, a place of rest and absolute beauty."[22] In light of the anecdote about Felix Gonzales-Torres's experience with this work (see footnote 20) and the juxtaposition with *Air Burial* outside the window, the work also connects with images of death. Could it be closer to the sheets that nestle around the slumbering figure of Venus in Giorgione's sensuous *Sleeping Venus* (1510)? Or are those the folds of the Old Testament tale told in Lorenzo Ghiberti's *Gates of Paradise* (1452)?

Ringed by the six bars of *Bouquet of Emily* that, with quotations from the letters of Emily Dickinson, exalt the transitory brilliance of the fleeting lives of flowers, *Gold Field* is like a tombstone, or a fountain wreathed in the soft glow of natural light. Standing before this golden fountain, placed across from a window overlooking the forest, there is a bizarre feeling as if one were in the forest. Walk slowly around the work, and diffuse light is reflected on the undulating golden surface gleams like foam, speaking beautiful and ceaseless words. Beneath the fountain there must lie a place of rest, warmed by the light of the sun, which we can always find by silently gazing into the particles of light.

18.

> "It comes to seize
> even the faint breath
> that I sigh out,
> my awe of the blue and golden ripples of water,
> the sky, the forest,
> and the roses of the water..."[23]

—Paul Valéry, *The Narcissus Cantata*

19.

> "A BLOSSOM PERHAPS IS AN INTRODUCTION, TO WHOM—NONE CAN INFER—"[24]

—Emily Dickinson

[Curator, Pola Museum of Art]

Ross and Felix (1994–1995) employing the same gold foil, in two layers. The work generates a sense of intimacy and a flame-like glow between the two softly layered mats. The close friendship between the artists, sparked by the encounter with *Gold Field* in 1990, continued until the death of Gonzales-Torres six years later.

21 Roni Horn, "Production Notes," in *Artforum*, October 2007, p. 310.

22 Felix Gonzalez-Torres, 1990: L.A., "The Gold Field", in *Earths Grow Thick*, Ohio: Wexner Center for the Arts, 1996.

23 Paul Valéry, *The Collected Works of Paul Valéry: Plays*, New Jersey: Princeton University Press, 1960, p.315.

24 From *The Letters of Emily Dickinson*, quoted in Roni Horn's *Bouquet of Emily*.

エミリの花束

朝比奈緑　下村伸子　武田雅子

《エミリのブーケ》(2006–2007年、pp.60–69)のタイトルにある「エミリ」とは、19世紀のアメリカを代表する女性詩人エミリ・ディキンスン (Emily Dickinson, 1830–1886) のことである。マサチューセッツ州アマストの町で生涯を過ごした隠遁詩人であり、没後出版された詩集によって知られるようになった。2020年度ノーベル文学賞を受賞したアメリカの詩人ルイーズ・グリュックなど、多くのアーティストに影響を与え続けている。この作品において、ホーンは『エミリ・ディキンスン書簡集』から、花に関する文を6つ選び出し、言葉の花束を創り上げている。ディキンスンにとって、手紙は外の世界との交流の手段であり、詩の発表の場でもあった。庭や温室で、多くの花々を栽培していたディキンスンは、しばしば近隣の友に、手紙とともに花束を贈った。

THAT A PANSY IS TRANSITIVE, IS ITS ONLY PANG
パンジーは移ろいゆく、ただそれゆえに胸が痛むのです

アマスト大学学長夫人オリーヴ・スターンズへの手紙より（1875年早春頃?）

萎れることなく無事に届きますようにという願いを込めて、咲き始めのパンジーの花束とともに送られた言葉。"pansy" と "pang" で頭韻を踏み、リズミカルな響きがある。長い冬を経て、やっと雪の下から芽吹いたパンジーの花に、神々しい尊さを感じながらも、その生命が永遠ではないことを嘆いている。

アマスト大学学長夫人オリーヴ・スターンズ
夫ウィリアム・スターンズは、1854年から亡くなる1876年まで学長を務めた。ディキンスンの祖父はアマスト大学の創設（1821年）に尽力し、父と兄は財務理事としてその経営に携わっていたことから、スターンズ家とは深い親交があった。

THE CAREER OF FLOWERS DIFFERS FROM OURS ONLY IN INAUDIBLENESS
花々の生涯が私たちと異なるのは、その声が聞き取れないということだけです

従姉妹ルイーザ・ノークロスとフランセス・ノークロスへの手紙より（1873年4月?）

この手紙では、春の訪れに心が躍り、この世の天国とも言える自然の美しさを享受する喜びを伝えている。この引用部分は、蜜蜂を受け入れ、散っていく花々の姿を見ての言葉であるが、さらに続けてこう語っている。「私は長じるにつれて、これらの無言の生き物たちへの敬意を深めています。彼らの方が、私よりも不安や恍惚を感じているかもしれません」。

従姉妹ルイーザ・ノークロスとフランセス・ノークロス
母方の従姉妹。10歳以上年下ということもあり、もっとも心を許した文通相手であったと言えよう。死の直前に、彼女たちに送った言葉「神に召されて」(Called back) は、ディキンスンの墓碑銘となっている。

MY FLOWERS ARE NEAR AND FOREIGN
私の花々は、身近にある異国です

エリザベス・ホランドへの手紙より（1866年3月初め）

温室の花々に陶酔する喜びを伝える言葉。温室へと向かう高揚感を「廊下を渡っていきさえすれば、香料諸島に降り立ちます」と続けて語っている。戸外よりも早く、春の花々の開花を楽しむことができたし、ニューイングランドでは珍しい品種も栽培していたという。ディキンスンにとって、温室は、日常生活を営む屋敷内における異空間であった。没後取り壊されていたが、2017年に復元され、一般公開されている。

エリザベス・ホランド
夫ジョサイア・ホランドは、文芸誌『スクリブナーズ・マンスリー』の創刊者。その孫娘セオドラ・ウォードは、トマス・ジョンソンと共に『エミリ・ディキンスン書簡集』(1958年) の編集に携わった。

BLOSSOMS HAVE THEIR LEISURES—
花々は咲いて、余暇を過ごしています—

コーネリア・ベック・スウィーツァーへの手紙より（1880年秋）

開花という成就を遂げた花々は、この世から姿を消す間までの時間を「余暇」として過ごす。球根を送ってもらうなど、園芸仲間としても親しかった隣人が、アマストを離れた後に送った手紙の最後に置かれた言葉。返信を心待ちにし、ともに過ごした夏の思い出の余韻に浸る、ゆったりとした時が流れている。

コーネリア・ベック・スウィーツァー
ディキンスン家の隣人。夫はアマスト大学卒業後、ニューヨークで卸売業を営んでいたが、夏には子どもたちと一緒にアマストの実家に滞在した。ブラックケーキのレシピや、花に詩を添えて送り届けた夏の日々は、晩年のディキンスンの暮らしに彩りを与えた。

TO COWER BEFORE A FLOWER IS PERHAPS UNWISE—
花を前にして立ちすくむなんて、おそらく愚かなことですが—

ジェイムズ・クラークへの手紙より（1883年3月中旬）

この引用部分の前には、「その愛らしさゆえに、こちらが恥ずかしくなってしまうほどのヒアシンスをお見せできたらと思います」とある。戸外では花が咲いていない時期、温室で育てたヒアシンスを披露することで、いち早く春を感じてほしいと願っている。さらに続けてこう語っている。「けれども、美はしばしば臆病者であり、さらには、おそらく痛みそのものとなるのです」。近寄りがたいほどの美しい花を前にして怯むのは、その命が永続的ではないことを悟り、刹那の美に圧倒されるからである。有限の時の中で、臆病者のように震える美は、限りなく愛おしく、滅びゆく運命を透視する痛みを私たちに与える。花の生命への畏怖を吐露した言葉。

ジェイムズ・クラーク
若い頃のディキンスンの恋愛の対象については今も確証はないが、候補の一人と考えられているチャールズ・ワズワース牧師の親友。1882年にワズワース牧師が没し、クラークが亡くなるまでの約2年間に書簡を交わす。晩年のディキンスンにとって、ワズワース牧師との思い出や敬愛の念を語ることができた貴重な文通相手となった。

A BLOSSOM PERHAPS IS AN INTRODUCTION, TO WHOM—NONE CAN INFER—
咲く花は、おそらく紹介状となりましょう—どなたに対してかは、誰も推し量ることはできません—

フォレスト・F・エマソン牧師への手紙（1883年初旬?）

アマストの教会を去る牧師へのお別れの言葉。おそらく花とともに送られたと思われる。ディキンスン自身は、文通相手であった文芸批評家トマス・ヒギンスンに、アマストの自宅で初めて会ったとき、「これが私の自己紹介です」という言葉とともに、デイ・リリー［一日で萎れてしまう百合］の花を差し出したと伝えられている。夏の盛りの8月のことであった。ヒギンスンは、没後出版の詩集の編集者として、ディキンスンの詩を世に紹介する重要な役割を担うことになった。

フォレスト・F・エマソン
1879年6月から1883年2月までアマスト第一教会で牧師を務めた後、ロードアイランドのニューポートに移った。その後ディキンスンの晩年まで、牧師夫妻とは短い手紙による交流が続いた。

[あさひな・みどり／慶應義塾大学教授]
[しもむら・のぶこ／京都女子大学名誉教授]
[たけだ・まさこ／大阪樟蔭女子大学名誉教授]

Bouquet of Emily

Asahina Midori, Shimomura Nobuko, and Takeda Masako

The Emily in the title of *Bouquet of Emily* (2006–2007, pp.60–69) is Emily Dickinson (1830-1886), one of the preeminent 19th-century American poets. The reclusive poet, who lived in the town of Amherst, Massachusetts, first gained recognition for a collection of poems that was published after her death. Dickinson has continued to influence a multitude of artists, including the poet Louise Glück, recipient of the 2020 Nobel Prize in Literature. In *Bouquet of Emily*, Roni Horn selected six phrases and sentences related to flowers from *The Letters of Emily Dickinson*, and used them to create a bouquet of words. To Dickinson, writing letters was a means of communicating with the outside world as well as a place to self-publish her poems. Dickinson grew many flowers in her garden and conservatory, and she often presented neighborhood friends with a bouquet along with her letters.

"That a pansy is transitive, is its only pang."

—Excerpt from a letter to Olive Stearns*, wife of the president of Amherst College (early spring 1875?)

Dickinson sent these words along with a bouquet of pansies, which were just starting to bloom, with the hope that they would arrive safely without withering. "Pansy" and "pang" are alliterative, and the line has a rhythmic quality. While sensing the divine dignity of the flower, which has at last sprouted up from beneath the snow after a long winter, she laments the fact that the pansy's life is not eternal.

*Olive Stearns
Stearns' husband William served as the president of Amherst College from 1854 until his death in 1876. As Dickinson's grandfather helped found the college in 1821, and her father and brother worked as treasurers at the school, she had a close relationship with the Stearns family.

"The career of flowers differs from ours only in inaudibleness."

—Excerpt from a letter to Dickinson's cousins Louise and Frances Norcross* (April 1873?)

In this letter, Dickinson conveys her excitement at the arrival of spring, and the rapturous delight she takes in the beauty of nature, which might be seen as heaven on Earth. This passage deals with watching the flowers receive the bees and their scattered petals, and it continues with the following line: "I feel more reverence as I grow for these mute creatures whose suspense or transport may surpass my own."

*Louise and Frances Norcross
The Norcross sisters were Dickinson's first cousins on her mother's side. Due in part to their being more than ten years younger than Dickinson, the sisters were perhaps her most trusted correspondents. Not long before her death, Dickinson sent them a note reading, "Called back." These are the words that are inscribed on her tombstone.

"My flowers are near and foreign…"

—Excerpt from a letter to Elizabeth Holland* (early March 1866)

These words capture the intoxicating joy of flowers in a conservatory. Dickinson continues by describing the sense of elation she feels when she goes to the conservatory: "…and I have but to cross the floor to stand in the Spice Isles." In other words, she could enjoy the spring flowers earlier than usual inside, and she was also growing varieties of flowers that were rare in New England. To Dickinson, the conservatory was like another dimension inside the house where she conducted her daily affairs. The conservatory was torn down after her death, but it was rebuilt in 2017, and is now open to the public.

*Elizabeth Holland
Holland's husband Josiah was one of the founders of the literary journal *Scribner's Monthly*. And Holland's granddaughter Theodora Ward assisted Thomas Johnson in editing *The Letters of Emily Dickinson* (1958).

"Blossoms have their leisures –"

—Excerpt from a letter to Cornelia Peck Sweetser* (autumn 1880)

Flowers that have succeeded in blooming enjoy a period of leisure before they vanish from this world. Dickinson used these words to end her letter to Sweetser, a neighborhood friend and fellow gardening enthusiast, who sent the poet bulbs and other things after she moved away from Amherst. While anticipating Sweetser's reply, Dickinson basks in the afterglow of her memories of the summer they spent together suffused with the slow passage of time.

*Cornelia Peck Sweetser
Sweetser was a neighbor of the Dickinsons. After her husband graduated from Amherst College, they moved to New York, where he ran a wholesale business, but in the summer the Sweetsers would return with their children to their house in Amherst. In Dickinson's later years, the summer days, in which she sent a recipe for black cake and flowers accompanied by poems, added spice to her life.

"...to cower before a flower is perhaps unwise – ..."

—Excerpt from a letter to James Clark* (mid-March 1883)

This quote is preceded by the following phrase: "I wish I could show you the Hyacinths that embarrass us by their loveliness...." Here, Dickinson hopes to give Clark an early taste of spring by presenting him with some hyacinths, which she is growing in her conservatory at a time when the flowers have yet to bloom outside. She ends the sentence with this thought: "...but Beauty is often timidity – perhaps oftener – pain." The reason we shrink away from a flower that is so stunning as to be unapproachable is that we realize that life is not eternal, and we are overwhelmed by its transient beauty. The letter expresses a sense of awe at the life of a flower.

*James Clark
Although we still do not know who the object of Dickinson's romantic affection was when she was younger, her close friend Rev. Charles Wadsworth has been suggested as one possibility. After Wadsworth died in 1882, Dickinson began exchanging letters with Clark for roughly two years until his own death. To the aging Dickinson, Clark was an invaluable correspondent, as he enabled her to share her memories, and her love and respect for Wadsworth.

"A blossom perhaps is an introduction, to whom – none can infer –"

—Excerpt from a letter to Rev. Forest F. Emerson* (early 1883)

These words were included in Dickinson's farewell letter to a minister who was leaving the church she attended in Amherst. Apparently, when another one of Dickinson's correspondents, the literary critic Thomas W. Higginson, visited her house on their first meeting, she handed him two day-lilies (so called because they only last for a day) and said, "These are my introduction." That was in August at the height of summer. By editing a posthumous collection of Dickinson's poetry, Higginson played a crucial role in introducing her work to the world.

*Rev. Forest F. Emerson
After serving as a minister at the First Congregational Church in Amherst from June 1879 to February 1883, Emerson moved to Newport, Rhode Island. Dickinson remained in touch with him and his wife via short letters until late in her life.

[Asahina Midori / Professor at Keio University]
[Shimomura Nobuko / Professor emerita at Kyoto Women's University]
[Takeda Masako / Professor emerita at Osaka-Shoin Women's University]

作品リスト｜List of Works

［凡例］
作品情報は、掲載頁、タイトル、制作年、素材・技法、寸法（平面作品の場合：縦×
横cm、立体作品の場合：高さ×幅×奥行cm、もしくは直径cm、厚さcm、映像の場合：上映
時間 分·秒）、所蔵先、クレジット（英文のみ）の順に記載した。特に記載のないものは
全て「courtesy of the artist and Hauser & Wirth」。解説のあるものは作品情
報の後に掲載した。

[Explanatory notes]
The listed details pertaining to each artwork are: page numbers, *artwork
name*, year of production, technique/media, and dimensions (two-dimen-
sional work: height × width in cm; three-dimensional work: height × width
× depth in cm, diameter in cm, or thickness in cm; video or film: duration
in minutes and seconds). All works courtesy of the artist and Hauser &
Wirth, except as noted. Explanatory texts, if included, follow each respec-
tive caption.

|p.43|

水による疑い（どうやって）
2003-2004年
12点のピグメント・プリント（6組）、メッキされたアルミニウムの支柱、
アクリルのグレージング
42.0×56.0cm（両面）アルミニウムの支柱：179.0×直径35.5cm

Doubt by Water (How)
2003-2004
12 pigment-printed photographs produced as 6 double-sided units,
6 anodized aluminium stanchions, acrylic glazing
Photographs: 42.0×56.0 cm / stanchions: 179.0× ø 35.5 cm

|pp.44–47|

死せるフクロウ
1997年
2点のアイリス・プリント
各73.7×73.7cm

Dead Owl
1997
Two iris-printed photographs
73.7×73.7 cm each

|pp.46–47; 49|

無限の瞬き
1991 / 1997年
オフセット・リトグラフィー／非塗工紙
106.7×147.3cm

Brink of Infinity
1991 / 1997
Offset lithography on uncoated paper
106.7×147.3 cm

|pp.50–51|
左から右／From left to right

|p.55|

無題（「…最新の新聞記事より：地方に暮らす女性が病院で手術を受け男性になった。彼女
　の名前は『ヴェロニカ』であったが、手術後に彼女、いや彼は『ジュリアス・シーザー』
　という名前を選んだ。」）
*Untitled ("...the latest newspaper item: a woman in a remote state went to the hospital and
　turned into a man. Her name was 'Veronica,' but after the transformation she,
　or he, chose the name of 'Julius Caesar.'")*

無題（「必要なニュースはすべて天気予報から手に入れる。」）
Untitled ("I get all the news I need from the weather report.")

無題（「事故の最中にしか、速度は生じない。」）
Untitled ("Speed only happens when you're having an accident.")

|p.55|

無題（「魔女は山雨の中で想像していたよりもずっと素敵だ。」）
Untitled ("A witch is more lovely than thought in the mountain rain.")

|pp.56–58|

無題（「…どの家でも、土間の上、敷物の上、板寝床の上で、村人たちは動かず、黙って横
　になっていた。その顔は汗だらけ。村全体がさながら深海の底の潜水艦であった――確
　かに存在はしているのに、声も、動きもなく、生きているしるしがない。」）
*Untitled ("... In all the dwellings, on the earthen floors, on mats, on bunks, lay silent, inert
　people. Their faces were bathed in sweat. The village was like a submarine at the
　bottom of the ocean: it was there, but it emitted no signals, soundless, motionless.")*

無題（「車で［チェルノブイリの］郊外にでると、道路沿いにかかしのようなものが見えます。
　ビニールですっぽりおおわれた雌牛が放されているのです。となりには、これまた全身をビ
　ニールにくるまれたおばあさん。」）
*Untitled ("If you drove out of town [Chernobyl] you'd see these scarecrows: a cow all
　wrapped in cellophane and then an old farmer woman next to her, also wrapped
　in cellophane.")*

|pp.4; 52; 56–57|

無題（「私の社会的な意識は、ほんの数十年前までは未開拓だった土地で形成された。寂寥
　感、なにもない土地、広々とした空、どこまでも続く地平線、そして、ほんのわずかな人々。
　これらが私の最初の事実であり、長い間、支配的なものであった。」）
*Untitled ("My social awareness was formed in a place that had been virgin land only
　a few decades earlier. Emptiness, space, vast skies, long horizons, and few people
　were my first facts, and for long, the dominant facts.")*

無題（「実際には、巧みな恩恵がある。」）
Untitled ("The actual is a deft beneficence.")

2018–2020年
鋳放しの鋳造ガラス
27.9×直径121.9cm

2018–2020
Solid cast glass with as-cast surfaces with oculus
27.9 × ø121.9 cm

物理学的には「固体」でも「液体」でもないガラスの曖昧さは、ホーン作品
の両義性、多義性を象徴するものだろう。水を湛えた器のように見える
この作品は、実は数百キログラムものガラスの塊である。ガラスが途方も
ない時間をかけてゆっくりと鋳造される過程は、溢れ出る灼熱のマグマ
が流れて固まり地面を形成したアイスランドの大地、あるいは融解と凍結
を繰り返し、地層のように時を重ねた氷河の氷をも想起させる。窓から
自然をとりこむ空間に設置された8つのガラス彫刻は、周囲を映し出しな
がら、また巨大なレンズとして光を拡散しながら、静と動、穏やかさと荒々
しさ、表層と深淵、透明感と重量感といった、相反する性質を内包して
いる。タイトルには、文学作品や歌詞などから引用した多様なテキストを
冠し、作品に新たなレイヤーを加えている。

The unresolved nature of glass, as a substance that from the
perspective of physics is neither solid nor liquid, echoes the
ambiguous and open-ended nature of Horn's work. Each of these
pieces, whose surfaces can evoke the appearance of water, is
actually a block of glass weighing hundreds of kilograms that is
slowly annealed in molds over great lengths of time. This process
is reminiscent of the geology of Iceland, where red-hot lava wells
up from underground, flows and solidifies to form the soil, and
the ice of glaciers accumulates to form strata as it repeatedly
thaws and freezes over the centuries. Eight glass sculptures,
installed in a gallery with a view of the forest outside, reflect
their surroundings and diffuse light while simultaneously containing contradictory qualities—static and dynamic, gentle and
rough, surface layer and abyssal depth, transparency and massive
volume. The titles, incorporating diverse quotations from sources
including literature and song lyrics, add new layers of meaning
to the works.

|pp.60–69|

エミリのブーケ
2006-2007年
アルミニウム、成形した白いプラスチック
6点組
146.7×5.1×5.1cm – 313.7×5.1×5.1cm

Bouquet of Emily
2006–2007
Solid aluminium and cast white plastic in 6 parts
Variable dimensions: 146.7×5.1×5.1 cm to 313.7×5.1×5.1 cm

Text from *The Letters of Emily Dickinson*:

THAT A PANSY IS TRANSITIVE, IS ITS ONLY PANG
(height: 206.4 cm)

THE CAREER OF FLOWERS DIFFERS FROM OURS ONLY IN INAUDIBLENESS
(height: 310.5 cm)

MY FLOWERS ARE NEAR AND FOREIGN
(height: 162.6 cm)

BLOSSOMS HAVE THEIR LEISURES—
(height: 146.7 cm)

TO COWER BEFORE A FLOWER IS PERHAPS UNWISE—
(height: 223.5 cm)

A BLOSSOM PERHAPS IS AN INTRODUCTION, TO WHOM—NONE CAN INFER—
(height: 313.7 cm)

|pp.60–61; 68–71|

ゴールド・フィールド

1980／1994年
焼鈍した純度99.99％の金箔
0.002×124.5×152.4cm
個人蔵

Gold Field

1980 / 1994
99.99% gold foil, fully annealed
0.002 × 124.5 × 152.4 cm
Private collection

ホーンの作品には、純粋な形と抒情的な物語性という、相反する性質がどちらも備わっている。壁面に立てかけられた6本の角柱からなる《エミリのブーケ》は、アメリカを代表する詩人、エミリ・ディキンスンが書いた手紙の言葉から選んだ一節を引いた作品である。しかしながら、引用された言葉は側面から見ると言語の体をなさず、文字は純粋な形として解体されている。一方の《ゴールド・フィールド》は、金という物質が持つ文化的なコンテクストを取り払い、形へと還元しながらも、波立つ水面や山脈のような風景を想起させ、抒情的な雰囲気を漂わせている。そのスケールから床に横たわる人をも思わせる本作は、光を放ち絶えず微かに揺れ動きながら、私たちに何を語りかけているのだろうか。

Horn's work paradoxically encompasses qualities of pure form and lyrical narrative content. *Bouquet of Emily* is a group of six aluminum bars leaning against the wall, each featuring a fragment of text from letters sent by the renowned American poet Emily Dickinson. However, when viewed from certain angles, the phrases and letters of the alphabet are deconstructed into pure forms. Meanwhile, *Gold Field* is suffused with a lyrical atmosphere, evoking perhaps, an undulating water surface or a mountainous landscape. This work, a mat made of pure gold foil, removes the material from its loaded cultural context and reduces it to form. What does this work, which in terms of scale recalls a person lying on the floor, say to the viewer through its luminosity and ceaseless subtle rippling?

|pp.72–77|

トゥー・プレイス

1989年–
布装丁の本、オフセット・リトグラフィー
各26.67×21.907cm

To Place

1989 – ongoing
Clothbound books, offset lithography
26.67 × 21.907 cm each

1975年に北大西洋の島国アイスランドを初めて訪れてから、ホーンはこの土地に魅了され、定期的に滞在して制作を行っている。現在も刊行を続けているシリーズ「トゥー・プレイス」は、彼女とアイスランドとの関係の集大成とも言える作品群である。アイスランドの灯台の中に2ヵ月も滞在して制作された水彩ドローイング集『ブラフ・ライフ』をはじめ、風景や動物、人々など、アイスランドで撮影した写真が収められている。また、地図などのアイスランドにまつわる印刷物を素材として、火山活動によって

形を変え続けるこの島の形を、流動する思考の軌跡であるドローイングになぞらえた作品を制作している。

Since her first visit to Iceland in 1975, Horn has been fascinated by its environment and regularly stays and works there for extended periods. Her ongoing series of artist's books, *To Place*, can be said to encapsulate her relationship with Iceland. The first of the ten current volumes contains reproductions of the watercolor drawing series *Bluff Life*, which she created while residing for two months in a lighthouse. Subsequent volumes present numerous photographs of landscapes, animals, people and other subjects taken in the country. She also produces works on paper comprised of printed matter related to Iceland, such as maps, which through the act of drawing trace the trajectory of her thought as it shifts and evolves, just as the island's shape changes due to volcanic activity

小さな包みの方は、ぎっしり詰まっている。

1990／2010年
黒鉛とコラージュ／『ブラフ・ライフ』特別版を印刷し水洗いしたラグ・ペーパー
25.4×30.5cm〔両面〕

Smaller Bundles Cram

1990 / 2010
Graphite and collage on washed rag-paper special edition print from *Bluff Life*
25.4 × 30.5 cm

|pp.82–83|

北極の自信 v.1

1990／2016年
『ブラフ・ライフ』特別版の地図、スナイフェルス氷河の画像（『ユニバーサル・ロールシャッハ』より）、『溶岩』の活版印刷のコラージュ／水洗いしたラグ・ペーパー
55.9×54.6cm

Arctic Confidence, v. 1

1990 / 2016
Collage of washed rag-paper special edition print from *Bluff Life*, Snæfellsjökull from *Universal Rorschach*, and letterpress print from *Lava*
55.9 × 54.6 cm

北極の自信 v.2

1990／2016年
『ブラフ・ライフ』特別版の地図、スナイフェルス氷河の画像（『ユニバーサル・ロールシャッハ』より）、『溶岩』の活版印刷のコラージュ／水洗いしたラグ・ペーパー
35.6×38.1cm

Arctic Confidence, v. 2

1990 / 2016
Collage of washed rag-paper special edition print from *Bluff Life*, Snæfellsjökull from *Universal Rorschach*, and letterpress print from *Lava*
35.6 × 38.1 cm

合理主義者はソンブレロ帽をかぶるだろう

1990年
インク、黒鉛／『ブラフ・ライフ』特別版を印刷し水洗いしたラグ・ペーパー
25.4×30.5cm

Rationalists Would Wear Sombreros

1990
Ink and graphite on washed rag-paper special edition print from *Bluff Life*
25.4 × 30.5 cm

|p.78|

人生について考える…

1990年
インク、黒鉛／『ブラフ・ライフ』特別版を印刷し水洗いしたラグ・ペーパー
25.4×30.5cm

I Think About Life ...

1990
Ink and graphite on washed rag-paper special edition print from *Bluff Life*
25.4 × 30.5 cm

島　イエス
1990/2012年
黒鉛、修正液／『ブラフ・ライフ』特別版を印刷し水洗いしたラグ・ペーパー
26.0×31.1cm

Island Yes
1990 / 2012
Graphite and white-out marker on washed rag-paper special edition print from
Bluff Life
26.0×31.1 cm

|pp.80–81|
溶岩島 v. 2
1990/2012年
『ブラフ・ライフ』特別版を印刷し水洗いしたラグ・ペーパーと『溶岩』の活版印刷のコラージュ
26.0×57.8cm

Lavaland, v. 2
1990 / 2012
Collage of washed rag-paper special edition print from *Bluff Life*
and letterpress print from *Lava*
26.0×57.8 cm

|p.79|
島、島 v. 1
1990/2012年
『ブラフ・ライフ』特別版を印刷し水洗いしたラグ・ペーパーのコラージュ
39.4×29.8cm

Island, Island, v. 1
1990 / 2012
Collage of washed rag-paper special edition print from *Bluff Life*
39.4×29.8 cm

島、島 v. 2
1990/2012年
『ブラフ・ライフ』特別版を印刷し水洗いしたラグ・ペーパーのコラージュ
40.0×29.2cm

Island, Island, v. 2
1990 / 2012
Collage of washed rag-paper special edition print from *Bluff Life*
40.0×29.2 cm

島、島 v. 3
1990/2013年
『ブラフ・ライフ』特別版を印刷し水洗いしたラグ・ペーパーのコラージュ
33.0×30.5cm

Island, Island, v. 3
1990 / 2013
Collage of washed rag-paper special edition print from *Bluff Life*
33.0×30.5 cm

火山現象 v. 6
1990/2014年
『ブラフ・ライフ』特別版を印刷し水洗いしたラグ・ペーパーと
『溶岩』の活版印刷のコラージュ
37.5×40.6cm

Volcanic Phenomenon, v. 6
1990 / 2014
Collage of washed rag-paper special edition print from *Bluff Life*
and letterpress print from *Lava*
37.5×40.6 cm

|pp.84–93|
円周率
1997/2004年
45点のピグメント・プリント
51.4×69.2cm (22点) / 51.4×51.4cm (13点) / 51.4×41.3cm (10点)

Pi
1997 / 2004
45 pigment-printed photographs on Somerset satin paper
51.4×69.2 cm (each, 22 prints) / 51.4×51.4 cm (each, 13 prints) /
51.4×41.3 cm (each, 10 prints)

「循環し繰り返される出来事の集積」と作家が語る《円周率》は、北ア
イスランドで7年にわたって撮影した45点の写真からなる作品である。野
生の鴨の巣跡から手作業で羽毛を集めることを生業とするビョルンソン
夫妻を中心に、彼らの家や、窓から見える風景、鴨の巣跡、この地の
野生動物の剝製、夫妻が毎日のように見るアメリカのメロドラマを映した
テレビ画面などが登場する。壁面の少し高い位置に展示された作品を
見渡す鑑賞者は、この空間のなかでぐるりと円を描き、もとの場所に戻っ
てくる。巡る時間と繰り返す命、そしてその美しい退屈さに捧げられた本
作は、北極圏の生への祝福のようだ。

Pi is a set of 45 photographs, taken over seven years in northern
Iceland, which the artist describes as "a collection of circular
and cyclical events." It focuses on Hildur and Björn Björnsson,
a couple who make a living by harvesting down from the
abandoned nests of wild ducks, presenting images such as
the interior of their home, views from their windows, ducks'
nests, taxidermy of local wildlife, and a TV screen showing an
American soap opera the couple habitually watches. Surveying
the photographs, hung slightly above eye level on the wall, the
viewer makes a circle around the space and returns to his or her
point of origin. This work, dedicated to the cycles of time and
life and the beauty concealed within tedium, is a paean to life in
the Arctic.

|pp.94–101|
静かな水 (テムズ川、例として)
1999年
15点の写真と文字のオフセット・リトグラフィー／非塗工紙
各77.5×105.4cm

Still Water (The River Thames, for Example)
1999
15 offset lithographs on uncoated paper
77.5×105.4 cm each

ロンドンの中心部を流れるテムズ川の水面を写した15点。私たちが一言
で「水」と呼ぶものの、驚くべき多様性を捉えている。よく見ると画面には
点のように細かな数字が配置され、下部の文章と「脚註」のように結び
ついている。ここには水の深みや波立つ水面が呼び起こす様々な感情
や問いかけ、そこから連想される不穏な物語、ディキンスンらの詩文から
の文学的引用などを織り交ぜながら、ホーンの言葉が散文のように綴ら
れていく。この作品の中で、彼女は「水に映るあなたを見るとき、あなた
の中に水を感じる?」と私たちに問いかける。水という身近なようで、不確
かで異様な物質が、私たちの体を流れ、満たしているのだ。

This is a set of 15 images of the surface of the River Thames,
which flows through central London. It captures the astounding
diversity in what people often think of as simply a single body
of water. Look closely and you will find the images dotted with
tiny numbers, which connect to footnotes below the photographs. In the footnote text, Horn's ideas are interwoven with
various emotions and questions evoked by the depth and rippling surface of the water, disturbing tales associated with the
river, literary quotations from Emily Dickinson and more. In
this work, Horn asks us: "When you see your reflection in water,
do you recognize the water in you?" Water is an indeterminate
substance, both familiar and strange, which flows through and
fills all our bodies.

水と言う
2012年5月、ルイジアナ近代美術館 (フムレベック、デンマーク) でのパフォーマンス
ヴィデオ 39分11秒
日本語字幕 | 石井麻希、良知 暁

Saying Water
Performance at the Louisiana Museum of Modern Art (Humlebæk, Denmark),
May 2012
Video 39′ 11″
Japanese subtitles: Ishii Maki, Rachi Akira

「考え続けること」は、苦痛を伴う。それが答えのない問いや自問であれ
ばなおさらである。日々生み出すことをやめない、思考を止めないホーン
の驚異の一つは、その圧倒的な思索の持久力と強度にある。ジョル
ジュ・ペレックの詩的な内的独白を思わせる《水と言う》は、「水」につい
ての思考をめぐる散文詩である。ポップ・ソングの歌詞や事件のニュース
を挿入しながら、人を闇に引き寄せる水の恐ろしさ、様々な色や形を映
し出す水の魅惑、その不可知性について、作家の思索は自在にたゆた
い連綿と続いてゆく。彼女らしいユーモアを織り交ぜながらも、結末や閉
じることに向かわないあり方、深い川に潜りこむような思索の旅は、分かり
やすさや予定調和を求めがちな現代の私たちに贈られた想像力のト
レーニングのようだ。

To persist in thinking about something can be challenging,
especially an unanswerable question or a question to oneself. One
marvelous aspect of Horn, who never stops working and thinking,
is the overwhelming endurance and power of her thought process.
Recalling the poetic interior monologues of Georges Perec, *Saying
Water* is a prose poem on the subject of "thinking about water."
Interspersed with pop music lyrics and news reports of incidents,
the artist's thoughts—on water's fearful power that beckons
people into darkness, the pleasurable sensation of seeing color and
form reflected in water, water's essential unknowability—flow
like an unending stream, freely shifting and transforming. Interwoven with Horn's characteristic humor, the text is a meditative
journey that evades closure and questions preconceived notions of
understanding and harmony.

または 7
2013／2015年
粉末顔料、黒鉛、木炭、色鉛筆、ワニス／紙
278.1×257.8cm
グレンストーン美術館

Or 7
2013 / 2015
Powdered pigment, graphite, charcoal, colored pencil and varnish on paper
278.1 × 257.8 cm
Glenstone Museum

または 6
2013–2014年
粉末顔料、黒鉛、木炭、色鉛筆、ワニス／紙
273.1×259.1cm
グレンストーン美術館

Or 6
2013–2014
Powdered pigment, graphite, charcoal, colored pencil and varnish on paper
273.1 × 259.1 cm
Glenstone Museum

ほか 4
2009年
粉末顔料、黒鉛、木炭、色鉛筆、ワニス／紙
250.8×271.1cm
グレンストーン美術館

Else 4
2009
Powdered pigment, graphite, charcoal, colored pencil and varnish on paper
250.8 × 271.1 cm
Glenstone Museum

または 1
2013–2014年
粉末顔料、黒鉛、木炭、色鉛筆、ワニス／紙
234.3×248.9cm
グレンストーン美術館

Or 1
2013–2014
Powdered pigment, graphite, charcoal, colored pencil and varnish on paper
234.3 × 248.9 cm
Glenstone Museum

まだ 5
2013／2017年
粉末顔料、黒鉛、木炭、色鉛筆、ワニス／紙
246.4×325.1cm

Yet 5
2013 / 2017
Powdered pigment, graphite, charcoal, colored pencil and varnish on paper
246.4 × 325.1 cm

ほか 9
2010年
粉末顔料、黒鉛、木炭、色鉛筆、ワニス／紙
235.0×243.9cm

Else 9
2010
Powdered pigment, graphite, charcoal, colored pencil and varnish on paper
235.0 × 243.9 cm

おく 3
2012–2013年
粉末顔料、黒鉛、木炭、色鉛筆、ワニス／紙
266.7×246.4cm

Put 3
2012–2013
Powdered pigment, graphite, charcoal, colored pencil and varnish on paper
266.7 × 246.4 cm

ドローイングは、ホーンにとってもっとも身近な表現手段であり、1982年か
ら今日まで「日々呼吸するように」、一定して継続されている唯一の形式
である。抽象的な線や形、あるいは引用された言葉などモティーフは
様々だが、それは手の運動であるとともに、彼女の思考や記憶と結びつ
いている。本展に出品された7点の巨大なドローイング作品は、大きいも
のでは高さ約3メートルにおよぶ。細部に目を凝らすと、手書きの記号や
印、紙の切れ目があり、それらが一度ばらばらに切断され、繊細な手作
業によって再び組み合わせられたものであることが分かる。

Horn describes drawing as her primary activity, comparable to
breathing, and it is the only practice she has pursued continually
from 1982 to the present. The content of her drawings ranges
from abstract lines and shapes to text quoted from a variety of
sources, and while they convey movements of the hand, they
also allude to the artist's thoughts and memories. The seven
monumentally sized drawings are as large as approximately
three meters in height. Close examination of the drawings
reveals handwritten symbols, marks, and incisions in the paper,
indicating that the works have been cut into pieces and then
reassembled using a delicate manual process.

水彩で描かれた慣用句や文学作品からの引用文が細かく裁断され、別の語句と組み合わさり、あざやかな色彩を伴う視覚的要素へと変化している。画面を分断し再び繋ぎ合わせるコラージュの手法は、パウル・クレーやエルズワース・ケリーといった過去の画家たちに連なるものである。ホーンはここに、シュルレアリスムの作家たちのような言葉遊びの要素を加えている。「犬のコーラス」ではシェイクスピアの戯曲『ジュリアス・シーザー』の「let slip the dogs of war（戦争の犬を解き放て）」というドラマティックな台詞や慣用句を用いた「Let Slip From the Frying Pan into the Fire（フライパンから解き放ち、火の中に放り込め）」などの言葉が、複雑な画面の中で、ユーモラスで活き活きとした表現を生みだしている。

In this series, phrases and literary quotations painted in watercolor are cut and combined, synthesizing language with vivid color and visual form. The collage technique of cutting up and reconfiguring the picture is in the vein of earlier artists such as Paul Klee and Ellsworth Kelly, while Horn here adds an element of wordplay that recalls the Surrealists. The *Dogs' Chorus* works reference "let slip the dogs of war," a dramatic line delivered in the Shakespeare play *Julius Caesar*. In *Dogs' Chorus—Let Slip From the Frying Pan into the Fire*, this quotation is combined with other words and idioms to convey humorous and vibrant messages in a work with a complex and dynamic structure.

| pp.170–181 |

あなたは天気 パート2
2010-2011年
64点のCプリント、36点の白黒印刷、PVCボードにマウント
各26.5×21.4×1.0cm

You are the Weather, Part 2
2010–2011
64 C-prints, 36 black and white prints, mounted on Sintra
26.5 × 21.4 × 1.0 cm each

1980年代前半から、写真はホーンにとって主要なメディアとなっている。真っ直ぐ視線を投げかける100枚ものポートレートは、アイスランドの温泉で6週間にわたって女性の表情の微妙な変化を記録し続けたものである。「曇った顔」「気が晴れる」「霞を食う」「称賛の雨」など、私たちは人間のあり方や経験を気象に見立てている。時に激しく、時に穏やかに、天気のように移り変わる、一人の女性が見せる唯一無二の100の表情を追いながら、同じように見えるものの中にこそ絶え間ない変化が潜み、私たちの「眼」こそが、代わり映えしない日常の中に心を打つものや驚きを見出すことに気づくのだ。

Photography has been a central medium for Horn since the early 1980s. The images in this installation, 100 close-up photographs of a woman's face, were taken at Icelandic hot springs over a six-week period and document subtle shifts in her facial expression. In everyday life, we often describe people's states of being or experiences in weather terms—someone can "have a sunny nature" or be "walking on air," or their face may "cloud over" when it "rains on their parade." As we view this sequence of one woman's 100 facial expressions, no two alike, we find that constant change lurks even within superficial sameness, and it is our own eyes that have the power to find significance in the unchanging routines of daily life.

| cover; pp. 1–3; 182–184 |

鳥葬（箱根）
2017-2018年
鋳放しの鋳造ガラス
131.4×直径142.2cm
ポーラ美術館

Air Burial (Hakone)
2017–2018
Solid cast glass with as-cast surfaces
131.4 × ø 142.2 cm
Pola Museum of Art

| p.217 |

水による疑い（何を）
2003-2004年
12点のピグメント・プリント（6組）、メッキされたアルミニウムの支柱、アクリルのグレージング
42.0×56.0cm（両面）アルミニウムの支柱：179.0×直径35.5cm

Doubt by Water (What)
2003–2004
12 pigment-printed photographs produced as 6 double-sided units, 6 anodized aluminium stanchions, acrylic glazing
Photographs: 42.0 × 56.0 cm / stanchions: 179.0 × ø 35.5 cm

Bibliography

Note: Author, Editor (ed.), *Title*. [exh. cat.] Place: Publisher, Year.

MONOGRAPHIC BOOKS & CATALOGS ON RONI HORN

– Roni Horn; Michelle White, *Wits' End*. Zurich: Hauser & Wirth Publishers, 2021.

– Roni Horn, *Island Zombie: Iceland Writings*. Princeton and Oxford: Princeton University Press, 2020.

– Michelle White, *Roni Horn: When I Breathe, I Draw*. [exh. cat.] Houston: The Menil Collection, and New Haven: Yale University Press, 2019.

– Briony Fer; Roni Horn, *Dogs' Chorus*. Göttingen: Steidl, 2019.

– Briony Fer, R*oni Horn: Remembered Words*, Seoul: Kukje Gallery, 2018.

– Gary Indiana, *Roni Horn*. [exh. cat.] (vol. 1: *Going North Roni Horn* / vol. 2: *Roni Horn*)
Munich; London; New York: DelMonico Books; Prestel, 2017.

– Fiona Elliot (ed.), Theodora Vischer, *Roni Horn*. [exh. cat.] Berlin: Hatje Cantz, 2016.

– Roni Horn, *Th Rose Prblm*. Göttingen: Steidl, 2016.

– Roni Horn, *The Selected Gifts (1974–2015)*. Göttingen: Steidl, 2016.

– Ardi Poels, *Roni Horn: Not this nor that*. Wassenaar: Voorlinden, 2016.

– Anne Carson; Roni Horn, *Hack Wit*. Göttingen: Steidl, 2015.

– Bice Curiger; Élisabeth Lebovici, *Roni Horn: Butterfly to Oblivion*. [exh. cat.] Arles: Fondation Vincent van Gogh, 2015. (French/English)

– Aveek Sen, *Roni Horn: The Sensation of Sadness at Having Slept Through a Shower of Meteors*. [exh. cat.] Seoul: Kukje Gallery, 2015.

– Marx Hollein; Kristin Schrader, *Roni Horn: Portrait of an Image*. Frankfurt: Schirn Kunsthalle; Munich: Hirmer Verlag, 2014.

– Roni Horn; Julie Ault, *Roni Horn. Everything Was Sleeping as if the Universe Were a Mistake*. [exh. cat.] Madrid: Turner Libros, 2014.

– Roni Horn; Julie Ault, *Roni Horn. Dormia tot com si l'univers fos un error*. [exh. cat.] Madrid: Turner Libros, 2014. (Catalan)

– Roni Horn; Julie Ault, *Roni Horn. Todo dormìa como si el universo fuera un error*. [exh. cat.] Madrid: Turner Libros, 2014. (Spanish)

– Briony Fer; Tacita Dean, *Roni Horn–153 Drawings*. Zurich: JRP/Ringier, 2013.

– Ingvild Goetz; Larissa Michelberger; Rainald Schumacher; Kirsty Bell; Christy Lange; James Lingwood, *Roni Horn*. [exh. cat.]
Ostfildern-Ruit: Hatje Cantz, 2012.

– Élisabeth Lebovici, *Roni Horn*. [exh. cat.] Seoul: Kukje Gallery, 2010.

– Yilmaz Dziewior; Gary Indiana; Julie Ault, *Roni Horn: Well and Truly*. [exh. cat.] Bregenz: Kunsthaus Bregenz, 2010.

– Dave Hickey; Roni Horn, *aka*. Göttingen: Steidl, 2010.

– Adrian Searle; Briony Fer, *VATNASAFN/LIBRARY OF WATER*. London: Artangel; Göttingen: Steidl, 2009.

– Éric Mézil, et al., *Roni Horn*. Paris: Édition Phébus, 2009. (English/French)

– Philip Larratt-Smith; Roni Horn, *bird*. Göttingen: Steidl, 2008.

– Julie Ault, *Roni Horn*. [exh. cat.] Seoul: Kukje Gallery, 2007. (English/Korean)

– Hélène Cixous; Roni Horn, *A Kind of You*. [exh. cat.] Melbourne: Australian Centre for Contemporary Art; Göttingen: Steidl, 2007.

– Fríða Björk Ingvarsdóttir; Roni Horn, *My Oz*. Reykjavík: Listasafn Reykjavíkur, 2007. (English/Icelandic)

– Hélène Cixous, *Roni Horn: Rings of Lispector (Agua Viva)*. Zurich: Hauser & Wirth; Göttingen: Steidl, 2006. (English/French)

– Tacita Dean; Angela Vettese, *Angie and Emily / Dickinson*. [exh. cat.]
Edinburgh: The Royal Botanic Garden; Bolzano: Museion, 2006. (English/German/Italian)

– Ute Eskildsen, *To Place: Postcards from the 1st 8 Books*. Essen: Museum Folkwang; Göttingen: Steidl, 2004. (English/German)

– Roni Horn, *Her, Her, Her, and Her*. New York; Göttingen: Steidl/Dangin, 2004.

– Roni Horn, *Cabinet of*. New York; Göttingen: Steidl/Dangin, 2003.

– James Lingwood; Fríða Björk Ingvarsdóttir, *Some Thames / Haskólínn á Akureyri*. Göttingen: Steidl, 2003. (English/Icelandic)

– Paulo Herkenhoff; Jonas Storsve, *Roni Horn, Dessins / Drawings*. [exh. cat.] Paris: Éditions du Centre Pompidou, 2003. (English/French)

– Thierry de Duve; Paulo Herkenhoff, et al., *If on a Winter's Night... Roni Horn....* [exh. cat.]
Winterthur: Fotomuseum Winterthur; Göttingen: Steidl, 2003.

– Roni Horn, *Dictionary of Water*. Paris: Edition 7L; Göttingen: Steidl, 2001.

– Jan Avgikos; Kathleen Merrill Campagnolo, *Still Water (The River Thames, for Example)*. Santa Fe: Lannan Foundation, 2000.

– Lynne Cooke; Louise Neri; Thierry de Duve; Clarice Lispector, *Roni Horn*. London: Phaidon, 2000.

– Laurence Bossé; Marie Laure Bernadac; Nancy Spector, *Events of Relation: Roni Horn*. [exh. cat.]
Paris: Musée d'Art Moderne de la Ville de Paris; Bordeaux: CAPC Musée d'Art Contemporain de Bordeaux, 1999. (English/French)

– Carla Schulz-Hoffmann, *Roni Horn: Pi*. Ostfildern-Ruit: Hatje Cantz; New York: Distributed Art Publishers, 1999. (English/German)

– Roni Horn, *You are the Weather*. Zurich; Berlin; New York: Scalo, 1997.

– bell hooks; Felix Gonzalez-Torres; Sarah Rogers-Lafferty, *Earths Grow Thick*. [exh. cat.]
  Columbus: Wexner Center for the Arts, Ohio State University, 1996.
– Felix Gonzalez-Torres; Roni Horn; Nancy Spector, *Felix Gonzalez-Torres — Roni Horn*. [exh. cat.] Munich: Kunstverlag Ingvild Goetz, 1995.
– Thomas Kellein; Roni Horn, *Making Being Here Enough; Installations from 1980–1995*. [exh. cat.]
  Basel: Kunsthalle Basel; Hannover: Kestner Gesellschaft, 1995. (English/German)
– Dieter Koepplin, *Roni Horn: Zeichnungen / Drawings*. [exh. cat.] Ostfildern-Ruit: Hatje Cantz, 1995.
– Lynne Tillman, *Gurgles, Sucks, Echoes*. [exh. cat.] Cologne: Jablonka Galerie; New York: Matthew Marks Gallery, 1995. (English/German)
– Jan Howard, *Inner Geography*. [exh. cat.] Baltimore: The Baltimore Museum of Art, 1994.
– Nancy Spector, *Roni Horn*. [exh. cat.] Tilburg: De Pont Foundation for Contemporary Art, 1994.
– Dieter Schwarz, *Roni Horn: Rare Spellings. Selected Drawings: 1985–1992*. [exh. cat.] Düsseldorf: Richter, 1993. (English/German)
– Rudi Fuchs; Hannelore Kersting; Roni Horn, *Things Which Happen Again*. [exh. cat.]
  Mönchengladbach: Städtisches Museum Abteiberg; Münster: Westfälischer Kunstverein, 1991. (English/German)
– Klaus Kertess, *Roni Horn*. [exh. cat.] Los Angeles: Museum of Contemporary Art, Los Angeles, 1990.
– Jeremy Gilbert-Rolfe, *Roni Horn: Pair Objects*. [exh. cat.] Paris; New York: Galerie Lelong, 1988.
– Helmut Friedel; Luise Horn; Barbara Hammann, *Roni Horn*. [exh. cat.] Munich: Kunstraum München, 1983. (English/German)
– Hermann Kern, *Roni Horn*. [exh. cat.] Munich: Kunstraum München, 1980.

RONI HORN: ARITST'S BOOKS

– *Th Rose Prblm*. New York: Roni Horn Studio, 2019. [Signed and numbered, limited edition of 125]
– *Remembered Words—A Specimen Concordance*. Göttingen: Steidl, 2019. [Published with two different covers]
– *82 Postcards*. Zurich: Hauser & Wirth Publishers, 2017. [Published with two different covers]
– *My Gifts, A Selection (1960–2015)*. New York: Roni Horn Studio, 2015. [Signed and numbered, limited edition of 300]
– Donna De Salvo; Carter E. Foster; Mark Godfrey; Briony Fer, *Roni Horn aka Roni Horn*. [exh. cat.]
  (vol 1: Catalogue / vol 2: Subject Index), Göttingen: Steidl, 2009.
– *Herðubreið at Home*. Göttingen: Steidl, 2007.
– *Weather Reports You*. Translated from the Icelandic by Bernard Scudder, 1st Edition: London: Artangel; Göttingen: Steidl, 2007;
  2nd Edition: Göttingen: Steidl, 2021.
– *Veðrið vitnar um þig*. (Introduction translated by Fríða Björk Ingvarsdóttir), London: Artangel; Göttingen: Steidl, 2007.
  [Icelandic version of *Weather Reports You*]
– *Index Cixous (Cix Pax)*. Göttingen: Steidl, 2005.
– *Wonderwater (Alice Offshore)*. (Annotated by Louise Bourgeois, Anne Carson, Hélène Cixous, John Waters. 4 vols.), Göttingen: Steidl, 2004.
– *This is Me, This is You*. Paris: Edition 7L; Göttingen: Steidl, 2001.
– *Another Water (The River Thames, for Example)*. 1st Edition: Zurich and New York: Scalo, 2000; 2nd Edition: Göttingen: Steidl, 2011.

VOLUMES OF *TO PLACE*

– *To Place: Haraldsdóttir, Part Two*. Book X, Göttingen: Steidl, 2011. [Special Edition of 100 + 25 AP]
– *To Place: Doubt Box*. Book IX, Boxed set, 28 two-faced cards; 56 images, Göttingen: Steidl, 2006. [Special Edition of 100 + 20 AP]
– *To Place: Becoming a Landscape*. Book VIII, 2 vols. Boxed set, Denver: Ginny Williams, 2001. [Special Edition of 100 + 25 AP]
– *To Place: Arctic Circles*. Book VII, Denver: Ginny Williams, 1998.
– *To Place: Haraldsdóttir*. Book VI, Denver: Ginny Williams, 1996. [Special Edition of 100]
– *To Place: Verne's Journey*. Book V, Cologne: Verlag der Buchhandlung Walther König, 1995.
– *To Place: Pooling Waters*. Book IV, 2 vols., Cologne: Verlag der Buchhandlung Walther König, 1994. (Icelandic/English)
– *To Place: Lava*. Book III, New York: Distributed Art Publishers, 1992. [Special Edition of 100]
– *To Place: Folds*. Book II, New York: Mary Boone Gallery, 1991.
– *To Place: Bluff Life*. Book I, New York: Peter Blum Edition, 1990. [Special Edition of 150]

Selected Exhibitions

2021   *A Rat Surrendered Here*. Château La Coste, Le Puy-Sainte-Réparade, France.
–   *Roni Horn: You are the Weather (Books, Drawings, Photographs)*. Kunsthaus Göttingen, Göttingen, Germany.
–   *Gold Field*. The Menil Collection, Houston, Texas.
–   *Roni Horn: Recent Work*. Hauser & Wirth, New York.
–   *Wits' End Mash*. Peder Lund, Oslo.
–   *Roni Horn: When You See Your Reflection in Water, Do You Recognize the Water in You?*. Pola Museum of Art, Hakone, Japan

2020   *Roni Horn*. i8 Gallery, Reykjavík.
–   *Roni Horn: You are the Weather*. Fondation Beyeler, Riehen, Switzerland.
–   *Roni Horn*. The University Museum of Contemporary Art at UMass Amherst, Amherst, Massachusetts.

2019   *When I Breathe, I Draw (Parts I and II)*. The Drawing Institute at the Menil Collection, Houston, Texas.
–   *Roni Horn*. Peder Lund, Oslo.
–   *Portrait of an Imag (Oslo),* Peder Lund, Oslo (outdoor installation).

2018   *Roni Horn*. Hauser & Wirth, Hong Kong.
–   *Roni Horn. Wits' End Sampler: Menil Drawing Institute Wall Drawing Project*, Menil Collection, Houston, Texas.
–   *Roni Horn: Wits' End Sampler / Recent Drawings*. Hauser & Wirth, Zurich.
–   *Roni Horn*. Kurimanzutto, Mexico City.
–   *Remembered Words*. Kukje Gallery, Seoul.
–   *Roni Horn: Pi*. Pinakothek der Moderne, Munich.

2017   *The Selected Gifts (1974 – 2015)*. Rat Hole Gallery, Tokyo.
–   *Roni Horn*. Nasher Sculpture Center, Dallas, Texas.
–   *Roni Horn*. Hauser & Wirth, New York.
–   *Roni Horn*. Glenstone Museum, Potomac, Maryland.

2016   *The Selected Gifts*. Fondation Beyeler, Riehen, Switzerland.
–   *Roni Horn*. Fondation Beyeler, Riehen, Switzerland.
–   *Roni Horn*. De Pont Museum, Tilburg, Netherlands.

2015   *Roni Horn. Butterfly to Oblivion*. Fondation Vincent van Gogh, Arles, France.
–   *Roni Horn. Butterfly Doubt*. Hauser & Wirth, London.
–   *Roni Horn*. Galleria Raffaella Cortese, Milan, Italy.

2014   *Roni Horn*. Peder Lund, Oslo.
–   *Roni Horn: Drawings*. Vigeland Museum, Oslo.
–   *Roni Horn. Everything was sleeping as if the universe were a mistake*. Fundació Juan Miró, Barcelona; "la Caixa" Forum, Madrid.
–   *Roni Horn*. Kukje Gallery, Seoul.

2013   *Roni Horn. Everything was sleeping as if the universe were a mistake*. Hauser & Wirth, New York.
–   *Roni Horn*. Hauser & Wirth, Zurich.
–   *Roni Horn* (Part 2). Sammlung Goetz, Munich.
–   *Roni Horn: Portrait of an Image*. Schirn Kunsthalle, Frankfurt.
–   *To Place: Roni Horn's Iceland*. Stanford University Libraries, Stanford, California.

2012   *Mirosław Bałka e Roni Horn*. Galleria Raffaella Cortese, Milan, Italy.
–   *Roni Horn* (Part 1). Sammlung Goetz, Munich.
–   *Roni Horn. Selected Drawings 1984-2012*. Xavier Hufkens, Brussels; Hauser & Wirth, Zurich.

2011   *The Wedding (the Walker Evans Polaroid Project) with Roni Horn*. Andrea Rosen Gallery, New York.
–   *Roni Horn: Double Mobius*. FLAG Art Foundation, New York.
–   *Roni Horn: Photographien / Photographic Works*. Hamburger Kunsthalle, Hamburg, Germany.
–   *Roni Horn: Recent Work*. Hauser & Wirth, London.
–   *Roni Horn*. i8 Gallery, Reykjavík.
–   *Roni Horn: Some Thames*. Galerie de l'UQAM Université du Québec à Montréal, Montreal, Canada.

2010   *Roni Horn*. Centre of Contemporary Art – Ujazdowski Castle, Warsaw.
–   *Roni Horn: Recent Drawings*. Hauser & Wirth, New York.
–   *Well and Truly*. Kunsthaus Bregenz, Bregenz, Austria.
–   *Roni Horn*. Rat Hole Gallery, Tokyo.
–   *Roni Horn*. Kukje Gallery, Seoul.

2009   *Roni Horn aka Roni Horn*. Tate Modern, London; Collection Lambert, Avignon, France; Whitney Museum of American Art, New York; Institute of Contemporary Art, Boston.
–   *The tiniest piece of mirror is always the whole mirror*. The Common Guild, Glasgow, Scotland.
–   *Paired Gold: Felix Gonzalez–Torres and Roni Horn,* Guggenheim Museum, New York.

2008   *Roni Horn*. CAC – Centro de Arte Contemporàneo, Malaga, Spain.
–   *Roni Horn*. Circulo de Bellas Artes (PhotoEspaña), Madrid.
–   *Roni Horn, Opposite of White & Opposite of White*. Gagosian Gallery, Los Angeles.
–   *bird*. Hauser & Wirth, Colnaghi; London.
–   *Portrait of an Image (with Isabelle Huppert)*. Overbeck Gesellschaft, Lübeck, Germany.
–   *This is Me, This is You*. Rat Hole Gallery, Tokyo.
–   *Roni Horn, Opposite of White & Opposite of White*. Xavier Hufkens, Brussels.

2007   *A Kind of You*. Australian Centre for Contemporary Art, Melbourne.
–   *Roni Horn*. Kukje Gallery, Seoul.
–   *My Oz*. Listasafn Reykjavíkur (Reykjavík Art Museum), Reykjavík.

2006   *Portrait of an Image*. Hauser & Wirth, Zurich.
–   *Roni Horn / Louise Bourgeois: Drawings*. Hauser & Wirth, Zurich.
–   *Angie and Emily / Dickinson*. Inverleith House, Royal Botanic Garden, Edinburgh, Scotland; Museion Bolzano / Bozen, Bolzano, Italy.
–   *Relaxness*. Safn, Reykjavík.

2005   *Portrait of an Image (with Isabelle Huppert)*. Matthew Marks Gallery, New York.
–   *Felix Gonzalez-Torres + Roni Horn*. Andrea Rosen Gallery, New York.

2004   *Roni Horn: Some Thames*. Art Institute of Chicago, Chicago.
–   *Roni Horn: In der Sammlung*. Museum Folkwang, Essen, Germany.
–   *Roni Horn: Rings of Lispector (Agua Viva)*. Hauser & Wirth, London.
–   *Roni Horn: Her, Her, Her, and Her*. Kjarvalsstaðir, Listasafn Reykjavíkur (Reykjavík Art Museum), Reykjavík.

2003   *Dessins / Drawings / Disegni*. Centre Georges Pompidou / Galerie d'Art Graphique, Paris; Fondazione Bevilacqua La Masa, Venice, Italy.
–   *If on a Winter's Night...Roni Horn....* Fotomuseum Winterthur, Winterthur, Switzerland.
–   *Roni Horn, Rings of Lispector (Agua Viva)*. Hauser & Wirth and Presenhuber, Zurich.
–   *This is Me, This is You*. i8 Gallery, Reykjavík.
–   *Roni Horn*. Raffaella Cortese, Milan, Italy.
–   *Roni Horn*. Xavier Hufkens, Brussels.

2002   *Blah, Blah, Blah*. (Part 2). Dia Center for the Arts, New York.
–   *Cabinet Of*. Galerie Yvon Lambert, Paris.
–   *Clowndoubt*, Matthew Marks Gallery, New York.

2001   *Roni Horn*. Hauser & Wirth and Galerie Eva Presenhuber, Zurich.
–   *Blah, Blah, Blah*. (Part 1). Dia Center for the Arts, New York.
–   *Still Water (The River Thames, for Example)*. i8 Gallery, Reykjavík.
–   *Key and Cues*. Jablonka Galerie, Cologne, Germany.
–   *Some Thames*. Museo Serralves, Porto, Portugal.
–   *Roni Horn*. Xavier Hufkens, Brussels.

2000   *Still Water (The River Thames, for Example)*. Whitney Museum of American Art, New York; Timothy Taylor Gallery, London; Lannan Foundation and SITE Santa Fe, Santa Fe, New Mexico; Castello di Rivoli, Museo d'Arte Contemporanea, Rivoli, Italy.

1999 *Roni Horn: Still Water.* Galerie des Projets du CAPC – Musée d'art contemporain de Bordeaux, Bordeaux, France.
–   *Roni Horn.* Jablonka Galerie, Cologne, Germany.
–   *Pi.* Listasafn Íslands (The National Gallery of Iceland), Reykjavík; Haus der Kunst,
       Bayerische Staatsgemäldesammlungen / Staatsgalerie moderner Kunst, Munich.
–   *Pi.* Matthew Marks Gallery, New York.
–   *Events of Relation.* Musée d'Art Moderne de la Ville de Paris, Paris.
–   *Roni Horn.* Raffaella Cortese, Milan, Italy.
–   *Roni Horn.* Zugspitze, Munich.

1998 *You are the Weather.* De Pont Foundation for Contemporary Art, Tilburg, Netherlands.
–   *Roni Horn.* Galleri Stefan Andersson AB, Umea, Sweden.
–   *Roni Horn.* Museum für Gegenwartskunst, Basel.
–   *Roni Horn.* Patrick Painter, Los Angeles.
–   *Roni Horn.* Xavier Hufkens, Brussels.

1997 *Roni Horn.* Raffaella Cortese, Milan, Italy.
–   *You are the Weather.* Fotomuseum Winterthur, Winterthur, Switzerland;
       Institut für Moderne Kunst / Schmidt Bank-Galerie, Nuremberg, Germany.
–   *Roni Horn.* i8 Gallery, Reykjavík.
–   *Untitled (Flannery) and Pooling — You.* Matthew Marks Gallery, New York.

1996 *Roni Horn.* Galerie Ghislaine Hussenot, Paris.
–   *Roni Horn: Five Installations.* Matthew Marks Gallery, New York.
–   *Earths Grow Thick: Works after Emily Dickinson.* Wexner Center for the Arts, Columbus, Ohio; Davis Museum and Cultural Center,
       Wellesley College, Wellesley, Massachusetts; Henry Art Gallery, University of Washington, Seattle, Washington (1997).

1995 *Roni Horn.* Alfonso Artiaco Gallery, Naples, Italy.
–   *Making Being Here Enough.* Kunsthalle Basel; Kestner Gesellschaft, Hanover, Germany.
–   *Gurgles, Sucks, Echoes.* Matthew Marks Gallery, New York; Jablonka Galerie, Cologne, Germany.
–   *Roni Horn: Zeichnungen.* Museum für Gegenwartskunst, Basel.
–   *Felix Gonzalez-Torres — Roni Horn.* Goetz Collection, Munich.
–   *Currents 61: Roni Horn.* St. Louis Museum of Art, St. Louis, Missouri.

1994 *Roni Horn.* De Pont Foundation for Contemporary Art, Tilburg, Netherlands.
–   *Drawings, Books, Photographic Suites.* Matthew Marks Gallery, New York.
–   *Roni Horn.* Texas Gallery, Houston, Texas.
–   *Inner Geography.* The Baltimore Museum of Art, Baltimore, Maryland; List Visual Arts Center, Cambridge, Massachusetts;
       Yale University Art Gallery, New Haven, Connecticut.

1993 *Roni Horn.* 2nd Floor, Reykjavík.
–   *Roni Horn.* Jablonka Galerie, Cologne, Germany.
–   *Recent Sculpture.* Margo Leavin Gallery, Los Angeles.
–   *Roni Horn.* Mary Boone Gallery, New York.
–   *Roni Horn.* Matthew Marks Gallery, New York.
–   *Rare Spellings: Selected Drawings 1985–1992.* Kunstmuseum Winterthur, Winterthur, Switzerland; Haags Gemeentemuseum,
       Den Hague, Netherlands; Secession, Vienna; Kölnischer Kunstverein, Cologne, Germany.

1992 *Roni Horn.* Annemarie Verna Galerie, Zurich.
–   *Roni Horn.* Jablonka Galerie, Cologne, Germany.
–   *Roni Horn.* Nýlistasafnið (The Living Art Museum), Reykjavík.

1991 *Roni Horn.* Mary Boone Gallery, New York.
–   *Things Which Happen Again.* Städtisches Museum Abteiberg, Mönchengladbach, Germany;
       Westfälischer Kunstverein, Münster, Germany.

1990   *Roni Horn.* Leo Castelli, New York.
–   *Drawings.* Margo Leavin Gallery, Los Angeles.
–   *Roni Horn.* Paula Cooper Gallery, New York.
–   *Temporary Contemporary.* Museum of Contemporary Art, Los Angeles.

1989   *Roni Horn.* Annemarie Verna Galerie, Zurich.
–   *Roni Horn.* Jay Gorney Modern Art, New York.
–   *Doubles.* Paula Cooper Gallery, New York.

1988   *Pair Objects I, II, III.* Galerie Lelong, New York; Detroit Institute of Arts, Detroit, Michigan.
–   *Roni Horn.* Mario Diacono Gallery, Boston.
–   *Roni Horn.* Susanne Hilberry, Birmingham, Michigan.
–   *Drawings.* Winston Gallery, Washington D.C..

1987   *Roni Horn.* Galerie Maeght Lelong, New York.
–   *Roni Horn.* Galerie Maeght Lelong, Paris.

1986   *Roni Horn.* Burnett Miller Gallery, Los Angeles.
–   *Roni Horn: An Installation of Sculpture: The Space Buttresses.* Neuberger Museum of Art, New York.
–   *Sculpture and Drawings.* Galerie Maeght Lelong, New York.

1985   *Roni Horn.* Burnett Miller Gallery, Los Angeles.

1983   *Roni Horn—Drei Arbeiten.* Glyptothek / Kunstforum / Kunstraum, Munich.

1980   *Roni Horn.* Institute for Art and Urban Resources (P.S.1, The Clocktower), New York.
–   *Roni Horn.* Kunstraum, Munich.

PERMANENT INSTALLATIONS

2021   *Air Burial (Hakone).* Pola Museum of Art, Hakone, Japan.
–   *Untitled ("I hated the mountains and the hills, the rivers and the rain. I hated the sunsets of whatever colour, I hated its beauty and its magic and the secret I would never know. I hated its indifference and the cruelty which was part of its loveliness.").*
        Installation in purpose-built pavilion, Havøysund, Norway.

2019   *Air Burial (Oslo).* Ekbergparken Park, Oslo.

2017   *Air Burial (Cairngorms, Scotland).* Cairngorm National Park, Scotland.
–   *Untitled ("One can recognize a great cold [in Yakutsk], she explains to me, by the bright, shining mist that hangs in the air. When a person walks, a corridor forms in this mist. The corridor has the shape of that person's silhouette. The person passes, but the corridor remains, immobile in the mist.").* Castello di Ama, Siena, Italy.

2007   *Vatnasafn / Library of Water,* commissioned by Artangel, Stykkishólmur, Iceland.
        Includes the installations: *You are the Weather (Iceland), Weather Reports You: Listening Room, Water, Selected.*

2003   *Some Thames.* Háskólinn á Akureyri (University of Akureyri), Iceland.

2000   *Yous in You.* Bahnhof Ost, Basel (destroyed).

1996   *You are the Weather (Munich).* Deutscher Wetterdienst München, Munich.

1988   *Things that Happen Again.* Chinati Foundation, Marfa, Texas.

1983   *Cobbled Leads,* Glyptothek Museum, Munich (destroyed).

謝辞 | Acknowledgements

本展開催にあたり格別のご協力を賜りました以下の諸機関、関係者の方々に深く感謝申し上げます。(敬称略)
We are deeply grateful to the following institutions and individuals who gave us their cooperation in making this exhibition possible. (Honorifics omitted)

ロニ・ホーン	Roni Horn
ロニ・ホーン・スタジオ	Roni Horn Studio
ハウザー＆ワース	Hauser & Wirth
グレンストーン美術館	Glenstone Museum
アメリカ大使館	United States Embassy
ヤマト運輸株式会社	YAMATO TRANSPORT CO., LTD.
キヤノンマーケティングジャパン株式会社	Canon Marketing Japan Inc.
アテネ・フランセ文化センター	Athénée Français Cultural Center
BEAMS DESIGN	BEAMS DESIGN
twelvebooks	twelvebooks
タカ・イシイ ギャラリー	Taka Ishii Gallery
朝比奈 緑	Asahina Midori
ルーカス・ウィレン	Briony Fer
佐藤 熊弥	Hayashi Takayuki
下村 伸子	Andrew Maerkle
キャサリン・セラーノ	Abby Merrick
武田 雅子	Yuta Nakajima
ユウタ・ナカジマ	Nishizawa Tezzo
西澤 徹夫	Sato Kumaya
林 卓行	Catherine Serrano
ブリオニー・ファー	Shimomura Nobuko
アンドリュー・マークル	Takeda Masako
アビー・メリック	Lukas Willen

ARTIST'S ACKNOWLEDGEMENTS

Thanks to Suzuki Kota for inviting me to Japan and producing the exhibition;
Shoji Yoh, Inami Ririko, and Ono Takayo from the Pola Museum of Art;
Fujimoto Miwako and her staff at Gōra Kadan, amazing;
Lukas Willen, Yuta Nakajima and Catherine Serrano from Hauser & Wirth;
Abby Merrick from Roni Horn Studio;
Briony Fer, Andrew Maerkle;
and the HIGURE crew.

水による疑い（何を）
2003-2004年

Doubt by Water (What)
2003-2004

ロニ・ホーンのスタジオ（オースターリッツ、ニューヨーク州）
Roni Horn Studio, Austerlitz, NY

ロニ・ホーン：水の中にあなたを見るとき、あなたの中に水を感じる？

Roni Horn: When You See Your Reflection in Water, Do You Recognize the Water in You?

展覧会
2021年9月18日［土］－2022年3月30日［水］
ポーラ美術館

主催：公益財団法人ポーラ美術振興財団 ポーラ美術館
後援：アメリカ大使館
協力：Hauser & Wirth／ヤマト運輸株式会社

［企画］
鈴木幸太（ポーラ美術館）
東海林洋（ポーラ美術館）

［会場構成］
西澤徹夫建築事務所

［施工］
株式会社東京スタデオ
HIGURE 17-15 cas
芹澤木材工業株式会社
合同会社サムサラ

カタログ
［編集］
鈴木幸太（ポーラ美術館）
東海林洋（ポーラ美術館）
湯原公浩（平凡社）

［デザイン］
川村格夫

［和文英訳］
クリストファー・スティヴンズ

［英文和訳］
石井麻希
林卓行
良知暁

［会場撮影］
来田猛
永禮賢

［校正］
栗原功
アドバンティジ・リンクス

2021年11月26日　初版第1刷発行

［編者］
公益財団法人ポーラ美術振興財団 ポーラ美術館
〒250-0631 神奈川県足柄下郡箱根町仙石原小塚山1285
www.polamuseum.or.jp

発行者　下中美都
発行所　株式会社平凡社
〒101-0051 東京都千代田区神田神保町3-29
電話　03-3230-6585（編集）03-3230-6573（営業）
振替　00180-0-29639

［印刷所］
株式会社東京印書館

［製本所］
大口製本印刷株式会社

Exhibition
September 18, 2021 – March 30, 2022
Pola Museum of Art, Hakone, Japan

Organizer: Pola Museum of Art, Pola Art Foundation
In association with: United States Embassy
Support: Hauser & Wirth / YAMATO TRANSPORT CO., LTD.

[Curators]
Suzuki Kota (Pola Museum of Art)
Shoji Yoh (Pola Museum of Art)

[Exhibition Design]
Tezzo Nishizawa Architects

[Construction]
TOKYO STUDIO CO., LTD.
HIGURE 17-15 cas
Serizawa Mokuzai Kogyo Co., Ltd.
SAMSARA

Catalog
[Editorial Team]
Suzuki Kota (Pola Museum of Art)
Shoji Yoh (Pola Museum of Art)
Yuhara Kimihiro (Heibonsha Ltd., Publishers)

[Design]
Kawamura Tadao

[Translation (Japanese/English)]
Christopher Stephens

[Translation (English/Japanese)]
Ishii Maki
Hayashi Takayuki
Rachi Akira

[Photo (Installation view)]
Koroda Takeru
Nagare Satoshi

[Proofreading]
Kurihara Isao
Advantage Links Inc.

First Edition: November 26, 2021

[Editor]
Pola Museum of Art, Pola Art Foundation
1285 Kozukayama, Sengokuhara, Hakone-machi
Ashigarashimo-gun, Kanagawa 250-0631 Japan
www.polamuseum.or.jp

[Publisher]
Heibonsha Ltd., Publishers
3-29 Kanda, Jimbo-cho, Chiyoda-ku, Tokyo 101-0051 Japan
www.heibonsha.co.jp

[Print]
Tokyo Inshokan Printing Co., Ltd.

[Book Binding]
Oguchi Book Binding & Printing Co., Ltd.

ISBN978-4-582-20723-1 C0070
NDC分類番号702.07
A4変型判（29.5×20.5cm）　総ページ220
落丁・乱丁本はお取り替えいたしますので、平凡社読者サービス係まで直接お送りください（送料小社負担）。
平凡社ホームページ　www.heibonsha.co.jp